MOVABLE TYPE
Biography of Legh R. Freeman

MOVABLE TYPE

Biography of
LEGH R. FREEMAN

Thomas H. Heuterman

THE IOWA STATE UNIVERSITY PRESS / AMES

TO THE MEMORY OF MY PARENTS,
who saw the potential for this work,
AND TO MY FAMILY,
who shared in its completion

PN
4874
.F64
H4

THOMAS HEUTERMAN has been a reporter for the *Yakima* (Washington) *Herald-Republic.* He holds the Ph.D. from Washington State University, where he is now chairperson of the Department of Communications. He began research on Legh Freeman in 1957.

© 1979 The Iowa State University Press. All rights reserved

Composed and printed by The Iowa State University Press, Ames, Iowa 50010

First edition, 1979

Library of Congress Cataloging in Publication Data

Heuterman, Thomas H   1934–
  Movable type.

  Bibliography: p.
  Includes index.
  1. Freeman, Legh Richmond.   2. Journalists—United States—Biography.   I. Title.
PN4874.F64H4   070.5′092′4 [B]   79-15511

ISBN 0-8138-0890-1

C O N T E N T S

Legh Freeman, probably at about the time he edited the Frontier Index. *(courtesy Western History Research Center, University of Wyoming)*

PREFACE

AT LEAST TWO historians of American journalism have commented on the frontier period of Legh Richmond Freeman's newspaper publishing career. "To my mind, this newspaper [*Frontier Index*] is among the most interesting in the history of American journalism," James Melvin Lee of New York University wrote in 1916.[1] "In all the annals of American journalism, I believe there is no more fascinating story . . . ," Douglas C. McMurtrie stated in 1943.[2] Lee and McMurtrie referred to the "Press on Wheels" which Freeman moved to at least sixteen publishing sites in the West following the Civil War. Even though Freeman and his newspapers became well known throughout the Midwest, the Rocky Mountains, and the Pacific Northwest, his "fascinating story" has largely remained untold in print.

For more than 100 years editors and authors have taken only superficial note of Freeman. Today some of his more colorful writing is taken out of context only to bolster accounts of the frontier press. His mobility across the North American continent prevented local historians from having a continuing interest in him. From his native Virginia he went to the Pacific Coast, stopping at more than a dozen places between Fort Kearny, Nebraska, and Anacortes, Washington, to write, explore, or engage in land speculation. The fact that a body of source materials was never assembled also prompted inaccuracies about his career. Biographical accounts largely ignore his early life and do not detail his more extensive postfrontier publishing experience which continued until 1915. The understandable but unrealistic concentration on Freeman's frontier exploits of 1865–1868 reflects a general problem defined by literary critic Robert B. Heilman, who wrote: "It has been the fate of the American West to beget the stereotypes that belong to pseudo art before it has yielded up the individualized types that belong to art proper."[3]

The West for Freeman was always a frontier of general opportunity, despite the disappearance of the specific railroad, Indian, or mining frontiers. It fed his opportunistic nature and offered him encouragement in the seemingly endless number of towns where he optimistically sought success. As a result, Freeman became well known, but he never became a figure of substance in a settled locale or a model of achievement in any of his various careers. Yet there is importance in what his life represented—what it tells of the West which allowed him, and thousands like him, to experience the fantasies which have become legend.

But while others dreamed of fortunes or open spaces, Freeman in audacious fashion lived out the life of a frontiersman whose temperament was little fettered even by the rapidly developing strictures of a western society. His imagination was shaped by the frontier and he was in turn all too willing to perpetuate its myths through his life and the columns of his newspaper.

The purposes of this work, therefore, are to draw together extant records in order to complete the "fascinating story" and to measure the journalistic, historical, and literary contributions of Freeman—as a western stereotype and as an individual.

ACKNOWLEDGMENTS

TRACING a figure as mobile as Legh Freeman necessitated assistance from numerous sources. Exceeding that of all others was the critical analysis and personal contribution by Professor David H. Stratton of Washington State University. His colleague, Professor George A. Frykman, provided similar help in assessing the context in which Freeman's activities took place.

Members of the Freeman family made available information which, of course, could not have been obtained from other sources. The late Varinia Freeman took much time to record personal recollections. Kemper Freeman, Sr., and Mr. and Mrs. William B. Freeman were most generous with the personal papers and family history they had compiled.

Providing critical reaction to portions of Freeman's record were Professors Oliver Smith of Brigham Young University, Warren J. Brier of the University of Montana, William Ames of the University of Washington, John Stevens of the University of Michigan, and Judith Leynse of Washington State University.

Responding to requests for specific information were C. Brewster Coulter, Bob Karolevitz, Ted Van Arsdol, Dee Alexander Brown, George W. Glass, Dumas Malone, and James Leach. The W. N. Dow, Nicholas DeBlasi, and Stanley Sevaldson families likewise generously assisted.

The staffs of numerous institutions aided the work by providing temporary work space or staff assistance. These agencies include the Yakima Valley, Washington, Regional Library; the Historical Society of Montana; the Kentucky Historical Society; the Culpeper County, Virginia, Circuit Court; the Western History Research Center of the University of Wyoming; the Nebraska State Historical Society; the *Salt Lake Tribune* and *Deseret News* of Salt Lake City, Utah; the *Washington Farmer* of Spokane and the *Skagit Valley Herald* of Mount Vernon, Washington; the *Yakima* (Washington) *Herald-Republic;* and the E. O. Holland Library at Washington State University. Administrators of the E. O. Holland Fund made possible part of the necessary travel.

Portions of this book form the basis for an article "Assessing the 'Press on Wheels': Individualism in Frontier Journalism," which appeared in *Journalism Quarterly* (autumn), 1976.

These professional contributions were matched only by the personal encouragement, patience, and support of Gretchen, Tom, and Karl.

OVERLEAF: *Bear River City, Wyoming,
where a mob burned the* Frontier Index *in
1868. (courtesy Union Pacific Railroad)*

1

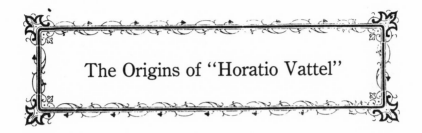

The Origins of "Horatio Vattel"

THE WORDS, "Horatio Vattel, Lightning Scout of the Mountains," were reputedly freshly carved in the doorpost of a Gordonsville, Virginia, railroad station when Legh Richmond Freeman's father demanded an explanation of his son. "That is the name I am going to take when I go out West to explore and write up the country," the child supposedly replied.[1] No doubt the story was embroidered to fit the adult life Freeman actually achieved, but fact and fancy are not opposites here. Legh Freeman did become Vattel the scout. For him, like many other Americans born in the 1840s and 1850s who later "went out West," fact caught up with fiction and even with childhood fantasy.

One source of Freeman's fascination with the West was a book his father brought back from a trip to Richmond. Filled with vivid pictures of Indians, the book told of explorations by early travelers and scouts. It became a valued possession and was one of the treasures he shared with playmates.[2] The interest in the frontier by residents of Culpeper, Virginia, where Legh Freeman was born, was not unusual. Stimulating the boy's imagination about the unseen West even more were the tales of his grandfather, John Hoomes Freeman, who told of early trips he had made to Virginia's western frontier. Legh Freeman chose to spend his adult life in the West, but the decision was not dictated solely by the lure of adventure. Equally important were a complex web of family and financial circumstances, and the Civil War itself.

The young Freeman maintained a lifelong pride in the rich heritage of Southern life, which he sought to appropriate for his own use. This was a pride only strengthened by the nation's sectional tensions which continually increased after his birth on December 4, 1842. Undoubtedly intrigued by the lore of Culpeper County, which included tales of George Washington, he allowed few to ignore his Southern birth. In laying out boundaries as county surveyor at the age of 17, Washington had termed the Culpeper townsite "a high and pleasant situation."

3

Freeman grew up, too, versed in yarns of the Culpeper Minute Men's fifer, drummer, and flag bearer who had given the nation one of its indelible images of the Revolutionary War.[3]

Freeman's pride in the South was not based on patriotic sentiment alone. He saw his family, and especially his paternal grandfather, as an embodiment of an aristocratic heritage—a dubious claim at best when carefully examined. But there is no doubt that the grandfather and grandson developed an intimate relationship. John Hoomes Freeman, at the age of ninety in 1869, singled out Legh from among his multitude of grandchildren to bequeath him a copy of the colonial laws of Virginia published forty-four years before the Declaration of Independence. On its flyleaf, Legh Freeman himself wrote:

> Presented to Legh R. Freeman by his Grandfather, John Hoomes Freeman, April 18, 1869, two hundred and forty-six years after our great, great, great[,] great, great Grandfather, Christopher Freeman, came over from England and settled at the confluence of Hazel and Rappahannock rivers, Culpeper County.[4]

In later life Freeman recorded more detail about this genealogy than he did about his own early life. He told how Christopher Freeman, an English landholder, had sailed from Liverpool in 1623 and, soon after the Jamestown massacre, landed at old Point Comfort, later to be known as Fortress Monroe. The first settler on the Rappahannock River, Christopher worked white convicts furnished and sold by the British government.

John Hoomes Freeman remained erect and alert well past his eightieth year, and in a voice "like a foghorn" was quick to reminisce with his grandson. As family lore has it, he told about when, garbed in silk stockings with knee buckles and his hair done in a queue, he was a "neighbor and intimate friend" of Thomas Jefferson. The grandfather is remembered displaying correspondence from the late president and telling about the Milton post office which he and Jefferson shared on the Rivanna River at an old mill a few miles below the University of Virginia.[5]

It is at this point that the credibility of Legh Freeman's Southern heritage begins to fade. The elder Freeman was associated with Jefferson, but not in the relationship that Legh Freeman carried away from their discussions. Other family reminiscences are equally inaccurate. Grandson F. K. Freeman wrote that John Hoomes Freeman was a private secretary to Jefferson, assisting in his escape from the British troops of Banastre Tarleton who invaded Monticello. Jefferson did take refuge with friends on June 4, 1781, when the raid occurred, but John Hoomes Freeman at that time was only two and one-half years old. Elizabeth Wright, who married into the Freeman family in 1929, more logically claims it was John Hoomes's father, Thomas Freeman, who aided Jefferson's escape, although Thomas Freeman is not mentioned in Jefferson's farm or garden books.[6] However, a "John Holmes Freeman" was mentioned in Jefferson's "Farm Book" and in correspondence as the overseer hired at Monticello on August 22, 1805, at a salary of 60 pounds per year just before he reached the age of twenty-seven.[7] In various places Jefferson details the slave transactions to which he assigned "John H. Freeman," but in correspondence from Monticello on August 10, 1806, he mentions Freeman's "constantly declining health." The president anticipated that this unspecified condition would "probably induce him to leave my service within a few weeks."[8]

Apparently more than illness forced a rupture in the relationship between Jefferson and his employee. On November 14, 1805, Jefferson wrote from Washington to George Jefferson, his agent at Richmond, Virginia:

> Mr Freeman[,] my manager at Monticello . . . being new in the business, has improperly applied to you for nail rods. I pray you not to supply it, as it's [sic] high price at Richmond would take away all profits from the manufacture. . . .

It is also indicated that the work of "John Holmes Freeman . . . was not satisfactory and he was replaced. . . ."[9]

Again emphasizing lineage, Legh Freeman's account of John Hoomes Freeman's marriage to twenty-four-year-old Ann Robertson, daughter of William and Elizabeth Robertson, includes the observation that his grandmother was "of the same stock as the mother of Lord Henry Brougham." The couple may have waited to marry until John Freeman obtained the position at Monticello; on November 27, 1805, three months after "John Holmes Freeman" began his employment for Jefferson, they were wed, the bride clad in a gown of white satin trailing a train of three feet.[10] On August 20, 1817, Ann died unexpectedly at the age of 36.[11]

Steeped, then in family lore and that of his native Virginia, it is not surprising that even as an adult, Legh Freeman wrote:

> Our ancestors were of the faith of the Cavalier High Church of England. All were tall, spare, straight, and aristocratic people. Every Freeman of our line has auburn hair and steel grey eyes. These features predominate in spite of intermarriages with black[-]eyed and corpulent people. Uncle Edward says he is impressed with the belief that such blood can belong only to nature's noblemen. . . . Although the most of our people have been wealthy slaveholders[,] the House has ever prided itself more upon honor than riches.[12]

According to a letter from George W. Glass (March 20, 1967), however, the reference to honor ignored the fact that John Hoomes Freeman's father was illegitimate. This penchant among many South-

6   CHAPTER 1

erners to include themselves in a Cavalier class has been termed a
"naive capacity for unreality," a phrase highly appropriate here.
Freeman was clearly of middle-class planter stock rather than of an
aristocracy, although his attempt at social elevation was typical.

Freeman descendants have been told that John Hoomes Freeman
was born at the family "mansion" in 1779, a reference further attempting to support the claim to high birth or wealth. But the Freemans
were not of the planter society of Tidewater Virginia any more than
they were among the indolent white trash. Life just east of the Blue
Ridge was less leisurely, opulent, and formal than that of the tradi-
tional Southern stereotype. The average planter there owned about five
or six slaves to tend to the major crops of grain, livestock, and tobac-
co, which were supplemented by corn, wool, potatoes, fruit, and hay.[13]

As early as 1825 John Hoomes Freeman sold five slaves and 230
acres of land in Culpeper County to erase a debt of $1,516. Seven
years later, perhaps to meet another debt, for $3,000 he sold to a son
the 230-acre tract on which he lived. This was not long-standing
Freeman property, but had been willed to John Hoomes's second wife,
Sarah, by her father. (John Hoomes married Sarah Grinnan, twenty-
nine, on September 4, 1821, shortly before his forty-second birthday.)
By 1835, however, this property east of Culpeper, bounded by the
Fredericksburg Road and the bank of the Mountain Run stream, 75
miles south of Washington, D.C., was back in John Hoomes's hands
for an identical sum of $3,000.[14] The son involved in the transaction
later became the steward of the county poor house.[15]

These property transactions fail to support aristocratic standing;
neither do the family's slave holdings. In 1840 John Hoomes Freeman
supported 8 slaves, only 3 of whom were males. It was not a significant number in a county where nine families each had 40 or more
slaves (two of these families 50 or more) and where the 6,060 slaves
outnumbered the white population of 4,933. In fact, one of John
Hoomes Freeman's sons had 18 slaves. The father and four of his five
sons in 1840 owned just 42 slaves among them on their individual
farms and only 10 of these were males over the age of ten.[16]

The fortunes of John Hoomes Freeman did not improve during the
remainder of the antebellum period. By 1850 his real estate was valued
at $6,000, but evidently included that property inherited from his
wife's family. Of the ten slaves he owned, only one male was neither a
child nor elderly. There is no evidence that any of his sons tended
Freeman property as their father aged, and ten years later, when
Freeman was eighty-seven, the value of his property had dropped to
$5,420. Of the ten slaves he owned then, only one was a male of work-
ing age.[17]

In attempting to substantiate a claim to Southern aristocratic
standing, Legh Freeman understandably ignored these difficulties that
John Hoomes Freeman posed. The genealogy dating back to 1623, the

Revolutionary aura, and the tie to Thomas Jefferson all overshadowed for childhood recollection realities of debts, declining properties, and small slaveholdings. But even as a fifty-four-year-old man in the Far West Legh Freeman wrote to a historian interested in his travels.

> I was born Dec. 4, 1842, on Arlington Heights overlooking the national capital and was thoroughly imbued from childhood with the high moral standard of the founders of this government whose sons and daughters were . . . playmates and companions. . . . My father . . . was a Virginia planter of the old school.[18]

In this letter Freeman claimed his father was a cousin of "Hon. Edward A. Freeman, the famous English historian and literateur."

The image of "nature's noblemen" abruptly ends in Arthur Ryland Freeman, Legh Freeman's father, born September 22, 1806. Hardly a Virginia planter of the old school, the oldest son of John Hoomes Freeman, with cropped beard and piercing gaze, could have walked inconspicuously among the Southern gentry. But he failed completely to reflect the qualities of courtesy, pride, and bearing those struggling toward aristocracy sought to appropriate from the higher planter class. Noticeably absent was the intense affection and respect for the wife of the family. Legh Freeman could not have been oblivious to these discrepancies. That he later ignored family conflict in favor of the Cavalier legend attests to the vigor with which he sought to uphold the image of Southern tradition. These contradictions help to explain, superficially at least, his own harsh concept of parenthood and his escape into the role of the dashing Horatio Vattel, Lightning Scout of the Mountains.

Arthur Freeman's marital problems may have stemmed from financial difficulties. According to the Glass letter, his first wife, Catherine Field, had died apparently before they had children. On January 20, 1835, he took as his second wife Mary Allison Kemper, the oldest child of the eight born to William Kemper, a leading citizen of neighboring Madison County (County Clerk's Records, p. 278). She was nine years younger than the bridegroom. Four sons were born during the first five years, the start of a family of nine sons and three daughters who were born within a nineteen-year period.[19]

Arthur Freeman became bankrupt four years after his marriage, but the burdens of early parenthood were apparently not the major contributing cause. About a month before he married Mary Kemper he had borrowed money, issuing bonds as collateral, and by mid-1839 his total debt reached approximately $7,000, including $3,300 which he owed a brother, Thomas C. Freeman. A "very heavy pecuniary loss" precluded his repayment, and he entered into an agreement to forestall bankruptcy proceedings. Another brother, Edward, was formally made trustee of Freeman's affairs and a two-year debt repayment schedule was established.[20] Edward Freeman was given title to all assets, including land Arthur owned in Rappahannock County, and even personal effects:

> . . . blacksmith tools and materials on hand; also seven beds, bedsteads and furniture; two bureaus; one secretary and book case and all the residue of his household and kitchen furniture; also two bay horses, one white mare and colt, two milch cows, three heifers, seven hogs, one yoke of oxen, one ox cart, one two-horse waggon [sic], seven McCormick ploughs, all the growing crops and all and every description of property. . . .[21]

The legal arrangement allowed Arthur to continue his blacksmith shop at Edward's pleasure as well as keep the household possessions and cows and horses "and take the profits thereof." No mention is made in the agreement about the status of slaves, but within a year the family had four young female slaves, at least one of whom was a child. There is therefore no justification for a later reference to Arthur Freeman as "a farmer and the owner of many slaves as were his ancestors on both sides."[22]

Freeman may not even have been a property owner. On January 1, 1850, the Kempers deeded to James L. Kemper, Mary Freeman's brother, a "flat ground" tract of 296 acres, known as the Greenfield estate, and a second parcel of the estate totaling 77 acres adjoining their home property. James Kemper was to hold the property in trust for the sole benefit of his sister and for the "maintenance and education" of her children, who by this time numbered seven, three others having died. The brother was charged with holding the property "free from all claims, demands, control, rights, interests, liabilities, encumbrances and engagements" which might be made by Arthur Freeman. The children were to have the property divided among them in the event of their mother's death.[23] Women in Culpeper County in 1850 owned property, thus the deed to James Kemper rather than to Mary Freeman was not because of a legal prohibition but because of the Kempers' obvious desire to keep the property beyond the reach of Arthur Freeman. There was no prohibition in the Virginia Constitution of 1850 barring women from owning property apart from their husbands.

It was on this property that Legh Freeman, age seven at the time of the execution of this deed, spent several of his childhood years. The Kempers included all household and kitchen effects for their daughter's use as well as the modest field inventory of plows, hoes, harrow, rake, and wagon. The livestock holding was equally modest, including three horses, fifty-one sheep, four head of cattle, and twenty hogs. Two male slaves, ages nineteen and forty, and two females, ages ten and thirty, probably owned by the

Freemans, were used to work the property, which was valued at $4,000.[24]

Freeman descendants have called this Kemper property the family plantation, a term perhaps technically correct, but one contributing further to the myth of high standing. This description of the farm is only speculation:

> Greenfield, Legh's plantation home, grew comfortably out of the tilled land surrounding it. The house was a wide, two-storied, white building, ample to receive and house a growing brood. A broad, high-pillared veranda ran across the front of the dwelling and provided room for expansion of the family's facilities during the long, mild season of the Virginia year. . . .[25]

Legh Freeman, although emphasizing his paternal forebears throughout his life, did not neglect his maternal genealogy which indeed strengthened his claim to the social standing he sought. The Kemper home, Mountain Prospect, was near Leon on the western Culpeper County border. William Kemper was a substantial middle-class planter[26] who traced his ancestry back to the families who immigrated to Virginia in 1713–1714 from Aldenburg, Germany, and were settled by Governor Alexander Spotswood at Germanna. Kemper was an elder in the Presbytery of Culpeper and reared his children in a stern Calvinistic environment which emphasized industriousness and the importance of education.

Legh Freeman's uncle, James Lawson Kemper, was about eight years younger than his sister Mary and had completed his law studies in 1846. In conflicts with her husband it was her brother to whom she turned in her business naiveté for legal advice and frequent loans. This aid continued while he was a five-term member of the Virginia House of Delegates (1853–1862), a major general of Virginia's Civil War Reserve Forces, and the state's first postwar, native-son governor (1875–1879). He stood by his sister when, in addition to the domestic trouble with Legh's father, she faced the wrath of her own family. Upon division of the estate after William Kemper died in 1853, three of her brothers and sisters felt that she should be charged rent for the time she had been living on family property. Mrs. Kemper's defense of her daughter, whom she called a "poor creature" in a helpless situation, gives an insight into the family's circumstances:

> . . . how could any one of you reconcile yourselves to such a thing when you recollect—her eight children to *support*, and to endeavour to give them some education; and I know she *has many hard* trials. . . .[27]

Mrs. Kemper said many of the servants at Mountain Prospect had an easier time than Mary Freeman. The mother of these children did not look like a poor creature in the sense that she was wasted or emaciated. She had a ruddy complexion and a round face above which she parted her hair in the middle. Her straight-lipped countenance was perhaps due to the dental problems she suffered, and she claimed to have other health problems. She frankly coveted having a household slave because "I am getting old, my constitution [is] shattered, and I want some relief, in the decline of life."[28] She was about forty-three at this time.

Arthur Freeman, prohibited from benefiting from the income of the Greenfield property, was another of Mary's problems. She had to turn to her brother for advice about a meadow which Freeman refused to mow. In fact, he failed to do anything "towards making the place yield any profit." He gave as a reason that he had no authority to do anything, but she added, "I don't think he would if he could."[29]

Mary admitted that she had thought her brother's original assessment of Arthur Freeman unnecessarily harsh, but she said she was then strangely infatuated and "willing to hope for better things." She had come to realize the same faults in her husband,

> to my hearts [sic] own bitterness[.] I fear you will say it is no more, than I deserve, and, that I ought not to have any one's sympathy. I hope you will not divulge what I have written, so that any thing will get back, for it would only make things worse. He has furnished the family with plenty to eat and wear, since he came back, which is more than he used to do. but [sic] seems to have no idea of good management here in any way, whatever. . . .[30]

It is obvious that the Freeman family's twentieth-century assessment of Mary Freeman's home life is sheer fabrication:

> . . . she was sensitive to the usual daily crises of their lives and moved by their childhood triumphs and tragedies. A hearty and happy person, she was steadfast in her ability to help them cope with either eventuality. She moved about her duties at the core of her home with her voice lifted high in song and sang in assurance that a benevolent God was at her right hand to guide her and her family. Her firm religious spirit pervaded and sustained her home.[31]

Arthur Freeman may not have abandoned his family as Mary Freeman's reference to his return could have implied. Perhaps because he needed the salary he became a railroad depot agent at Gordonsville, thirty-five miles south of Culpeper in Orange County, and may have been employed there before his family moved. The north-south Orange & Alexandria Railroad at Gordonsville crossed the tracks of the Virginia Central Railroad, which carried Shenandoah produce eastward to Richmond. Freeman was probably employed by the Orange & Alexandria; patrician John S. Barbour, Jr., the railroad president, was a native of Culpeper County, and the family was repeatedly a benefactor to Mrs. Freeman.[32] A family account of Arthur Freeman's move into railroad employment appears to have been overly romanticized:

> Arthur Freeman . . . had succumbed to the fascination of future possibilities of the railroad era, which was then bursting forth upon the land, sending numerous fingers of transportation throughout the South of the 1850s. Arthur Freeman was manager of one of the earliest of these lines in Virginia.[33]

Mary Freeman sold the Greenfield property in order to move her family to Gordonsville, but the sale and the move only served to exacerbate the family situation. The primary point of contention came to be whether Mrs. Freeman would control her share of the proceeds from the sale or whether they would be turned over to her husband with the interest earned. Freeman threatened to resign his position as railroad agent if she did not help to support the family. He further threatened to take the children out of school, stop renting their home in order to force her to support the family out of her income, and ignore past accounts and allow no new charges. In the midst of this trouble, she received a $25 loan from her brother.

Legh Freeman was twelve years old by the time the family was established in Gordonsville, but Arthur Freeman forbade his wife to take the children and visit their grandmother, forcing Mary Freeman to contrive a plan to make the trip in secret. Her husband ultimately consented to the trip, but not before his wife had discussed details for a secret departure with "some of the best people in the place," perhaps the Barbours. Freeman's continuing obduracy drew epithets of "irresponsible" and "louse" from James Kemper.[34] The situation threatened to climax in violence. Mary Freeman urged her brother not to act rashly toward her husband and oldest son, John William, her two antagonists, and she expressed the hope that time would mellow their threats.

She also hoped that a horse cart accident in which John William, then 18, fractured his elbow would make him a better boy. She believed such afflictions were sent as punishment, but she saw the cause of her son's belligerence also due to his father, who failed to provide "good employment and training."[35]

Mary Freeman's maternal affection thus had a limit. When her brother asked whether she had prepared a will, she replied that she planned to leave her effects to her seven youngest children because "the others have acted so towards me, and still do, that unless they change, I do not desire them to handle any of it."[36]

The sum of money Mary Freeman nurtured through these family assaults led by her husband, and upon whose interest she was dependent, totaled $3,150 in 1860, invested in "state stock." Fulfilling a wish for "a home of *my own*," she used the full sum and signed a note for an additional $625 to purchase property at Maywood, near Gordonsville.[37] Reference to her own home may have indicated a desire to leave railroad quarters rather than separate from her husband. The real estate investment was probably fortunate, considering the value of Southern securities by the end of the Civil War.

Within these meager and contested financial resources, Mary Freeman found funds for her family's education, expenditures that would result in discernible influences in Legh Freeman's life. His mother lavished the Kemper concern for education on her children; Freeman and an older brother, Frederick, both related that they had attended "old field" schools of the type commonly operated in the South. In addition, Mary Freeman probably tutored her sons just as her father had established a home school on his plantation. Legh and his brother attended Kemper College in Gordonsville, operated by a cousin. Later evaluation of Freeman as a self-educated man is, therefore, not literally true. He did become a telegrapher, probably at his father's hands in the railroad office. Yet certainly an adequate academic foundation had been laid for both brothers to profit later from extensive reading. Their formal education and intellectual development would prove to be, as was their mother's and her parents', far above the average educational achievements of even middle-class antebellum Southerners.

Mary Freeman's educational concerns extended to her daughters. One of the reasons she gave for wanting to expedite the move of her family from the Kemper-owned farm to Gordonsville was because "I want the children to be going to school." At Gordonsville, she was disappointed upon an indication from her brother that certain funds would not be forthcoming for a piano. She bemoaned these prospects, saying, ". . . the teacher has left. . . . I am very uneasy because my daughters have no teacher, and the lack of means, causes the future to look dark, with respect to them, however I hope some way will be opened for them." She postponed the purchase of her own coveted home near Gordonsville "until my daughters are educated, they now have the advantage of an excellent school, and I trust in a few years, they will be competent to teach, and can do without my further assistance. . . ."[38] The "excellent school" may also have been Kemper College.

This emphasis on education marked only one of the contrasts—and tensions—between the parents in Legh Freeman's family. The truth is diametrically opposed to the conclusion that "the anchor was firm in Legh's home as he grew. It added a base of security from which he developed outward to test the feast of life which lured him."[39] Rather, Legh must have faced the emotional problem of seeing his father break the image of the Freeman family as "nature's noblemen," if in fact he did not create the myth in later life because of his father's shortcomings.

As if this complex family problem was not enough of a liability, Freeman suffered from a physical handicap. As a youth he fell from an apple tree, suffering a leg injury that made him somewhat lame for life. With financial, familial, and physical difficulties, therefore, it would not be surprising that young Freeman entertained notions about going "out West." The additional trauma of the Civil War ironically provided the means by which the fictional hero Horatio Vattel could embody the physical and heroic traits that circumstances denied the real Legh Freeman.

2

"Galvanized Yankee"

FREEMAN faced no indecision in giving his allegiance to the Confederacy. Yet in later life in the North he claimed that he left home at the age of seventeen, before his military service, because of his distaste for slavery. Such contradictions became numerous. Actually, at seventeen, as a descendant of a family that he saw as an embodiment of the Southern way of life for nearly 250 years, he could hardly fail to be moved by the strident plea his uncle, James Kemper, made in the Virginia House of Delegates early in February 1860. In remarks carried throughout the state by the *Richmond Enquirer,* Kemper predicted that

> when Virginia rings the peal to arms, among the ranks of her cavaliers, when she prepares to face an enemy bristling with the improved weapons of the day, her immemorial pride will indignantly recoil from the proposal to throw her children upon the point of danger, with means of defense which are neither inferior [n]or liable to a suspicion of inferiority. . . . She will never stain her own honor by subjecting her troops to the ignomy [*sic*] of confronting well-armed invading fanatics, with uncertain arms in their hands. Her brave volunteers she will arm to the teeth; she will arm them with the completest weapons that can be fabricated by the skill of man; with weapons to match the spirit which animates them. . . .[1]

The address was one factor in the passage of Virginia's Militia Act of March 30, 1860, which called for the formation of volunteer companies and the enlistment of all able-bodied men between the ages of eighteen and forty-five. Virginia was, therefore, significantly ahead of its sister Southern states in preparedness for the outbreak of hostilities the following year.

On April 17, 1861, less than a week after the bombardment of Fort Sumter, the Virginia delegates voted 88 to 55 to secede from the

Union. By nightfall, although Virginia had not yet formally joined the Confederacy, fourteen volunteer companies from northern Virginia communities, including Gordonsville and Culpeper, were preparing to board three northbound trains for an early morning rendezvous at Strasburg in the Shenandoah Valley.

The exact date when Legh Freeman's Civil War service began is not known, but he probably did not join one of the companies boarding the creaking wooden railroad cars that night in the glare of the wood-burning locomotives. He waited and ultimately joined a cavalry unit, perhaps because of his injured leg. He never attained a rank higher than private, but he apparently served under the renowned military figure, Brigadier General John Hunt Morgan. How he found his way into a Kentucky cavalry regiment remains unexplained, although such interstate enlistments were not uncommon during the war; three of Morgan's companies were composed of Virginia infantry veterans whose enlistments had been completed. Divided Kentucky may have recruited beyond its own borders; General Braxton Bragg in 1862 decried the failure of Kentuckians to join the Confederate army, a problem, however, that the popular Morgan did not encounter.[2]

Freeman was a private in Company I of the Kentucky Cavalry's Third Regiment.[3] The unit was apparently Captain R. M. Gano's regiment in General Morgan's First Brigade, formed in 1862. But Freeman was a telegrapher rather than a dashing Cavalier cavalryman. At least one of his assignments was to learn of Union battle plans by tapping Northern military telegraph communications. In turn he transmitted false Confederate plans to confuse enemy forces. Such an assignment was similar to that carried out by the famed George (Lightning) Ellsworth, who became a legendary figure in the South for his telegraphic service for General Morgan. Freeman probably did not work personally with Ellsworth because, in publishing a news story in 1879 about Ellsworth and Jesse James being accused of a plot to capture Jay Gould for ransom, he made no personal reference to Ellsworth. He was never hesitant to tell about his associations with well-known persons or incidents.[4]

Freeman apparently came under Morgan's command following the general's famed raid into Ohio in the summer of 1863. Following that ill-fated raid, Morgan's forces regrouped at Morristown, Tennessee, in August 1863 to organize a cavalry regiment. Freeman may have participated in this reorganization, if not as one of the escapees and stragglers from the Ohio incursion, then possibly as one of 300 men who had not gone on the raid because of illness or other causes. This new unit fought on September 19, 1863, at Chickamauga and on November 23 in the Confederate defeat at Missionary Ridge. Freeman could also have enlisted during another reorganization that followed these battles and General Morgan's escape on November 27, 1863, from the Ohio State Penitentiary at Columbus.

Morgan, in the spring of 1864, was in charge of the Department of Southwestern Virginia, with headquarters at Abingdon, Virginia. The general sent scouts, apparently including Freeman, into Kentucky to obtain information about Union forces and the availability of cavalry mounts. Whatever his original regimental designation, Freeman, because of his telegraphic talent, could have been among Captain Tom Quirk's scouts on this and other assignments from Morgan.

Freeman was captured on May 7, 1864, by Union forces in Floyd County in the Appalachian country of eastern Kentucky. He was north of Pound Gap, through which the general moved out of Virginia on May 31, on Morgan's last Kentucky raid.[5] Following his capture, Freeman was apparently held at Louisa, Kentucky, on the West Virginia border. Perhaps because of news of Morgan's raid, Freeman was sent west to Lexington and then, on June 6, to the military holding prison at Louisville. Finally, on June 7, he was sent on the 375-mile trip to the Rock Island military prison in the Mississippi River between Davenport, Iowa, and Rock Island, Illinois, where he arrived on June 9.

The "bull pen," as the prisoners called the twelve-acre stockade on the north bank of the three-mile island, hardly looked to Freeman like the gateway to freedom it would become. He was among the 1,660 Confederate soldiers sent to Rock Island during that month, a number perhaps swelled by some of the 7,000 troops captured in May during the battle of the Wilderness. The prison population in June would thus reach its maximum concentration of 8,607 men, living in eighty-four identical barracks, each capable of housing 120 soldiers.[6]

While the prison could not be described as the harshest of the Civil War, Freeman found that stockade conditions did spawn illness and death. During the summer months of 1864, 287 prisoners died, a decrease from the toll of 860 during the first three months of the year. Although he did not contract smallpox as did some of the prisoners, Freeman was ill during at least some of his confinement and was treated, probably for some kind of fever. In later life he remained impressed by the medical ministrations of the women of the nearby communities and he credited them with aiding his recovery. This considerate attention may have been a factor in his return to the Rock Island community for a brief period of residence some years later.

While the concentration of prisoners was a problem to captor and captive alike, there were those who saw in the island's idle manpower an answer to one of the North's pressing problems. President Lincoln in 1864 sought recruits from among the Confederates at Rock Island to man forts in the West and he removed a previous restriction limiting such volunteers to persons of foreign and Northern birth.

When the Rock Island commander, Colonel A. J. Johnson, announced the president's plan, Legh Freeman faced a decision of myriad consequences. Volunteering would carry him hundreds of miles farther away from Virginia and his family, which could well utilize his services in recovering from the effects of the war. If he accepted a blue uniform he would be labeled a traitor by loyal Confederate prisoners, who had in fact organized a theoretical cavalry regiment of ten companies from among 1,300 veterans within the confines of Rock Island.[7]

Offsetting these disadvantages, Freeman could see evident advantages in the president's offer. In accepting, he would find camaraderie among hundreds in Rock Island disillusioned with the lack of major Confederate campaign successes during the summer fighting season. Volunteering could mean death at the hands of Indian hostiles, yet remaining in prison—exposed to various sicknesses—seemed to offer the greater possibility of death.

More general factors no doubt entered into his decision. One must have been the simple lure of freedom. Or, as the son of a railroad man, he may have wanted to be in the proximity of the fabled Pacific railroad. Groundbreaking ceremonies had been held at Omaha and grading and surveys were then under way. Perhaps of great influence in his decision was the West itself, where it would be possible to live out the fantasies of childhood. But above all else, Legh Freeman had a strong opportunistic streak in him, as many of his actions in the West would reveal; this was a chance for personal advantage that he could not refuse.

The transaction in which Freeman became one of the freed "galvanized Yankees" was formalized on October 27, 1864, when he raised his right hand and took the oath pledging support not only to the Constitution but congressional and presidential proclamations regarding slavery as well. Thus he must have been among the 1,797 recruits who were separated from the other prisoners by a high board fence and crowded into sixteen small barracks in an area known as the "calf pen." Three months went by and it was early February 1865 when the Union coordinated details to implement its plan.[8]

The volunteers were then divided into two regiments, the Second Regiment, United States Volunteers, which was sent to Fort Riley, Kansas, via Fort Leavenworth, and the Third Regiment, United States Volunteers, to which Freeman was apparently assigned. Freeman's group left Fort Leavenworth on March 11 for Fort Kearny, Nebraska, where troops were needed on the Oregon Trail stage line west of the fort. This was the "bloody year" on the Plains;[9] the Civil War had not sufficiently reduced overland traffic to make military protection less essential. In six weeks during the spring of 1865, a count showed that no fewer than 6,000 wagons, each loaded with from one to four tons of freight, passed Fort Kearny, 900 in the last three days of the count alone. Many wagons were laden with supplies for Forts Laramie and Bridger, while others were en route to Salt Lake City merchants.[10]

The Third Regiment did not sight Fort Kearny until April 9, the day fellow Southerners were forfeiting their arms at Appomattox.

News of the surrender reached the regiment's 800 troops that day; Freeman, as a telegrapher, undoubtedly noticed that a telegraph line had been threaded among the cottonwood trees and adobe and wooden buildings at the fort. In fact he found the telegraph office in the southwest area of the fort to be one of the most active places at the post. It was here that the news dispatches between San Francisco and New York newspapers were tapped, tying the isolated fort to population centers.[11]

Sometime after his arrival—it is not clear when—Freeman became the Fort Kearny telegraph operator. Neither is it clear whether he was initially a civilian operator or under military command. Yet at one time he was paid $150 a month to attend to the business of the Overland Telegraph, which was "considerable" at the fort because of the military dispatches. Freighters rendezvoused at the fort before heading west into Indian territory, and they, too, received orders from their employers by telegraph, directing them to the desired market. One of these employers was Edward Creighton, who in 1861 in partnership with Brigham Young had constructed the telegraph line along the Pony Express route. As general manager of Overland Telegraph, operating from Omaha, he was also Freeman's employer.[12]

One of Freeman's new associates was the fort's postmaster, Moses H. Sydenham, who had a book and stationery store in the telegraph office. To Sydenham, a native of England and at age 27 only four years older than Freeman, the new telegrapher appeared a "red-hot, unreconstructed 'secessionist' fresh from the southland."[13] Despite the loyalty oath, Freeman's galvanized Yankee veneer was not very thick.

Freeman and Sydenham must have had many lengthy conversations. Just as Freeman could tell of the circumstances that had taken him to this post, Sydenham could recount how, in conjunction with his position as postmaster, he had begun the *Fort Kearney Herald* in June 1862. He had obtained a large-sized Lowe handpress from Boston and other material from George P. Rowells of Chicago. Sydenham later reminisced about his printing venture:

> Of course the paper was published more to advertise the good qualities and most favorable features of what was then known as the "Great American Desert" than for anything else, and the expense came out of my earnings. . . . There were no settlers from whom to receive subscriptions and no businessmen to help with their advertisements. . . . At the head of my editorial column I had the picture of an aboriginal Indian on the war path, waving his long spear. . . . Beneath the Indian I had the words "Passing away." This picture was permanent for every issue.[14]

Sydenham had published the *Herald* for only about six months before selling it to Seth P. Mobley, a soldier in the Seventh Iowa Cavalry, and a man named Brundage, who was at the same time the

Fort Kearny telegraph operator. This may have been the Hiram Brundage who is given credit for setting up the first press in Wyoming to begin publication of the *Daily Telegraph* at Fort Bridger in June 1863.[15] Mobley did a considerable amount of printing for military officials and Brundage utilized telegraphic news for the columns of their weekly newspaper before they abandoned the enterprise.

Freeman saw the idle printing equipment and considered a similar printing venture. An alternative open to him was to return to Virginia with the Confederate volunteers being released from service with the end of the war. His decision loomed potentially as consequential, and perhaps as difficult, as the one he had made the previous year (1864) at Rock Island.[16]

He knew that if he returned to Virginia, even with the stigma of a former galvanized Yankee, he could undoubtedly be of aid to his family in overcoming the aftereffects of the war. Family letters, rumors, and newspaper accounts must have verified the physical, economic, and social ruin of Virginia, a condition depicted by Walt Whitman, who found the Culpeper countryside "dilapidated, fenceless, and trodden with war."[17] The observation was not exaggerated; Freeman's grandmother, Maria Kemper, the former mistress of the Mountain Prospect estate, described living conditions in the aftermath of the war:

> . . . we are reduced so low that we have to think of something *to live on.* We have been selling milk for a long time—and made out to live from *hand to mouth,* but now we get very little milk—sometimes we can sell a little; our provision is now very low—there is meat enough in the house to last perhaps three days, a part of a barrel of flour and some meal . . . my wardrobe is very low, since I've been living here [four years at Culpeper] I have bought three calico dresses—and very little else. . . .[18]

The ruin of the Orange & Alexandria Railroad route between Culpeper and Gordonsville resulted from the three major fighting seasons of the war. Generals John Pope, Thomas J. (Stonewall) Jackson, Robert E. Lee, Ulysses S. Grant, and George G. Meade alternately camped with their armies at Culpeper. Their campaigns had left Freeman's grandmother, an aunt, and her family in the fall of 1865 with only $30 and produce for trading for several months' subsistence.[19] The sum was a sharp contrast to the wealth envisioned by the veterans at Fort Kearny who repeated tales told along the Oregon Trail about the recent gold discoveries in Montana and elsewhere in the West. They awaited the bonanza that construction of the Pacific railroad would carry to them when it was due to reach Fort Kearny within a matter of months. Rolling from their tongues were magic names like Oregon and San Francisco, where other easterners bereft of resources had prospered as homesteading farmers and fledgling entrepreneurs.

The decision facing Freeman, therefore, was simplified. With justification he could rationalize that he could indeed aid his family more substantially with $150 a month amidst the resources of the West than in the waste of the Southern economy. Now that he found himself on the edge of the country's true frontier, it was difficult to retreat from the reveries of childhood and the more tangible opportunities lying in the West. By the time the Third United States Volunteers became civilians again at Fort Leavenworth on November 29, 1865, Freeman had irrevocably turned his back on the South, geographically if not philosophically.

The "Press on Wheels"

FREEMAN became the editor and publisher of the *Kearney Herald* in December 1865. In the fluid social state existing at the frontier outpost, Freeman, at age 23 and with no experience in printing, was drawn into his lifelong work.

Obviously using his telegrapher's salary to acquire the idle printing equipment at the fort, Freeman set out to establish an operable printing plant. He later wrote about how he collected pied type and whittled wooden letters with a jackknife where letters were missing from the type case. Printers were "detailed" from the ranks of the army, and the printer's devil was a drummer boy. The imposing stone was a two-inch oak plank obtained from the Quartermaster Department and the ink stone was donated by the government painter, who had used it in grinding and mixing paints. Freeman received official military sanction for use of government quarters.

Freeman set an annual subscription price of $6 for the four-page, semiweekly newspaper and a six-month rate of $4. He arranged the type in two columns on 9-by-14-inch pages. Sharing prominent space with the newspaper's name at the top of the first page was the motto: "Independence in All things, Neutrality in Nothing." Although it may have been an appropriate creed for a Confederate veteran and ex-galvanized Yankee, it did not originate with him. The same words had been incorporated as part of the masthead of the *Huntsman's Echo,* which had been published in 1860 and 1861 by Joseph Ellis Johnson at Wood River Center, Nebraska Territory, a Mormon community twenty-six miles from the fort.[1] Johnson then apparently took his printing equipment to Utah, where he published other newspapers, but copies of the *Echo* and its motto may have found their way to the fort and served as an inspiration to Freeman.

The first issue of the *Kearney Herald* circulated beyond the confines of the fort. The *Nebraska Republican,* published at Omaha by E.

B. Taylor, superintendent of Indian affairs for Nebraska, reported that its staff had seen the issue "published at Fort Kearney by Mr. Leigh R. Freeman, gentlemanly telegraph operator at that post."[2] The spelling variation of Freeman's first name was apparently copied correctly from the *Kearney Herald* itself. Throughout Freeman's writing are examples of typographical errors committed by typesetters, nineteenth-century spelling variations, words misspelled for effect, and errors in punctuation. Many of the latter were undoubtedly due to the difficulty typesetters had in distinguishing between single and double quotation marks, for example, on typefaces. Edward Creighton, Overland Telegraph general manager, had given Freeman permission to use telegraphic press dispatches free of charge. The front page carried dispatches from Sacramento, Washington, and New York, and the editor promoted this news:

> Persons wishing to obtain the earliest telegraphic accounts of the proceedings of the U.S. Congress, the Legislature of Nebraska, the progress of the Mexican and Chilian [sic] wars, and other excitable news, should subscribe at once to the Kearney Herald, which will furnish all items of importance at least two days in advance of any other means of intelligence.[3]

Freeman attended to the role of publisher as well as editor. In the same column that sought subscribers, he reminded the outfitters of Missouri River cities that they would find it "greatly to their interest" to advertise in the *Herald* "as all the freighters and passengers buy it."[4] To attract these customers, Freeman placed copies of the newspaper on sale at the telegraph and stage offices; the cedar log buildings, owned by Ben Holladay, several hundred feet west of the fort also housed an eating station, storehouse, barn, and stables. Freeman thus hoped to tap the resources of the stage men, passengers, wagon masters, and soldiers. He also distributed copies to the fort post office, and, two miles west of the fort, to the post office at Kearny City, a collection of mud huts and hovels better known as "Adobe Town" or "Dobytown." Begrimed travelers there, however, probably remained more interested in its whiskey than its reading matter; the town was inhabited by only six families but boasted fourteen saloons.

In contrast to the company, male and female, congregating beyond the military reservation were the ladies of the garrison itself. Freeman devoted a news item in his second issue to an afternoon ride some of the wives, escorted by officers, took beyond the fort. Protection was needed not because of Indians, but because of "a pack of prairie wolves and one timber wolf." The conclusion was a little anticlimactic: "The wolves were not hurt, however, and the wolves hurt nobody."[5]

If the fledging editor saw such insignificant incidents as being worthy of news space, he was also able to recognize legitimate news. When Jim Bridger checked into the Overland House at Kearny City,

Freeman was on hand to interview the aging fellow Virginian. Since he had become a minor celebrity in the East with publication of Washington Irving's *The Rocky Mountains* in 1837, Bridger had frequently been the subject of such attention. But at Fort Kearny he was unaware that he was being labeled a "hero" and scrutinized by Freeman as the virtual prototype of Horatio Vattel:

> He is perhaps sixty years old, fully six feet high, raw boned, blue eyes, auburn hair (now somewhat gray)[,] is very active and communicative. He has guided numerous military expeditions against the Indians and of these together with his own independent forays, he relates many interesting and thrilling incidents. . . .[6]

Bridger told Freeman that he was en route to Washington, D.C., "to tell the authorities how to manage the Indians." Hunting the savages with mounted men and wagon trains was "simply absurd," he related, because this strategy resulted only in heavy loss of animals and unnecessary exposure of troops compelled to return for rations or to halt for their supply train to overtake them. His solution was to follow the Indians on foot, week after week, overtaking and surprising their villages. Yet he admitted that an impending campaign against the Sioux by the 18th United States Infantry was being "planned more sensibly than any before fitted up in this country."[7]

This last comment would prove to be of interest not only to Freeman but also to the army. General Grenville Dodge urged Bridger to remain in the West, and on January 26, 1866, he was hired as chief guide for the spring campaign. Colonel Henry B. Carrington had assumed command of Fort Kearny and the 18th Infantry in the initial step of the federal government's attempt under mounting pressure to open the Bozeman Trail, sometimes called Powder River Road. Beginning at Fort Kearny, this road went northwesterly via Fort Laramie to the Montana mining communities of Virginia City, Bozeman, and Helena as an alternative to the longer South Pass and Mullan Road routes.

As telegrapher and newspaper editor, Freeman was at the center of activity as Colonel Carrington organized a force of 2,000 men and arranged for supplies for Bozeman Trail and Platte River duties. Civilian orders competed with the military's on the telegraph wires as surveying and grading parties prepared for the approaching Union Pacific Railroad tracks. As the weather warmed in the spring of 1866, freight and household wagon trains passed the fort in increasing numbers.

That the pace of activity was merely transient in nature, however, did not escape Freeman's attention. Within months the troops would largely vacate the fort. By the end of the construction season the rails would extend beyond the outpost and a new site would duplicate the activity of the Kearny town site and fort. Considering the major decisions he had made at Rock Island and then at Fort Kearny at the end of the war, Freeman's decision now to continue westward seems almost routine, but not without attending complexities. True, his continued proximity to the railroad and telegraph line would ensure him a steady income as a telegrapher. A completed rail route to the East would generate advertising and subscription revenue. But Freeman was also attracted by the Montana goldfields, as his later activities prove.

Perhaps a less apparent factor contributed to Freeman's decision to move beyond Fort Kearny. The young man who had grown up poring over pictures of Indians learned that Oglala Sioux leader Red Cloud had arrived at Fort Laramie on March 12, 1866. Red Cloud agreed to attend a peace conference which the government hoped would end in a treaty guaranteeing safe passage on the Bozeman Trail. A similar treaty had already been signed on the Missouri River in October 1865 with the Teton Sioux, but Red Cloud and his Sioux hostiles were at that time celebrating victories on the Powder River.

Freeman decided to attend the Fort Laramie treaty conference and to continue on to the Powder River country. He wrote to his brother, Frederick, asking that he go to Fort Kearny to assume publication of the newspaper, an apparent indication of the *Herald's* revenue potential. After Frederick's arrival, the two brothers were invited to a banquet for Major General William Tecumseh Sherman, who had arrived at Fort Kearny on May 16, 1866, to discuss the construction of forts to guard the Bozeman Trail. He was carrying out dictates inherent in the creation in April of the Department of the Platte with headquarters at Omaha, which was to afford "the best possible protection to . . . the region of Montana, and the routes thereto."[8] Colonel Carrington was placed in command of a newly created Mountain District.

At the banquet, General Sherman was asked to tell of his march to the sea. He related that when he heard through his scouts that Confederate President Jefferson Davis had removed General Joseph E. Johnston from command of the Confederate army, he "felt like jumping up and knocking his heels together three times" because Johnston was the only general whom he feared in the Confederacy. At this remark Frederick Freeman, who had served in the Signal Corps of Johnston's army, may have felt like jumping up among the banquet guests for a few additional comments, but Sherman never learned that two young ex-Rebels were among his listeners that night.[9]

Probably because he had no official connection with either the fort or the Overland Telegraph, Frederick Freeman moved the press to Kearny City. It was too early to call it the "Press on Wheels," but the newspaper soon earned this title as new publication sites multiplied (Table 3.1). The description referred to the newspaper's unusual mobility, not to any literal existence on wheels, such as publication in a railroad boxcar, as is commonly believed. Legh Freeman later attributed this initial relocation to an attempt by the military to muzzle the newspaper, an action which, he said, had resulted in the brothers' verbal bombardment of the fort.[10] If he did not confuse the incidents, this action was similar to the banishment of the *Frontier Index* in 1868 at Fort Sanders, Wyoming.

TABLE 3.1
ROUTE OF THE "PRESS ON WHEELS," 1865–1868

Publishing Site	Approximate Dates of Publication	Publisher
Fort Kearny, Nebraska Territory	December 1865–May 1866	Legh Freeman
Kearny, Nebraska Territory	May 1866–Fall 1866	F. K. Freeman
North Platte, Nebraska Territory	Fall 1866–July 1867	F. K. Freeman
Julesburg, Colorado Territory	July 1867–March 1868	F. K. Freeman
Fort Sanders, Dakota Territory	March 6, 1868–March 24, 1868	F. K. Freeman
Laramie City, Dakota Territory	April 21, 1868–July 7, 1868	F. K. Freeman
	July 7, 1868–July 21, 1868	Legh Freeman
Benton, Dakota Territory	August 1868–September 1868 ("Branch office")	?
Green River City, Dakota Territory	August 11, 1868–August 21, 1868	Legh Freeman
Green River City, Wyoming Territory	August 25, 1868–October 13, 1868	Legh Freeman
Bear River City, Wyoming Territory	October 30, 1868–November 17, 1868	Legh Freeman

NOTE: Following completion of the Union Pacific Railroad, Freeman's newspapers were still known as the "Press on Wheels," but the moves were less frequent. He published the *Ogden Freeman* in Utah Territory from 1875–1879; several newspapers in the vicinity of Butte, Montana Territory, 1879–1884; the *Frontier Index* at Thompson Falls, Montana Territory, 1884; and the *Washington Farmer* and other farm publications at Yakima City and North Yakima, Washington Territory, 1884–1889, at Anacortes, Washington Territory, 1889–1894, and again at North Yakima, 1894–1915.

Although civilians were included, Legh Freeman apparently did not ride from Fort Kearny with Colonel Carrington on May 19, 1866, in the long-planned expedition to the Bozeman Trail. Accompanying the column were wives and children, a factor in the unit's designation as "Carrington's Overland Circus."[11] The colonel's route led first to Fort Sedgwick (near Julesburg, Colorado), where 1,300 of his command relieved volunteers guarding mail roads and telegraph lines on the Oregon Trail. (The *Frontier Index* claimed that Julesburg was in Nebraska Territory although the three Julesburg town sites were all in Colorado.) Jim Bridger served as guide for the remaining 700 troops en route to Montana.

Freeman probably left Fort Kearny four days later. His stated objective was to report the Fort Laramie treaty conference for the *Kearney Herald,* yet he seems to have traveled with his two wagons that he would later use, probably for trading, in the country beyond Fort Laramie. The conference opened on June 5, and although he undoubtedly was still en route on that date, he completed the 351-mile trip while several thousand Indians were still encamped in the narrow valley at the fort. As the conference progressed, Freeman observed the buffalo dance, green corn dance, sun dance, and scalp dance performed by the Indians.

On one occasion Freeman went with government commissioners on a deer hunt on the Sabile and Chugwater creeks. When he went out alone from the camp and did not return by midnight, the consensus of the group was that he had fallen prey to hostile Indians. Thus convinced, Lieutenant John B. Furay wrote Freeman's epitaph:

> Here lie the remains of Legh R. Freeman.
> He lived and died a printer's demon.
> Stranger, tread lightly on this sod,
> For if he gapes you're gone, be [sic] g--d![12]

While Freeman saw multitudes of Indians at the fort, he did not encounter hostiles on the hunting trip, nor did he apparently ever see Red Cloud. According to a letter written by E. B. Taylor, Nebraska Indian affairs superintendent and one of the peace commissioners, Red Cloud left the post on June 8 before Colonel Carrington, and probably before Freeman, arrived.[13] The colonel and his troops continued northward on their mission on June 17. Fort Phil Kearny was established by July 15 near present-day Sheridan, Wyoming; between July 26 and December 21, when the Fetterman massacre occurred near that fort, Indians appeared there fifty-one times. They attacked nearly every person and wagon train attempting to use the road, yet emigrants and freighters were permitted by the military to go into the country without any warning that Red Cloud had refused to compromise.

Despite the critical situation, Freeman decided to move for the first time beyond the protection of the military. It was in Indian-controlled country that Horatio Vattel came alive, although his journalistic byline was yet to appear. In two years, Freeman had moved from the ranks of the Confederate army through a military prison and a publishing experience onto the Indian frontier—a chronological achievement he had not even imagined in childhood.

Freeman remembered in 1899 that with companions whom he did not identify he took three trained hunting horses and two 4-horse wagons of supplies, at least some of which were apparently intended for sale, on a mission ostensibly to explore the Yellowstone country, which he had heard described by Bridger and his partner, Lu Anderson. His activities reflected a blend of Horatio Vattel the adventurer and Freeman the profit-seeking war veteran, but the later account of these exploits published under Freeman's byline sounds more like the yarn-spinning Vattel.[14]

In the summer of 1866, twenty miles below present-day Livingston, Montana, he built a "fort" on the Yellowstone River in the shape of a cross so that cross fire could be aimed on assailants from any direction. A tunnel was run from the fort to the river, where a boat was kept for escape. When Indians did lay siege to the structure and drove off his horses, Freeman escaped into the boat, glided onto the river, and crossed overland to the "half-breed hamlet of Bozeman." There he bought oxen and began to drive them back to the river.

The second morning out from Bozeman, Freeman recalled, he met the wagon train of Hugh Kirkendall, containing household goods and merchandise for Montana. The train, from Fort Scott, Kansas, had survived an attack near Fort Phil Kearny and now had been joined by Jim Bridger and John Bozeman. They told Freeman that he could not reach his fort driving cattle afoot, inasmuch as war parties roamed throughout the country. He proceeded, nevertheless, and on the slope of Hunter's Hot Springs a mounted war party encircled him. As he told it, he got between two oxen that were yoked together, seized the ring in the yoke with one hand, and with the other prodded the cattle with his rifle, goading them into a gallop. After a running fight of several miles, one ox fell, pierced by arrows. Freeman killed the other with his pistol and, lying between them, slaked his thirst with their warm blood. As in the stereotyped tales of the West, a party of immigrants heard the shots and "came to the rescue."

When Freeman returned to the Yellowstone River, he found his fort in ashes. The companions he had left there to guard it had become alarmed and moved on. Later Freeman asked a Crow what the Indians thought of the white man who had built the fort, and the Crow replied:

> We think you were raised among the Indians, because you mount your horse on the right side, and because you practice Indian tactics. The hostiles say they have always been foiled in their efforts to take you, and they wonder where you got the red mare that runs like the wind. Their name for you is "Big Jaw," because you talk all the time.[15]

Freeman wrote as well as talked. He sent his brother accounts of "Yellowstone Hell" in 1866 and 1867 and provided the editor of the *Virginia City Democrat* in Montana with similar stories. He termed these reports the world's first published accounts of what is today the national park.[16] His were certainly among the first. Until Freeman's time, those who had stood in awe of the "Yellowstone Hell" were illiterate trappers such as Bridger, whose oral accounts were taken as tall tales, or others who were too intent on finding gold to record the natural phenomena they encountered. For example, a forty-two man prospecting party went through Lower Geyser Basin in 1863 but apparently failed to see any significance in the hot springs its members viewed.[17]

Freeman's claim of being the early writer of Yellowstone lore appears verified by an account published by an Omaha newspaper. It tells of "L. R. Freeman" (undoubtedly Legh), who in the summer of 1866 interviewed a party that was probably the first, aside from early trappers, to see the geysers of the upper Yellowstone basin.[18] This account preceded Lieutenant Gustavus A. Doane's 1870 Yellowstone exploration and subsequent report to the United States War Department, which, as the first official account, caused a sensation in the eastern states. Although earlier, Freeman's stories did not have the scientific scope nor the eastern circulation of the Doane party's.[19]

Freeman spent the winter of 1866–1867 on the Yellowstone and was camped there in April 1867 when John Bozeman and his companion, Tom Coover, passed him on their way to Fort C. F. Smith, on the Bighorn. On April 20 five Indians appeared at Bozeman's camp and killed him. Coover escaped and, according to Freeman's later account, made it back to Freeman's camp that night. Coover reported, however, that after leaving Bozeman dead, he came upon "McKenzie and Reshaw's camp,"[20] the names, perhaps, of Freeman's companions.

Following the incident, Freeman and his four companions proceeded to the Upper Yellowstone, but a band of seemingly friendly Crows, unsuccessful in drawing them into ambush, escaped with their horses and supplies. The men had nothing to eat for three and a half days except a curlew and one biscuit apiece. Coming upon a wolf hunter's abandoned camp, they boiled the strychnine out of poisoned elk and ate the meat. They went on to Bear Creek, near Mammoth Hot Springs, where they found placer gold. Indians attacked again while some of the partners were washing gold nuggets and burned the group's wikiup of green fir boughs. It was not until later that the whites found a Crow camp where they procured provisions and horses. This incident formed the basis for at least one tale of frontier humor that Freeman soon published.

Although Freeman did report certain activities, his purpose in the Yellowstone country appears not to have been primarily journalistic. He wrote of the Indian attacks he survived, but he cannot realistically be included among the correspondents of the Indian campaigns who attached themselves to military units to continue war reporting techniques perfected during the Civil War.[21] But Freeman's adventures prove the inaccuracy of the portrayal in twentieth-century fiction and film of the effeminate quill pusher in eastern clothes. His was more the swaggering, masculine writer's role exemplified by Mark Twain.

Freeman continued in the Yellowstone country through much of 1867. He later wrote that his activities included owning a "ranche" in the Gallatin Valley, another in Wyoming on the Yellowstone, and a half interest in a sawmill below the great falls of the Yellowstone. On five creeks of the river he "mined and sold goods to the miners."[22] Freeman, therefore, appears to have been in turn or concurrently a writer, miner, land speculator, incipient stockman, and, in the sawmill venture, exploiter of the timberlands.

In his endeavors Freeman was apparently moderately successful; his decision to start rebuilding his family's resources in the West had proved wise. His mother told her brother, James Kemper, late in 1868:

> . . . two years after the war or about that time Mr. [Arthur] Freeman was thrown out of his place on the rail road, he had no means of making a support for his family, he had not a horse or mule . . . during the two years, Legh sent to us, as much as $700. Fred, also sent a good deal, both have been sending ever since, occasionally as much as $25, $50, [$]75 and $100. $150 once. I do not know how on earth we would have made out, if it had not been for what they have done, and are still doing for us. . . . struggling so hard to maintain, this *helpless, dependent family.* . . .[23]

Frederick Freeman achieved political success, too, through the newspaper he edited at several sites pending his brother's return. He proved able to earn community acceptance, a task Legh Freeman always found difficult. In the relatively short period of two and one-half years on the railroad frontier, Frederick was a publisher, politician, hotel keeper, and urban land speculator.

Opportunity for political activity arose immediately for Frederick. On June 2, 1866, two days after Legh had left for Fort Laramie, Nebraska voted on a state constitution and state officers, and the *Kearney Herald* shortly became the county Democratic organ. Despite a county Republican majority at least partially provided by Iowa soldiers at Fort Kearny, Frederick was elected to the Nebraska Territorial Council in 1866, defeating George Francis Train. (William F. Schmidt, in a letter to the author, wrote: "I am certain that Mr. Frederick Kemper Freeman's brag about being elected will have to stand. We have . . . failed to find any returns pertaining to him. . . .")[24] Yet he did not remain long at Kearny. The Union Pacific tracks were laid past the adobe huts in late summer 1866. It became obvious the opportunity would lie at the winter terminus of the railroad, North Platte, and not at the bypassed town. An estimated 4,000 people rushed to the new site for the winter's revelry, taking their makeshift buildings with them by rail.

Frederick Freeman replaced the old roller press with a new Washington handpress; for the 100-mile trip to North Platte he loaded the equipment on three ox-drawn wagons driven by Mexicans. The caravan was held up at Plum Creek, but the would-be robbers left in disgust upon finding that the freight was only a printing outfit.

It was on this move that the newspaper, renamed the *Frontier Index*, earned the permanent sobriquet of the "Press on Wheels," a designation that would be accurate well into the twentieth century. Likewise, its new home, North Platte, would be known as the Union Pacific's first "Hell on Wheels" because of its wild character.[25]

There were advantages in such an untamed setting. The newspaper was rushed with advertising and job printing orders, getting from $10 to $20 for striking off 100 words in small circulars or posters. The price per line in local advertising columns was 25 cents on the inside of the paper. No one haggled over prices. Despite the transient nature of the community, business lots sold for $2,000 to $3,000 apiece, a rate that motivated the Freeman brothers to add real estate speculation to their later ventures.

The brothers' financial activities were of some success and provided relief for their dependents in Virginia. The newspaper's revenue probably did allow for such support. The forty-five extant issues show that of the 1,076 columns printed, 728.5 were taken up by advertising, a 67.7:32.2 advertising-editorial ratio.[26] But Legh Freeman was better known in the West for his humorous frontier literature than for any financial achievement. This was Horatio Vattel's more constructive contribution to American journalism.

4

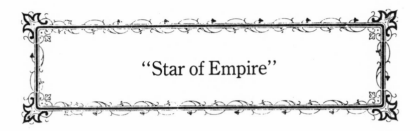

"Star of Empire"

"GENERAL HORATIO VATTEL" was a name better known in the West than Legh Freeman. A còrrespondent for the *Omaha Republican* sought out for an interview

> that great western genius whose genuine witticisms, peculiarly expressed prophesies, sensible profundities and wise sayings generally, are so extensively copied and quoted throughout this western country and California.[1]

As Legh Freeman traveled southward in 1867, from the Yellowstone to Arizona and then to California and Nevada before returning to the newspaper in Wyoming in 1868, he wrote constantly. Each story was dispatched to his brother. As the Omaha correspondent recognized, readers of the *Frontier Index* looked forward to a mixture of Vattel's tall tales, anecdotes, humorous essays, and travel narratives in columns adjacent to conventional news that Frederick Freeman penned of the army's Indian campaigns, railroad construction, stage line schedules, weather, illnesses, and booming towns. Legh Freeman's writing demonstrates that spellbound since childhood by the stereotyped West of Indians and adventure, he now sought to further this stereotype. He knew what pleased his western readers, so he catered to their literary tastes and traditions and then characteristically reveled in the notoriety he earned.

The dual nature of Legh Freeman and Freeman-as-Vattel appears to have overcome in writing, 100 years before it was articulated, one problem that critics of frontier literature have always faced in seeking the meaning of the "western experience": whether this experience may better be understood as "factual anecdotal history" or as a "metaphorical parable" of that history. Freeman wrote as the factual frontier journalist. Freeman-as-Vattel, "Lightning Scout of the Mountains," wrote of a West larger and more heroic than life.[2] Freeman was thus

31

one of those who unconsciously recognized the necessity of reflecting the West through mixed levels of expression long before Bernard DeVoto wrote, "The novelist can have the Old West myth or the historical West . . . but not both at the same time." DeVoto also commented that if the eastern dude wanted to romanticize the West, then this "sanctions the Westerner to act out his dramatic fantasy artfully . . . with the heady knowledge that he is getting away with it."[3]

Many examples of Freeman's frontier humor were lost or destroyed. Yet the surviving samples are probably representative of his work. The foundation of his reputation lay in the Yellowstone country, which by its nature prompted tall tales. The earliest of these remaining today was displayed on the front page of the *Frontier Index* early in 1868.

A TALL TALE OF LEGH R. FREEMAN

The Greatest Bear Story yet. . . . I observed a short distance from me a number of long legged Jack Rabbits, amusing themselves by jumping across a hole that we had dug some days before to build a fire in, that the coals might not blow away. To have some pastime I placed myself in the hole; scraped leaves over my body, and soon captured a leaping rabbit; into the breast of this I inserted a stick so as to hold him above the level of the hole, and his comrades, having returned, commenced jumping over his back. Presently my rabbit disappeared, as a large object darkened the sun, and looking to my left I saw a Rocky Mountain Grizzly, not eating, but fondling with the rabbit, and alternately he would lay it down, cross and flap his paws, gazing intently at me, and presently he seemed determined to find out what manner of varmint [*sic*] I was, when suddenly he swallowed the rabbit whole, (I believe he could have swallowed an elephant as easily,) thrust one paw under me and threw me about a mile to one side, where I lay insensible some time, and upon consciousness returning, I felt that I had been brought about by the monster blowing a current of reviving breath upon me sufficiently strong to have turned a wind-mill for a Union Pacific Railroad water station. I moved slightly, and bruin ran behind a butte, which, however, was not large enough to hide both his extremities at once, so his head peeped around the opposite side, then he turned and peeped around the other side. After repeating that maneuver several times, and gradually prolonging the periods of time between his peeps to five minutes, I jumped up and ran for a quaking asp grove, and just as I climbed a tree, I saw the old fellow peep, then cunningly drew back his head and peeped quickly from the same side. Then satisfied that I was really gone, he sprang to where I had lain and, scenting around, discovered my trail and bounded to the tree that I was up. He gnawed, the tree reeled, tottered, and I directed its falling course to another tree, to which I clung until it to[o] was cut down and lodged on another. The bear kept up this cutting until he had cleared away about eight acres of thick timber, when the last tree lodged against one that was petrified, and he even tried his teeth on it, but thinking they had become dull, he went to a cliff near by and whetted them on its side. "Well," says I to myself, "old fellow, I would like to get a wood contract for the U.P.R.R. and persuade you to fill it." His second attempt at the petrified tree proved useless, and he seemed puzzled, and again went to the butt [*sic*] and began peeping. I looked up the petrified tree, and out on a petrified limb saw a petrified bird singing a petrified song, sticking out his mouth about ten petrified feet. Looking down, I saw that the ground was covered with petrified balls like sycamore balls, and from these a considerable forest was growing up and stretching away to the east.

I had heard from the Cheyennes that on the Arkansas river, there is a great petrified buffalo, weighing many tons, which changes its head alternately from north to south every six months and that it sometimes assumes the form of a buffalo with mane like unto a lyon [*sic*], and devours many warriors; and I not knowing but that it might have strayed off among the mountain buffalo here and assumed the form of a great bear, I resolved to resort to some strategy tò out wit him. So I stripped, stuffed my clothes with twigs, and sliding down, supported the effigy against the foot of the tree, then ran a streak. I looked back and saw bruin crush the figure to attoms [*sic*], then scenting my track, came bounding furiously after me. I knew that he would soon reach me, so I crawled into a petrified log, upon which he lit, the concussion of his mighty weight cousing [*sic*] it to resound like a clap of thunder. He then picked up one end of the log and looked as if looking through a field glass, then slammed it down, but as it would not break he ran to the other end and repeated the maneuvre, though finding these attempts vain, he commenced an operation that produced a great crashing noise and at the same moment the air was filled with stifling, sulphurous fumes. O, Lordy! thinks I, he is the demon that controls the fiery vaults of these volcanic steam-boat springs and has caused a new eruption from the bowels of the earth. I became giddy and presently senseless; but soon consciousness returned and I found myself in the middle of the great Yellow Stone lake! and now understood that the bear had rolled the log over high precipices, brimstone, buttes and steamboat springs, kerslosh into the Lake, the log, the bear and I. This is the largest and strangest mountain lake in the world. It being sixty by twenty five miles in size and surrounded by all manner of large game, including an occasional white buffalo, that is seen to rush down the perpetual snowy peaks that tower above, and plunge up to its sides into the water. It is filled with fish half as large as a man, some of which have a mouth and horns and skin like catfish and legs like a lizard [*sic*]. The earth trembles with the evolutions of the surrounding Star Bolt, Geysers and Steamboat Springs, that shoot ashes, water, steam and many kinds of molten minerals into the air, and when the minerals cool they crystalize in the form of soda, alum, copperas, borax, brimstone and various species of salts and other composition.

But this is disgressing. As we came to the surface, the bear the log and I, the great monster commenced raising [sic] first to one end of the log and then the other, treding [sic] water on his hind feet while he looked through and slammed it under water, but finding that he could not drown me out in that way, he placed his whole weight (supposed to be about eleven thousand pounds,) on the center of the log and sunk it deeper than a bell diver ever went into the sea. I slid out and swam under water about six hundred yards, and as I came up, swam on my back, and saw that bruin too was up at his old trick of peering through the log, and in a moment more he slammed it under water, and walked erect on the surface of the lake, looking sharply around, and catching sight of my face, made rapidly for it, but just before he neared me, I dived under and swam several hundred yards, then coming up, I saw the bear swimming rapidly for the lower neck of the lake to where a cross mountain closes up the valley between the ranges of high peaks that divide the Yellowstone from Wind river on the east and those that divide the Yellowstone from Gallatin valley on the west. This cross range backs up the water, and from the head tributaries of the Yellowstone, and thus the lake is formed; and where the water of the lake breaks over the northern face of this cross ridge, there is a perpendicular wall of fifteen hundred feet over one cliff, which is by far the highest fall of any large river, and considering the surrounding scenery, is the most sublime spot on earth. Well, the bear had no sooner reached this cliff than he commenced scratching and tearing away the rocks, so as to drain the lake, perceiving which I swam nearly to him, then dived under and where the fifteen hundred foot fall had been, I now passed over nothing but rapids. Just before reaching the three hundred foot falls, below, I landed and ran for life down the banks, past the first seventy foot fall, and glancing back, saw the bear running over the dry bottom of the Lake and kicking up such a cloud of dust that I am sure a fresh eruption of the earth had taken place, but I soon changed my mind when the bear spied me and came so near overtaking me that I bearly [sic] reached camp, grabbed my rifle and was joined by the boys and the "Sheep Eaters," in firing on the monster whose hash we succeeded in settling in about forty eight hours; and the meat of that bear lasted the whole camp all last winter. So I told Maj. Campbell, at Gallatin City. "Ha, ha, ha," says he, "then all of this strange volcanic region, the meriads [sic] of large game, white buffalo, legged fish, the great Montana lake and grandest of all falls, are all humbugs?" No humbug about it sir. The monster of the adventure just related was only a cub! The old bear came along and threw the rocks back into the canyon, thus causing the lake to back up again and the water to fall all over the great cliff, leaving all things as nature originally constructed them except that every huge block of stone thrown back had the print of the bear's great paws deeply imbedded into them; and I cut out one of these tracks and deposited it in my cabinet of select minerals, where it now is at my old trading post, fifty miles east of the settlements.

LEGH[4]

Undoubtedly borrowed from staple frontier lore, the chase in this story is similar to the charge of the bull buffalo Mark Twain recounted three years later in *Roughing It.* James R. Dow says the *Frontier Index* was no doubt one of the first contributors to the spread of much folklore in the Wyoming Territory.[5]

Freeman drew heavily from other frontier sources in the tale describing the petrified tree. Tales of petrified objects dated back at least to the autumn of 1823 when Jim Clyman, a partner of Jedediah Smith, supposedly found a grove of petrified trees. Tales of petrified forests, trees, branches, and "peetrified birds a s-ttin' on the branches a' singin' peetrified songs" abounded thereafter around western campfires.[6] Mark Twain even told of a petrified man. Freeman, however, apparently adapted the story of the petrified bird from Jim Bridger's tale, perhaps hearing it first-hand from the mountain man in 1866 at Fort Kearny or Fort Laramie. Freeman's account is strikingly similar to the following story Bridger supposedly told Narcissa Whitman:

> . . . up in the Yellowstone country—petrified trees a-growin' with petrified birds in 'em! I knowed it for a fact. An old Crow medicine chief, he put a curse on the place a long time back and everything was frozen t'stone. Grass and sage, bushes and animals too. They's streams up there with falls and spray and everything, all froze t'stone![7]

The petrified forest, bird, or song motif is also described in other writings.[8] Freeman ends his tale with an anticlimax (cutting out a bear track and depositing it in his cabinet of select minerals), a device typical in humorous writing of the day.[9]

Another literary similarity exists in an adventure Freeman related which parallels an encounter of Obed Bat's in James Fenimore Cooper's *The Prairie,* published in 1827. Hearing "the most unearthly sound" while traveling in the Humboldt Valley, Freeman discharged each of his revolvers toward the noise. The "ghost" immediately rent the night air with death agonies. A search the next morning disclosed that he had killed a young donkey which was found stiff in the sagebrush.[10] Dr. Bat, however, did not shoot the jackass that frightened him.

Freeman drew, too, on the well-known literature of Sir Walter Scott, which remained in high esteem in Freeman's native South. Playing on the incongruities of the genteel and the western traditions, Freeman fashioned a tall tale which the *Frontier Index* headlined, "Scott's Lady of the Lake vs. Gen. Horatio Vattell's [*sic*] Squaw." It set out to deprecate everything European. Freeman claimed that "Walter" had appropriated a narration of Vattel's:

> He contracts everything so as to apply to dimunitive Scotland's dimunitiveness. He compares the great Yellowstone Lake and its island to the frog pond of Katrine and its bog sods—Fremont's

peak to the hill of Benvenue. The fifteen hundred foot perpendicular fall of the [Y]ellowstone river to an insignificant cascade—
The seven great rivers of America rising and flowing in contrary
directions to the different seas, to babbling brooks. The roaring of
the great falls and of the volcanoes to the music of the waterfall—
The red glare and escaping smoke from the craters—to misty
floating clouds and the reflection of a setting sun. . . .[11]

"Most absurdly," Freeman wrote, Scott called a squaw "Lady
Ellen" and described her rawhide canoe a "fairy shallop." He completed the tale in verse, claiming that

> Scott's muses couldn't
> Grasp the magnificent scenery
> And primitive novelty, or wouldn't
> Of fair Wyoming Territory.
> Reared in Scotland's cramped mountains,
> Tutored by her little fountains,
> It's truly not very surprising
> That in their vague, dreaming surmising,
> The muses should so far miscontrue
> My thrilling narrative so untrue. . . .
> We will sue him in Yellowstone Hell.
> The jury empaneled of ghosts;
> The court, infernal hobgoblin hosts;
> There in midst of volcanic craters,
> We'll prove Scotland's bard sma'l potatoes,
> And force him to crawfish and subscribe,
> Never again to speak, write or sing,
> Of deer, dog, or hunter's wilkin ring,
> Of mountain waterfall, glen or brake,
> Other than those of Yellowstone Lake.
> Nor of island, boat, bag, pipe, ladies nor
> Of else than Horatio Vattel's squaw. . . .[12]

If other tales of Freeman's were not frankly derivative, they still
did not depart significantly from often told western lore. Drawing upon
the incident when the band of Crows drove off his horses and supplies,
leaving his party without food, Freeman wrote that he had spied a
huge buck sheep with "tremendous" horns:

I fired at his breast, but he being above me, the ball fell just
enough to slit his belly from one end to the other, and down he
tumbled, his guts rolling out, and he rolling on into a boiling
spring, the water of which was salty, and by the time we could get
to him and drag him out our breakfast was all prepared. . . .[13]

This story also echoes one told by Jim Clyman of Jedediah Smith's party, but Freeman set the tale in the Yellowstone to add the detail of the boiling spring.[14]

Yet the tall tale could be so brief as to be slipped into the *Frontier Index* almost unnoticed among its varied fare: "The Yellowstone Lake, in Wyoming Territory, is so clear and so deep, that by looking into it you can see them making tea in China."[15]

Freeman's anecdotes were spun at an equally fast pace. He noted from his travels in the West that people in various places had different ways of expressing the same thing "to avoid the truth":

> For example, in Montana, when a man asks you to take a drink, he says: 'Let's try some of the molten lead and brimstone of Yellowstone Hell.' In Idaho, 'Let's have a little extract of Kamas [*sic*].' In Utah, 'Let's take the Sacrament.' In Arizona, [']Let's take a scalp.' At Sacramento, 'Let's reduce the flood.' In San-francisco, no regular toast, but a constant drink. In Virginia City, Nev., 'Let's take so'thin to timber your lower level.' At Carson City, 'Will you help to take the profits off my craps?' About the Mud Volcanoes on the Humbolt, it[']s 'Suppose we blaze?' At Ft. Churchill, we say, [']Let's innoculate [*sic*] with the measles,' and everybody is innoculated around here. . . .[16]

These descriptions are remarkably similar to those H. L. Mencken later made in a categorization of western American terms for strong drink.[17]

Freeman utilized another form, the humorous essay, which, in the case of "The Bull Whacker's Revenge," is of interest only because of the literary devices it employed. The work was "Written for the Frontier Index . . . By Chance." This byline raises the question of whether Freeman was the author. Chance L. Harris was an agent assigned to solicit advertising, subscriptions, and job work at Bear River City, Wyoming, where the *Frontier Index* had been moved. Yet certain words and the hero's name, Jim, are similar to Freeman's technique in his "Lady of the Lake" poem. There is reference to crime at Bear River City, a matter which proved to be of paramount concern to Freeman. Whoever the original author, it was Freeman who edited the piece and must be given the credit for placing it in the newspaper's columns. He had by then relieved his brother of the editor's position. Certainly the essay furthered the reputation of the newspaper, created by Horatio Vattel, as a purveyor of humorous western lore.

"The Bull Whacker's Revenge" ran in the *Frontier Index* (Bear River City, Wyoming Territory) in two installments in November 1868. The subheading below the title probably guaranteed readership among the railroad workers and townspeople, but also displays the quality of humor employed: "A-nawful Tale of the Rocky Mountains. A Little on the Thrill and Excite, but more on the Gush! A Jurl and some Feller in It!"

The narrative is set in the upper edge of Wyoming Territory near Fort Bridger and immediately satirizes the military, a frequent Freeman target. The hero of the tale is Jim, an officer of the post command, who visited the "she-ro" of the story. The "dark cloud" on the horizon was a mule skinner from "Varmount," M. Uley. To seek revenge for the intrusion of Uley, Jim decides to turn bull-whacker and "outshine the brute," which he successfully does.

The tale displays the author's familiarity with literary devices humorous writers of both the Far West and the East were employing to amuse their readers. Identifiable in the course of the tale, to use the categorizations of Walter Blair, are cacography ("committ suaside"), anticlimax, as in the tall tale ("went silently to the stream and washed his feet; his feelings had come over him"), Shakespearian quotation in an incongruous context ("Accursed be the tongue"), and play on words ("M. Uley")—all devices that had helped ensure the success of Artemus Ward, Bill Nye, and others.[18] Thus where Freeman-as-Horatio Vattel had embellished the tall tale or rephrased European literary works, now as writer or editor he exhibited familiarity with techniques of humor prevalent throughout the country. Here the regional tall tale was combined with the romantic serial which was becoming popular in eastern newspapers.

In at least one of his many travel narratives, Freeman also wrote in a slightly ironic vein. After traveling from Montana to Arizona by horseback, he described the site at the confluence of the Virgin and Colorado rivers where he hoped to found Freemansburg:

> This is a barren, rocky, cactus waste, extending south into the Mexican states of Sonora and Chihuahua. The sand storms are equal to those of the Platte, and the heat is so intense that vegetation withers before it. In mid-summer the thermometer stands about 110 and sometimes reaches 120 accompanied by suffocating siroccos! The sky is ever brassy, and the birds dare not exert themselves to a song, after spring is gone, until the cool breezes of fall again bring the myriads of water fowl from the north to winter here! Even wild geese know enough to travel south upon the approach of winter, but poor, groveling, gold seeking, man, "holes up" like the grizzlies. . . .[19]

Freeman abruptly altered the image of the countryside, but the irony increased in intensity:

> Wheat was only twenty inches high on the Muddy—a near tributary of the Virgen [sic]—last November. They only make upon an average, five hundred pounds of lint cotton to the acre, from inferior seed. Sweet potatoes, melons and "sich like," of course do not startle the denizens of these sandy bottoms. The thousands of pitch pine drift wood [sic] is perfectly worthless. You can't raise more than two good crops a year here and that won't pay for running the risk of losing your hair by Walupah Utes and Apaches.

Keep away from here all of you, if you don't you may be served as that poor thick skulled Aztec Indian—a full blood of the Montezuma tribe—Juarex [*sic*] (War-rez) by name—served the aspiring agents of Napoleon. I am not a Virginian. No, somebody else is one of the despised 'chivalry.' I would not know how to treat a man decently if he were to come to this embryo city. I don't know what good old fashioned hospitality means. No, it[']s somebody else. I couldn't advise any of you to come, for fear you might get shot with one of old Chee-rum's silver bullets. Perhaps you think some other Indians than these shoot silver bullets.

LEGH[20]

While the subject matter of this travel narrative was similar to that described by hundreds of other frontier observers, few captured in one story the contrast of the West as the Great American Desert and at the same time the potential Garden of the World. Nothing became of Freemansburg, Arizona, but it was not because its sponsor failed to believe deeply in the agrarian potential that would help to raise his settlement out of the desert sand. Although this was his earliest attention to agriculture, the affinity increased with passing years and ultimately dominated not only his business activities but his political interests as a Populist as well. In seeing agriculture as one financial basis for his Arizona enterprise, following his Indian encounters and prospecting ventures, Freeman was merely typical of many Americans who recognized the adjustments they had to make. The end of the railroad frontier meant they had to be content in the less volatile settings of the farm and the agrarian community.

But this change did not end the romance of the westward movement for Freeman. As the "Press on Wheels" made its final trip to Bear River City, Wyoming, Freeman saw the *Frontier Index* as the "Star of Empire taking its way westward." Here in only slightly modified form was Bishop Berkeley's 1720 observation that "Westward the course of empire takes its way."[21]

The Far West of the day called for romantic treatment, and his readers relished such fare; thus the tall tales of Horatio Vattel were born. The literary demands that had fashioned a fictional Leatherstocking out of the exploits of Daniel Boone were now copied in the Lightning Scout of the Mountains who was fashioned to some extent after Jim Bridger. Yet it is difficult to determine whether Vattel was a spontaneous creation of Freeman's pure joy with the West or whether Freeman was merely contriving an effect in his writing. He imitated the subjects and style of popular western themes. Certainly the selection of the name *Frontier Index* itself indicated a romantic consciousness. Freeman claimed that 2,000 editors sought exchange issues from him and that his total circulation was 15,000 copies. The paper was read as far east as New Hampshire.[22]

As it turned out, Freeman's contribution was only western. Momentarily he enriched the humorous literature of the West. The *Frontier Index* became associated in the western public's mind with the Pacific railroad frontier as the Omaha reporter indicated, and the newspaper dutifully reflected the flavor of the West. Yet Freeman was not provincial in outlook. He displayed a familiarity with the national strain of American humor, as when he proposed the 1868 presidential ticket of Brigham Young and Brick Pomeroy.[23] Had Freeman not antagonized his readers, as will shortly be examined in detail, had he developed his humor beyond the completion of the railroad and struck out into creative work, he might have become well known nationally. Certainly Mark Twain and Bret Harte had started in similar fashion. Characteristically, Freeman even believed that he could improve upon Twain's writing. During a trip to San Francisco, Freeman complained:

> "Mark Twain," (Clemens) was trying to raise an excitement, just before I left about his Holy Land Tour; but why should we pay any attention, for if he has been to the old Holy Land, thats [sic] played out, am I not just from the new Holy Land [California] that is still in its day of prosperity? I leave it to our readers to judge which is the most interesting correspondence, of the things that were, or the things that are,—dead things or live ones?[24]

Freeman's readers did judge him, violently so, as it turned out. But Freeman at least disproves the twentieth-century assessment that "no writer who lived in the West found much to say about it; and indeed, except as it came to exist in men's minds and imaginations, there was little to say."[25] The very fact that his readers wanted him to further the stereotyped lives they were living says a great deal.

5

The "Filthy Rebel Sheet"

As Freeman spun his tall tales, roaming the canyons, forests, and plains of the West, he also baited Negroes, Chinese, and Indians. The contrasting strains of Horatio Vattel's humor and hatred were not incompatible in his view. His racism stemmed partly from his Southern heritage, but in the West he was also playing to the popular sentiment about these racial groups. In a widely held western view Chinese coolies threatened the labor markets and Indian depredations justified the Red Man's extinction. Even as he chuckled over the tall tale, the westerner looked to subjugation of the other races as a practical matter of survival.

Yet Freeman carried the reputation of being a firebrand beyond these popular themes of racism. In dispatches sent to the *Frontier Index* and in columns he wrote in 1868 from the editor's chair, he vehemently fought the election of Ulysses S. Grant. Also among his editorial forays, he attacked the lawless element of the frontier by supporting vigilantes. Some of those condemned ultimately rose up against him, precipitating one of Wyoming's major early civil uprisings.

There was a hint of Freeman's potential for violent rhetoric in a profile of him printed *Omaha Republican* and copied in the *Frontier Index*. While he still roamed throughout the West, he clipped the article "to furnish our mountain people with an idea of the way things work east of the mountains." He was described as being

> of medium stature, rather wiry and physically strong on the Kit Carson order, but larger; a head well balanced; deep blue eyes, with a pleasant look about them, set rather wide apart, denoting energy of purpose and intellect; a mouth a little large, with a constant smile about it except when in earnest conversation. You then see that firmness which says, "Don't run over me." A broad

forehead, not too high, and hair that stands on end "like quills upon the fretted porcupine;" complexion generally light, but now a trifle browned by exposure to the sun and western winds. The "Gen.l" [Vattel] is a decidedly good conversationalist, well read and extensively traveled; has a remarkable memory; is well posted on politics and history; enjoys his own or another's puns; is quick witted, clear sighted, a thorough Democrat, but with all [sic] liberal in his views.[1]

But actually Freeman's views were hardly liberal. He was already demonstrating that he was biased and intolerant. For instance, under the byline of Horatio Vattel, "general in chief, and Editor of the official organ of the armies of Masonic Democracy," Freeman had written, "Grant is too much nigger—too much GAR for us!"[2] But other than with the usual byline, Freeman's opinions were never specifically labeled editorial fare.

Freeman was only twenty-five years old when he wrote this impiety, sitting as editor of the *Frontier Index* in Laramie because his brother had gone to New York as a Dakota Territorial delegate to the 1868 Democratic National Convention. In the twenty-five months since he had left Fort Kearny, Freeman, by his own account, had traveled on horseback from the Yellowstone to his Freemansburg (Arizona) venture; gone on a raft trip through "the Great Canyon of the Colorado"; and visited Los Angeles, San Francisco, and Sacramento (California), Reno and Fort Churchill (Nevada), and Salt Lake City (Utah). According to his description, his raft trip was in 1867, two years before John Wesley Powell's descent of the Colorado River on May 24, 1869. It is highly unlikely that Freeman traversed the entire Grand Canyon route as he hinted.[3]

Freeman now penned his stories in a portable frame structure attached to Laramie's Frontier Hotel, two buildings owned by his brother. He worked at a desk next to a bed and a case of leather-bound books. Just outside the door of his room six typesetters worked amid their type cases, two presses, and two imposing tables. Decorating the walls of this fifth publishing site were repeating rifles, two banjos, and two silver-keyed flutes. This description of the Laramie office appeared in the *Frontier Index,* August 25, 1868, after the newspaper had been moved to Green River City (Wyoming Territory).

Previously, from Fort Kearny and North Platte, Frederick Freeman had moved the newspaper to Julesburg, Colorado, in July 1867 and then to Fort Sanders near Laramie during the winter of 1867–1868. It was on this move, with the temperature at 20 degrees below zero, that Frederick Freeman was run over by a wagon carrying 6,700 pounds of printing equipment. He was hospitalized at Fort Sanders for two months for treatment of internal and spinal injuries. He credited his overcoat and heavy winter clothing with saving his life.[4]

The transfer of the newspaper from the fort to Laramie was made in late March or early April 1868. From this temporary location Freeman sent forth the newspaper which he labeled

> the emblem of American Liberty . . . now perched upon the summit of the Rocky Mountains; [it] flaps its wings over the Great West, and screams forth in thunder and lightning tones, the principles of the unterrified anti-Nigger, anti-Chinese[,] anti[-]Indian party—Masonic Democracy!!!!![5]

Donald W. Whisenhunt stated that it was not uncommon for frontier newspapers to be racially oriented against Indians.[6]

These nativistic principles prompted the motto of the *Frontier Index:* "Only WHITE MEN to be naturalized in the United States. The RACES and SEXES in their respective sphere as God Almighty originally created them." The imprint of Freeman's upbringing in Virginia is unmistakable here. In the same issue of the newspaper, he told of a conversation with a merchant who thought a Negro was as good as, "and a darned sight better than," some white men. Freeman told the merchant that he did not dispute him "as regards himself, for we thought a ring tailed monkey was better than any white man who seeks to degrade anglo-saxons by comparison with any inferior race." Freeman's actions, in his view, were consistent with his philosophy. He claimed that while he was in Montana he was appointed a notary public by Governor Thomas Francis Meagher's "reposing special confidence in me." But Freeman resigned when he noticed a newspaper item reporting that Governor Pierpont of Virginia had reposed similar "especial confidence in one stable, gumbo, gizzard-foot, Americano-Africano citizen of the old dominion."[7]

Later he bragged:

> Our office sign is being painted not by a Nigger[,] Chinaman, Indian nor ringed tailed monkey, but a white Mormon. . . . Our Columns are headed by the magic names SEYMOUR and BLAIR[.] And we mean business. Up with white men, down with the devil. Give us Freedom in these Rocky Mountains, or give us hell if you can! HORATIO VATTEL. Lightning Scout of the Mountains.[8]

This preference shown to "white Mormons" would stand in sharp contrast to Freeman's attitude only a few years later when he attacked them, too, with equal fervor. But he was only typical of millions of Americans who believed deeply in the inherent inferiority of Negroes, Chinese, and Indians:

> Before the disunion, the dismemberment of the United States, and the hellish corruption of the Government by self-agrandising

[*sic*] political fiends, white polygamists were as good as those who have black, yellow or red skins, with only the brutal organs of the back part of the head developed, and who worship idols such as the Sun, the Chinese wooden Joss in San Francisco, and the Idols of African Mithology [*sic*].[9]

Illustrating the influence westerners had in altering the view of Indians he held from childhood books, Freeman's attacks on Indians were now no less virulent than those on Negroes:

It would be unnatural to believe that treaties made with creatures, whose all absorbing phrenological organs are predominating treachery, theft and blood thirstiness, can last. Do the scape-goat tools expect to level those bumps from the savage head? Was a Hyena ever domesticated? Can you fraternize the Iichneumon [ichneumon] with a dog so that he will not spring at him and cut his throat unawares? Does the eagle ever cease to seek his prey, or the lion his onslaught? Are those grades of the man species of the animal kingdom, whose craniums are developed most prominently by grovelling instincts and savage passions, capable of fraternising [*sic*] with the white race? Verily no! They are naturally inveterate enemies. Then war to the knife. Attack the treacherous blood hound, now, before new grass fattens his weak ponies. Disregard the pow-wows of the old women conspiracies against you and your property. . . .[10]

Indian agents who dealt with the tribes deserved hanging, Freeman said. His characteristically western solution through extermination to the racial problems extended to the Chinese as well as Negroes and Indians. He saw 400 million Chinese "knocking at our national door," threatening "our white laborers and their wives and children. . . ." Americans would have to subsist, not live, he said, "on rats,[*sic*] and rice and drink tea made from the grounds emptied from Chinamen's teapots." Once again the column was signed, "Horatio Vattel."[11]

Freeman noted the poem Oliver Wendell Holmes read at a dinner given by Boston officials for Chinese diplomats. He reprinted portions of it, including a concluding stanza:

Open Wide, ye gates of gold[,]
To the Dragon's banner-fold!
Builders of the mighty wall,
Bid your mountain barriers fall!
So may the girdles of the sun
Bind the East and West in one.[12]

Had Holmes been a California Democrat, Freeman wrote, he would have produced a much more popular poem—"Something in this style":

Long-tailed, bicar-eyed coolies, git!
Vamose! we don't want you a bit;

Make tracks! go back, straight whence you came
Dod rot my oats if t'aint a shame
The legislature will consent
To have such vermin hither sent.

White men will not let, by gosh!
You cussed heathens worship Josh
In this here free and Christian land.
So leave at once! B'ye understand?
Our little boys shall break your bones,
With pistol-shot and clubs and stones.

Rat-eating, dirty yellow skins,
Whenever one of you begins
To make a pile we'll quickly see
Who owns this country, you or we—
We'll quick make you obsquatulate,
And padlock up the Golden Gate.[13]

Freeman saw his own family as "nature's noblemen"; any possible degradation of Anglo-Saxons was unthinkable to one who attributed America's greatness to its European derivation. He made frequent references to "ring tailed monkeys" or "creatures," and their "bumps from the savage head" and "grovelling instincts and savage passions." The descriptions displayed how widespread the belief either in the theory of phrenology or natural selection had become nine years following publication of Darwin's *The Origin of the Species,* although there is no evidence that Freeman was familiar with Darwin's book at this time. Freeman's concern for "our white laborers and their wives and children" is a further example of a common belief in a period when American labor opportunities appeared limited.

These "species of the animal kingdom"—Negroes, Chinese, and Indians—were not in a position to challenge their journalistic adversary. Ironically, Freeman's abandon in writing was abruptly terminated by his fellow Anglo-Saxons, who reacted with the savagery he had attributed to the three other racial groups. The riot that ultimately broke out had its roots in the general lawlessness of the Union Pacific Railroad frontier. But Civil War veterans and Republican sympathizers, goaded by the criminal element—which had also felt the sting of Freeman's acrimony—forcibly stopped publication of the *Frontier Index.*

The newspaper had for some time jousted with the military. Before Legh returned as editor, friction with the army had begun when the newspaper was published at Fort Sanders, a two-year-old post near Laramie. By April 1868 the newspaper was being published in the town and General John Gibbon commanded Frederick Freeman "to make himself scarce" around the fort. The older Freeman brother claimed that the real reason for the order was that the *Frontier Index* had charged General Gibbon with being at heart a North Carolina "tar heal [*sic*]" and Southern sympathizer and only a Grant man because of expediency. Frederick Freeman claimed that newspaper editors in Cincinnati, Baltimore, Washington, Philadelphia, and Chicago, as well as in the West, copied and commented about his exposé of General Gibbon's "general conduct." Because the *Frontier Index*, when published at the fort, did not devote "every line" to General Gibbon, Frederick Freeman contended, it was denied the "privilege" of remaining.[14]

Legh Freeman joined the attack upon his return, claiming that before the days of "nigger radicalism," the Grand Army of the Republic, and "Beast Butler," the press was at liberty to criticize the conduct of civil or military servants "as a free right and as an inherent liberty in justice to the people." Under the new regime, he contended, "it is death" to use the name of a military lord in an open trial of equity. He went on to specify other "crimes" committed by the general:

> Gen. Gibbon's bridge across Laramie river, built by the government, is an impositition upon tax payers; the idea of charging two dollars a team for one single team going over that bridge—sixty or eighty yards long! Feeding sheep upon a government reservation, and fining citizens for doing the same thing. Taking in a big income from his beer saloon, (in the old Frontier Index office) from the soldiers. . . .[15]

Not only was the method of beer distribution criticized, but the *Frontier Index* righteously claimed, "If we could possibly be persuaded to accept any military office . . . we would be above building houses of ill fame."[16]

Grant came under attack by the Freemans not only as a military man but as a Republican and as a Negro sympathizer before he became president. Initially the criticism was relatively mild:

> All that we can say of poor Grant, is that he is a *magnificent* fool; he has allowed himself to be butchered by a set of shameless political vagabonds, who have robbed him of all respect and decency; we wouldn't give a hill of beans for his hide and tallow from today thro' eternity. Grant, you are to be pitied; your father tried hard to teach you sense, but he couldn't[;] you were too far gone. . . .[17]

By early summer, when it became apparent that Grant was heading for the presidency, Legh Freeman signed his name to an article headed, "TOMMY GRANT AND HIS SISTER":

> Scions of General Ulysses, served the people of Knights Ferry [California] as wood-choppers, watercarriers &c. They are the progeny of a Digger Squaw, kept by Ulysses when a barroom bummer of Knights Ferry, in the early days of this country. The boy, like his father, is remarkably fond of cigars, talks horses and is not at all adverse to indulging frequently in copious draughts of bran-

dy. "Tommy" was badly beaten a few days since by a gentleman of African odor, and is not expected to recover. The bottom rail is truly getting on top. The difficulty arose from a desire of the freedman to more closely commingle the blood of races, by becoming a son-in-law of our future President. He was enamored of "Tommy's" sister, who claims the General for her father. The negro has been examined and committed to await the action of the grand jury. The General has our tender sympathy, in this truly solemcholly mishap in the California branch of his family. It seems that even if we fail in electing Brigham Young, we are to have a polygamist for President.[18]

Grant had visited Knight's Ferry, California, in 1853 or 1854 while he was stationed at Fort Humboldt, California. He apparently went to see his wife's brother, Lewis Dent, who ran a ferryboat on the Stanislaus River at Knight's Ferry. Grant expressed his loneliness in California, but resigned his commission while there partially in order to return to his family. An additional factor in the resignation was pending misconduct charges for alleged drinking.[19]

In the columns of the *Frontier Index,* the general was referred to as "Useless Slaughter Grant" or "Horse Useless Grant." He was seen as an instigator of a congressional plot to block passage of the Wyoming territorial bill and thus defer the appointment of territorial officers:

> . . . it was all a preconcerted piece of villany [*sic*] between Grant, his boot-licker, Pat Connor, and the Rump-Hell Congress, so as to create a false pretext for bayonet rule along the line of the railroad towns. . . . It was done to prevent Wyoming from being settled by conservative white men. The hundred beautiful valleys to the northeast of us . . . were abandoned to the Indians for the same purpose. A few more such planks in Grant's platform will Africanise and Indianise our whole mountain region. . . .[20]

Rather than to "circumvent appointment of territorial officers" as Freeman charged, Grant's role in the "plot" appears primarily to have been to fulfill the obligations of a treaty he had signed in July 1868 at Fort Laramie closing the Bozeman Trail, Fort Phil Kearny, and Fort Reno and turning the Big Horn country back to Red Cloud. At the same time railroad construction could continue unhindered.[21]

Before Legh Freeman could deliver an even stronger attack against Grant, the *Frontier Index* was labeled "that filthy rebel sheet" in a counterattack by the *Reveille,* probably a western military newspaper. Freeman reprinted the charges that the *Frontier Index*

> is always filled with ribaldry and gross abuse of the government or some of its agents. It seems to gloat and grow fat with the lowest billingsgate it can command in ministering to its vulgar appetite by pouring out abuse upon anything or any person who stood by our

country in the time of her trial. From the tone of the *Index* we should judge the editor would make a good member of the Ku Klux Klan. . . .[22]

Certainly the Ku Klux Klan could not have used stronger words than Freeman in protesting the election of Grant:

WHAT WE EXPECT—PREPARE FOR THE WORST. Grant, the whisky bloated, squaw ravishing adulterer, monkey ridden, nigger worshiping mogul, is rejoicing over his election to the presidency. On the fourth of March next, the hell-born satrap will (if he be alive) assume the honors (?) and robe of a DICTATOR. The scepter he already holds (in his sword) to be wielded with a tyrant's hand, in some cruel perpretrations [*sic*] as may be suggested by a Usurper['s] vicious brain. The road to the White House which Grant has traveled over during our last campaign is paved with the skeletons of many thousand soldiers whom he slaughtered Uselessly during his western and southern military career. A blindly infatuated people seem to have rejoiced over the actual murder of their friends and kindred, at least appearances indicate it from their endorsement of the murderer, in elevating him, by their votes, to the pinnacle of his demoniac ambition. The tanbark, stinking aristocrat and double-dealing hypocrite will give them all the taxation and blood they want. His supporters will see the day when they will howl for peace, and hide their heads for very shame. Their honor and the memory of the noble dead has left their hearts forever.

Thank God, we are in a region where the presence of such a cesspool of rottenness and corruption is not constantly under our nostrils, where the filthy fumes are not continually rising to poison the mind.

Eastern mothers must tremble for the safety of their daughters['] virtue, knowing that the gaudy military uniform of their President and *ruler* covers the filthy, lecherous carcase [*sic*] of a libertine, seducer, and polygamic squaw keeper. Fathers must be proud to know that the leather-headed, brawling debauchee, and California barroom-bummer, is their leader and an example for their sons.

The leading Radical politicians and vampires have made their bed, however, and our prayer shall be that their necks may be brought to the guillotine with that of the Dictator; for we can assure these scheming Jacobins that if Grant attempts to carry out his ambitious, nefarious plans, the streets of our eastern cities will run more blood than did the unfortunate Paris in the reign of Robesperrie [*sic*]. Time only will tell how this "elevation of one of the mob" will end, and in the meantime we advise our friends to be prepared for the worst. Booth still lives. *Sic semper tyranis!*[23]

Freeman did see blood run, but it was in the streets of Bear River City, where he narrowly escaped having his own blood shed. The inflammatory ideas espoused in the columns of the *Frontier Index* had met an enthusiastic reception on the inherently violent railroad frontier. Now these violent impulses got out of control and were turned back upon Freeman. This interaction of journalism and lawlessness had continued since the inception of the "Hell on Wheels" at North Platte, Nebraska Territory. Many of those who were lawbreakers at Bear River City were the same who had been subdued during the 1867 Fourth of July celebration at Julesburg on the Colorado-Nebraska border. Railroad officials there brought a boxcar of construction crews to town to enforce order. Then, at Cheyenne, merchants and railroad employees called for soldiers from Fort Russell, who instituted martial law. When this edict expired, a "Citizens' Committee" of vigilantes operating with black masks continued to enforce order even though some elements of the community opposed such activity.

Frederick Freeman made it clear in the *Frontier Index* he opposed the outlaws when they resumed operations at Laramie following his move there:

> Our citizens should support a strong police force and help them to put down crime and rowdyism. We were told yesterday of two bands of horse thieves and highwaymen that have their dens on Crow and Dale creeks, each numbering thirty or forty men. They are circling around Laramie, playing Indian. We say go for 'em.[24]

But the outlaws organized before the law did in Laramie, intimidating citizens and prompting a period of anarchy and terror. Again, a vigilance group banded together and by fall 500 armed vigilantes had carried out numerous raids. There was no similar disorder at Green River City, Wyoming Territory, the next stop of the *Frontier Index*, but only because the town was not a winter terminus of the railroad construction crews and their camp followers. By the time editor, workman, and outlaw all reached Bear River City, however, the mode of operation of the lawbreakers had been honed to perfection.

Legh Freeman termed Bear River City "the liveliest city, if not the wickedest," in America. As a real estate speculator, however, he had a special motive for wanting law and order. In fact, Freeman claimed that he had "built up" Green River City and Bear River City, where he was the postmaster, in competition with the Union Pacific–developed communities of Bryan and Evanston, respectively.[25] He naturally supported formation of a vigilante committee at Bear River City, too, although a replacement had been appointed following the sheriff's resignation. Vigilantes took over law enforcement and inserted a warning in the *Frontier Index:*

> WALKING PAPERS—The gang of garroters from the railroad towns east, who are congregating here, are ordered to vacate this city or hang within sixty hours from this noon. By order of
> ALL GOOD CITIZENS[26]

The "good citizens" felt no compunction to hide their extra-legal activities:

NOTICE—Most of the cut-throat gang ordered to leave here have vamosed, though there are several here yet who have the mark of the beast in their forehead, who had better make the cap fit themselves before Saturday at midnight, or climb a telegraph pole. *This means business.*

VIGILANCE COMMITTEE[27]

Freeman technically may not have been the chief of the vigilantes, as was publicly hinted, but it was no coincidence that he became the first target, following destruction of the jail when a mob attacked Bear River City. He was certainly a party to the vigilantes' inner councils and his writing at least hastened the conflict. Describing four recently arrived outlaws, he wrote that they were known and marked by the vigilantes: "Bear River City will be made hot for this class of desperadoes." The perpetrator of an attempted strangling attack on a Bear River City woman, Freeman added, "would make another good subject for the Vigilantes to practice upon."[28] The anonymous citizens group already had practice; it was understood that its members were from the Laramie organization.

Freeman saw it expedient to disclaim any formal association with the vigilantes:

We have never been connected with the vigilantes at any time, though we do heartily endorse their action in ridding the community of a set of creatures who are not worthy [of] the name of men, and who cause our town to be shunned by the thousands of honest laborers in the timber and on the railroad grade, who would otherwise come here to spend their money and enrich our tradesmen. . . .

It is well known that wherever we have sojourned in the Territories, we have opposed violence in any form, and given the common law priority, but when very fiends assume to run our place of publication, there are plenty of men who rather delight in doing the dirty work of hanging without us, as was evidenced Tuesday night, and as will be witnessed again if the ring leaders are found in town by midnight of this, Friday, November the 13th.[29]

Freeman assured "men who have clear consciences" that they need not fear the vigilantes. "It is only the guilty who quake in their boots." That the vigilantes were effective, he said, was proved by the fact that "honest men can now walk our streets in safety, provided they keep sober and are armed to the teeth." He reported the hanging of "three notorious robbers," ages 21, 22, and 23, in front of the city's jail. A "justice dealing band" had entered the jail to invite the three "to take a walk" and they were ultimately hung in the cold, freezing air. They were cut down about seven o'clock A.M., and in the afternoon a wagon conveyed their bodies to the cold, frozen graves, from whence it should be hoped that they may be resurrected to ascend to a cool and delightful haven instead of descending to Brick Pomeroy's "red hot" place.[30]

Freeman's description is hardly less graphic than James Chisholm's account of the Cheyenne vigilantes' work: ". . . the spectacle of a human being suspended in the air, with blue, swollen features, tongue and eyes protruding in a horrible manner, and fists clenched in the last convulsive struggle, is not a pleasing object to encounter in your morning ramble."[31]

A deceptive quiet settled over the community following the hangings. But on November 20 the vigilante committee made further arrests, imprisoning several men in a temporary jail built of logs. An employee in the railroad grading crews, brother of one of the hanged or jailed people, supposedly incited fellow workmen to retaliate. They were joined by workers from neighboring camps. The vigilantes had burst into the jail just days before to hang its three occupants, but the railroad workers now freed the inmates, setting fire to the building. The mob headed next for the *Frontier Index* office, ransacked the premises, destroyed all equipment, and burned the structure.

Because of the resulting confusion and the distance of Bear River City from newspapers in population centers, details reported about the riot varied, but, except for casualty reports, largely were not contradictory. A contemporary newspaper account reported that Freeman was captured by the mob and was threatened with instant death if he did not reveal the names of the vigilantes:

Mr. Freeman at once drew his "iron" but found a dozen at his head and breast in a second. "Hang him! Shoot him! Death to the Chief of the Vigs!" was rung in "Horatio Vattel's" ears for five minutes. When he got the ear of Tom Smith, one of the leaders, Patsey Marley quieted the crowd, and attracted their attention for a moment, when Mr. Freeman made his escape through a saloon. . . . The mob became incensed . . . and began the search. . . . Freeman [was] disguised and taken out of town.[32]

Another version attributes Freeman's escape to a Frenchman, Alex Topence, who was a slaughterhouse operator for the railroad crews. Seeing the mob heading for the printing office, Topence supposedly rode to Freeman and gave him his horse for the escape.[33] The accounts agree, however, that Freeman escaped on horseback to Fort Bridger "so fast that you could have played checkers on his coattails," according to a physician returning to the town at the time. Freeman himself, in a tone characteristic of Horatio Vattel, later claimed that he merely "went to Fort Bridger for troops" and had the town put under martial law.[34] Troops from the fort did arrive, but not until the next morning. By then the mob, largely unarmed, had been driven from town by armed citizens, undoubtedly including vigilantes, who had initially barricaded themselves behind sacks and bales of merchandise in a store.

There is disagreement as to the number of casualties. The *Salt Lake Telegraph* initially reported that twenty-five were killed and sixty wounded, but three days later revised the figures downward to fourteen dead and thirty-five wounded. Freeman afterwards claimed that forty rioters and one citizen died. One historian indicates that there were no deaths, but the previously mentioned physician, who was there, listed fourteen dead with a greater number wounded. An eyewitness in his old age claimed that fifty-three died. Part of the confusion stemmed from the fact that all contemporary newspaper accounts published differing casualty figures.[35]

It has been generally accepted that the cause of the riot was the lawlessness of Bear River City and that the *Frontier Index* was destroyed because it was an exponent of law and order. While not inaccurate, the assessment seems a simplistic explanation. It ignores the temper of the railroad crews, who, as will be seen, had no outlet in the *Frontier Index* for their grievances. It ignores resentment over the vigilantes' continuing activities in Wyoming and general reaction to the presidential election. Yet Freeman had editorialized on each problem in a way that could have triggered the destruction.

A decade and a half after the riot, established at Butte, Montana Territory, Freeman saw an even more malevolent motivation behind the destruction of the newspaper:

> Our press had always been remarkably bold and fearless in behalf of the right. . . . And in the course of human events when we thought we had a right to lay out towns independent of the Credit Mobilier ring, we did so, and for this, and for exposing the frauds of that hydra-headed monster, its chief had a riot brought on us at daylight Nov. 20, 1868, composed of several thousand graders, headed by cut-throats of the most desperate type who were paid $15,000 to head the mob. Our office was burned to a grease spot, the marble imposing stones were reduced to lime and the type ran down the hillside as a molten mass. Counting the number killed by the citizens and those slain at the wakes, thirty-nine of the mob bit the dust, while only one citizen gave up the ghost.
>
> Like an avenging nemesis, we proceeded to New York, entered complaint against the Credit Mobilier ring, for frauds perpetrated on the American people, had the directors arrested, their safe blown open, and proved by the contents, the charges we made, then carried the war into Africa, by bringing out of the expose in Congress—camped on the trail until Oakes Ames was in his grave, from nervous prostration resulting from the excitement of the investigation. . . .[36]

This account must be considered mere braggadocio. No twenty-five-year-old frontiersman could have so successfully and single-handedly defeated the Credit Mobilier, even if historians were not destined to record other factors as being responsible for its dissolution. This is not the only claim of Freeman's that is without confirmation in this period. He contended in the *Ogden Freeman,* April 3, 1877, that he gave Wyoming its name. Elsewhere he claimed that he was the first to use the name in correspondence he sent from the 1866 Fort Laramie peace conference. C. G. Coutant discusses Freeman's claim, but says that Congressman J. M. Ashley of Ohio used the name, perhaps taken from the Wyoming Valley of Pennsylvania, in introducing a territorial bill. Coutant says that Freeman "undoubtedly did more to popularize the name, Wyoming, than any other man."[37]

Frederick Freeman also attributed destruction of the printing plant to machinations of the railroad, but his reasoning ironically contradicted his brother's account. He said that the two had opened "immense veins" of coal at Rock Springs, Wyoming, and initially received the cooperation of the Union Pacific's construction company for transportation. When the construction company turned a portion of the completed road over to the Union Pacific's operating unit, the railroad owners supposedly told the brothers to get off the profitable property or "they would shoot them off." Consequently, Frederick Freeman contended, the railroad called its laborers to Bear River City, made them drunk on "bad whiskey," and incited them to burn the newspaper office. A New York attorney supposedly advised the Freeman brothers to abandon their fight. They were told it would take many thousands of dollars to regain their coal claims.[38] It is true that Legh Freeman took note of the Rock Springs coal beds in the *Frontier Index* (Green River City, Dakota Territory, August 11, 1868) and that he later returned to the vicinity to engage in coal mining operations, but unlike his brother he did not attribute the Bear River City riot to this factor.

Both Freeman brothers appear to have been writing from face-saving retrospection. Apparently no evidence supports animosity between the *Frontier Index* and the Union Pacific prior to the riot. In April 1868 the newspaper announced appointment of W. B. Bent as the railroad's real estate agent in Laramie:

> Those in search of lots in this new Chicago, will find Mr. B always ready and happy to serve them. He is a gentleman of apt business qualifications; you can approach him at any hour in the day, and will be treated with courtesy and prompt attention. Mr. B has the tact of knowing how to deal with the world; he has studied human nature, and appreciates the power of common politeness and possesses a remarkably pleasant address; he never fails to make a kind impression upon all with whom he has any business or personal transaction. In a word, the company has shown its usual wisdom in selecting Mr. Bent as real estate agent at this very important point. We know of no

one more competent to subserve the interests of the great corporation, and at the same time accord to the public universal satisfaction.[39]

Part of the high esteem expressed here may have stemmed from the fact that Bent had also purchased an advertisement announcing his appointment. In addition, the railroad had been running a standing one-column advertisement in the newspaper. If the brothers had been thwarted in laying out independent town sites, as Legh Freeman charged, the Republicans and the military could attest that the *Frontier Index* would not have been reticent in objecting. But the congeniality expressed toward the Union Pacific real estate venture does seem incongruous with the competing standing advertisement the *Frontier Index* (May 5, 1868) printed while located at Laramie: "Freeman Bros., Real Estate Agents. Business on Wheels. Buy and sell real estate at the successive terminal towns of the great railroads across the continent. . . ."

Immediately after the riot Legh Freeman was more concerned with rebuilding than assessing blame. Three days after his enforced trip to Fort Bridger, he told the *Salt Lake Telegraph* that his printing office would be rebuilt at once. He said he had telegraphed Chicago for a new press and equipment and he promised that the *Frontier Index* would be "on wheels" again in three weeks. "The Institution shall rise, Phoenix-like, from her ashes, to still advocate the cause of right and truth, to denounce tricksters and mobocracy, uphold the good and faithful," he asserted. In December he predicted, "A few more weeks will find us hotter than red, in the vicinity of Ogden. . . ."[40] The site mentioned in this prediction, if not the timing, would prove accurate.

6

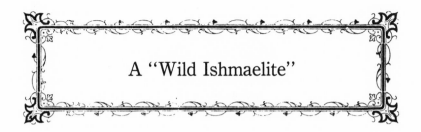

A "Wild Ishmaelite"

FIVE MONTHS after the Bear River City mob sent Freeman fleeing to Fort Bridger in defeat, Horatio Vattel sought his triumph in Virginia. Residents of Culpeper were handed flyers announcing "A Rare Treat!":

> COME AND HEAR the author of "Ten Years on Horseback in the Indian Wilds, Mining Camps and Mormon Backwoods of the Western Territories." At Culpeper Court House, Va., Tuesday evening, May 2, 1869. HON. LEGH R. FREEMAN, Editor of the Frontier Index, published at each successive hundred mile terminus of the great "National Iron Band"—the Union Pacific railway—"The Press on Wheels," as the "Star of Empire," leading the vanguard of civilization westward to the Occident.
>
> He is familiarly known through the territories under the nom de plume of General Horatio Vattel, Lightning Scout of the Mountains.
>
> He will describe graphically and humorously: The Characteristics of the various Indian Tribes; The Curious Habits of the Game[;] Singular atmosphere phenomena and grandeur of natural scenery; the American desert; death valley; Yellowstone Hell; the Mormon Beliefs and practices, what they have done and what they are doing; what the Chinese are good for and how they live on the Pacific Slope; Present developments of the agricultural and mineral lands—How the Precious metals are Found and saved; progress of the Union, central, northern & Southern Pacific Railroads and their branches; What a Young Man and Woman may honorably and profitably do along the lines of these great continental thoroughfares.
>
> Doors open at 7 o'clock. Speaking commences at 8 o'clock. Tickets 50 cents.[1]

Thus when returning to his birthplace, far removed from the fluid social state of the West where every man was free to select his own identity, Freeman maintained the role of Horatio Vattel. He swaggered onto the speaking stage in buckskin coat and fringed leggings as he had swaggered into his adulthood, purposely enjoying a role larger than life. It was now obvious that his three years in the West, which had allowed his fantasies to be played out without restriction, had only whetted his appetite for such a life-style. From now on, he would live out his life with no perceptible modification of his personality.

The dashing figure was reunited at Culpeper with a girl whose acquaintance he had made a few years earlier and with whom he had maintained a correspondence. Ada Virginia Miller, a native of Strasburg, Virginia, a Shenandoah valley community, had apparently met Freeman while he was in the army during the Civil War. She was seventeen months younger than Freeman, having a background similar in some ways to his mother's. The daughter of an apothecary, she had studied German at Notre Dame Convent at Columbus, Ohio, before the war, although her family was Lutheran. Virgil and Tacitus were among the classics read to the family by her father, and her education included training in piano, art, and needlework. During the last year of the war she had taught fourteen students, including her brothers. She subsequently became the assistant to the principal of Strasburg Academy, a school established after the war in the absence of public education. She wrote articles for a newspaper at neighboring Winchester and had translated a German folktale for publication in the *Shenandoah Herald* at Woodstock. In addition to being a young woman of cultural background, she had qualities that attracted the Horatio Vattel side of the complex figure of Legh Freeman. Her father had taken her on fishing and hunting trips, and she knew how to handle a shotgun—a skill she had demonstrated in driving Yankee soldiers out of the family garden.[2]

Four days after his Culpeper address, Freeman and Miss Miller were married at Strasburg. They left in a buggy on a honeymoon trip to Gordonsville to visit Freeman's mother, who still lived on the Maywood place she had bought before the Civil War.[3] There Freeman also visited the grave of his father, who had died in June 1868. He had already held a reunion with John Hoomes Freeman, who by then was ninety-one years old. On April 18 he had received the copy of the laws of colonial Virginia from his grandfather.

The couple returned to the Shenandoah Valley for a leisurely summer following the wedding trip. Freeman went fishing and hunting with his wife's brothers and joined them in their swimming holes. The family went to picnics, camp meetings, and spelling bees until late in the fall, but even if this bucolic life appealed to his bride, it could not hold Freeman. When he received an offer of employment from a telegraph agency at Rock Island, Illinois, he chose to again become a telegrapher. He and his wife moved to the vicinity of his Civil War imprisonment, where they built a home. It was here that their first child,

Legh Freeman, taken at Rock Island, Illinois, about 1870. (courtesy Western History Reasearch Center, University of Wyoming)

named Randolph Russell for a maternal uncle, was born in March 1870. In the Miller family Bible the boy's name is listed as Legh Randolph Russell Freeman, but since a later Freeman son was named Legh Miller Freeman, the initial Legh is probably in error.

Although Freeman never furnished details to his children in later years, his wife's family remembered that he invested much of his salary at Rock Island in unspecified stock in Chicago, losing most of what he speculated.[4] Perhaps because of this failure, Freeman finally decided to return to Wyoming. That he could take his wife and infant son to a community near the site of the Bear River City debacle indicates how much the completion of the transcontinental railroad had transformed Wyoming community life.

Although details are sketchy, it is known that the family moved to Rock Springs, where in 1868 Freeman had become aware of, and perhaps laid claim to, coal-producing properties. He may have been motivated by the knowledge that since 1871 Union Pacific locomotives were being converted to coal. He sought capital to develop his claims and, in order to file on additional land, even raised $75 from one of his wife's brothers after writing to Virginia about the certainty of future property values. However visionary Freeman may have been about the demand for coal, such meager investments were insufficient to compete with the resources of the Union Pacific. The railroad went into the coal business for itself and by the end of the decade was mining 200,000 tons of coal and shipping 20,000 carloads annually from Rock Springs alone. It was undoubtedly this one-sided competition that later prompted Freeman family tradition to blame the railroad for running Freeman out of Bear River City in 1868. Despite Freeman's lack of success in this venture, his wife expressed only contentment and hope in the letters she sent to her family at Strasburg. And, in January 1873, she became the mother of a second son, Hoomes Kemper.[5]

Earlier, when faced with failure at Freemansburg and Bear River City, Freeman had resorted to the mobility open to a single man in his optimistic search for a new start. Now, although encumbered by a family, he decided on yet another move in order to return to newspaper work, which had given him the only success he had known. Ignoring the potential hardships for a wife and infant sons, Freeman showed that the responsibility of marriage had not affected his wanderlust. Not surprisingly, he selected another site on the Union Pacific Railroad in 1875. It had taken more than the few weeks he had originally estimated, and he was no longer "hotter than red," but he now fulfilled the prediction made after the Bear River City riot of making his journalistic comeback at Ogden, Utah Territory.

With some logic, Freeman counted on his previous amicable relations with the Mormons to ensure his financial success at Ogden. In 1868, at the same time he was blasting Negroes, Indians, and Chinese, he had taken a sympathetic stance on the

"Mormon question." He had proudly advertised that the *Frontier Index* was

> the only "Gentile" paper that is conducted in such a conciliatory manner as to have secured a general circulation among the widespread business element of the Mormons!!!!!
>
> It does not advocate sending an army of "Spoonies" to plunder and lay waste the peaceful mountain homes—ravish the women; and entail starvation upon the orphaned children of an harmonious brotherhood—a brotherhood which has converted a savage sage brush desert into the happiest community in America!!!!!![6]

Freeman reinforced this position in his editorial column:

> A man . . . wanted to know HOW FAR WE FAVOR THE MORMONS? We replied . . . we favor them because they are white people, who have improved a savage desert waste, when they were isolated thousands of miles from the necessaries and comforts of life; and because they are white we want to see their one hundred thousand people, who have done so much for a country that we would not have settled at all, admitted to the rights of citizenship before the polygamy-practicing Chinese, Indians and negroes are given the right of suffrage. . . .[7]

Freeman's motivation for lavish praise of the Mormons in 1868 seems to have been again characteristically opportunistic. Displaying his oversized ego, he interpreted Brigham Young's interest in Mormon colonization in southern Utah as being tantamount to endorsement of his Freemansburg, Arizona, venture. Horatio Vattel seemed to be speaking when he said that the interest of the "Lion of the Lord" extended to an agreement to

> pay the passage of the 14,000 factory girls of Lowell, Mass. . . . to Freemansburg. The result would be that the 28,000 batchelor [*sic*] miners of Arizona would rush up and take two apiece . . . that would increase the population of Western Dixie so rapidly that we would organize—the region . . . into the new Territory of Aztec—with Freemansburg as the capital and myself as delegate to Congress, and eventually Governor, eh?[8]

Mormons did settle in the vicinity of Freemansburg, but before Freeman arrived. On January 23, 1865, in his gubernatorial message, Brigham Young announced construction of a warehouse and landing "at the head of navigation on the Colorado River." The description of the site is similar to that given of Freemansburg by Freeman: "At the head of steam navigation on the Great Colorado River."[9] Both the Freeman and Mormon enterprises failed, but before this happened, Freeman and the Mormons may have taken some steps to cooperate. The Saints did import machinery for a cotton factory, if not the factory girls. But Freeman might well have become a full partner in Mormon Zion if his account of a historic meeting between Horatio Vattel and Brigham Young could only be taken at face value. Assuming the role of the heroic buckskin-clad figure, Freeman said he was

> hoisted on the shoulders of the populace [in Salt Lake City] and seated on the right hand of the throne with Brigham and his twelve Apostles; and now we hear the silvery tones of this most high proclaiming amid loud hosannas, welcome! welcome!! thrice welcome!!! For thou did'st visit us when in distress, and extended the hand of sympathy when all gentiles hated us because they knew us not. And again from Solomon No. 2 [Young] we hear this: ["]*From what I have known of you, Mr. Freeman, I think you are a pretty good Mormon, but not much Saint;*" and then came from his Holiness, the blessing, *"well, I wish you all success!"* which being interpreted after the manner of men, means, that as I have suffered under mongrel rule, and the impeachers are being hissed by all white men out into outer ignominy, our glorious portion shall be to build up the city of Freemansburg and organize the Territory of the Aztecs. Hallelujah! Hallelujarum!! Selah!!!
>
> HORATIO VATTEL
> Telegraph Scout of the Mountains[10]

Frederick Freeman in 1916 wrote of his visit to Brigham Young in 1868:

> He was very cordial and friendly, "[*sic*] carried us into his private Council Chamber, asked us to shake hands with his twelve Apostles, and granted us the freedom of the City. He informed us that he was strictly moral in his habits, declaring that he never had but one wife during her natural lifetime, that all of the hundreds of others were spiritual wives married to him in the holy Temple, hoping to get to Heaven by holding on to his coat-tail; that many of them were from 70 to 80 years old."[*sic*] He gave the *Frontier Index* a big send-off, giving the editor a big subscription list and extensive advertising contract.[11]

Legh Freeman had gone so far as to propose a presidential ticket of Brigham Young and Brick Pomeroy in 1868, but probably for oblique reasons. Rather than primarily ridiculing Young, it appears that Freeman's proposed ticket was printed merely to illustrate how ludicrous he regarded the manipulations of the Radical Republicans in their attempt to impeach Andrew Johnson. However full of hyperbole his proposal may appear in retrospect, it was apparently taken at face value by the Mormon *Deseret News* at Salt Lake City:

> Legh R. Freeman . . . can lay claim to advancing the most sensible idea on statesmanship that we have seen for some time, in raising the name of President Young as candidacy for the Presidency of the U.S.[12]

Because of such past amicable relations with the Mormons, Freeman had good reason to be optimistic regarding his prospects in Ogden. There was further encouragement when Ada Freeman visited the Salt Lake City office of the *Deseret News* early in June 1875 to announce plans for the new Ogden "gentile" newspaper. Freeman himself did not make the announcement only because he remained in Wyoming to mine his coal claims. The editors treated Mrs. Freeman with professional courtesy:

> This morning we were called upon by Mrs. A. Freeman, wife of L. R. Freeman . . . who it will be remembered, was editor and proprietor of the Frontier Index. Mrs. Freeman proposed publishing a semi-weekly paper in Ogden, to be known as the Freeman. She will manage and edit it herself until the arrival of Mr. Freeman, who is at present residing in Wyoming territory. She expects to issue the first number about the first of this month.[13]

The first issue of the *Ogden Freeman* on June 18, 1875, therefore, was the work of Mrs. Freeman, who was nearly eight months pregnant with her third child. With her in Ogden were her two-year-old and five-year-old sons. (Legh Miller Freeman was born on July 20, 1875.) The *Deseret News* (June 19, 1875) noted approvingly that the new publication had "a neat and newsy appearance. . . ."

It is apparent that Freeman sought more than this perfunctory Mormon blessing; he also hoped to be identified with the early Mormon press. The *Ogden Freeman* carried not only a current volume and number appelation but also a *"Frontier Index* series" designation dating back to 1850. Freeman later rationalized that he had counted from the time the Mormon emigration first started a newspaper office on Wood River—in the Platte Valley—"where the present editors came into possession of the paper."[14] He was obviously referring to the *Huntsman's Echo,* published by Joseph Ellis Johnson, but how he hoped to claim legitimately the 1850 date as a part of his publication's origins—especially since Johnson, too, now lived in Utah—is unexplained. Perhaps he decided on use of the date because the *Deseret News* had been established in that same year. Johnson had started his first paper at Council Bluffs in 1852. Some authors and journalists who have written about Freeman have uncritically accepted the 1850 date, although Freeman was only eight years old at the time. For example, the *San Francisco Chronicle* on March 25, 1885, reported that Freeman was the one who took the first printing press across the Missouri River above St. Louis to Fort Kearny in 1850. Freeman reprinted the story without correction in the *Washington Farmer* (North Yakima, Washington Territory), April 11, 1885. Frederick Freeman, in apparent confusion, even went so far as to say that the *Frontier Index* "was published on an old time hand-roller press, which had been abandoned by General Joseph E. Johnston, who, prior to 1861, was in command of the United States troops in the far western territories."[15]

For the time being, however, Freeman remained in Wyoming while his wife began the newspaper because his coal claims were producing enough to demand his attention. He later stated that during the first ten weeks the *Ogden Freeman* was published, a $100-a-week deficit was offset by income derived from the mining activity.

Freeman apparently sought to realize the possibility he saw for Mormon advertising, subscriptions, and commercial printing when he arrived in Ogden. Emphasizing his earlier cooperation with the Mormons, he went so far as to be an apologist for the Mountain Meadows Massacre. But he was not destined to share in the resources of the Mormon empire in Utah despite his earlier good relations with the Saints. He received nothing more than a perfunctory welcome from Mormon interests in Ogden. In fact, with the influx of gentiles into Utah after completion of the Union Pacific, Brigham Young had instituted a boycott of non-Mormon business. For example, Zion's Cooperative Mercantile Institution was established to serve only Mormon consumers and, of course, it advertised in the *Deseret News*.

Rebuffed in his attempts to enter the circles of Mormon trade, Freeman turned next to non-Mormon businesses in Ogden. But the outlook was equally dim for solicitation of revenue from gentiles. A period of depression in Utah had followed the Panic of 1873. The gentiles, excluded from the Mormon economic system, were especially hurt, and bank deposits dropped by one-third. In any case, Freeman could expect to draw on no significant volume of gentile business. It has been estimated that of 86,786 people in Utah in 1870, only 5 percent were gentiles. In the election of 1870, the Mormon-dominated People's party polled 21,656 votes to 1,444 for the gentile Liberal party. The railroads to the north and south of the Union Pacific were also initially Mormon-owned and were designed to profit primarily church-controlled businesses.

In his problems of obtaining support from the Mormons and the gentiles, Freeman found that he was no longer in a monopoly position such as he had enjoyed with the *Frontier Index*. Advertising, subscription, and commercial printing income had all flowed then to the Freeman brothers, but now this lucrative trade was kept by the Mormons and was not available to the limited gentile community. Freeman was forced to take steps to offset this economic disadvantage. By entering into a newspaper partnership with an H. M. Bond, he gained the advantage of a reduced capital outlay necessary in such a precarious financial situation. Bond, who became manager of the plant's "machine department," contributed his job printing business and equipment to the venture.[16] But the partnership was dissolved within three months, a duration which proved typical of many of Freeman's subsequent business associations, since controversy always seemed to attend his private business as well as his community relations.

Freeman managed to find some business revenue by reaching far beyond Ogden, where most of that city's 3,000 residents were under Mormon control. Ogden was a budding commercial center for the Pacific Northwest and the Rocky Mountains. Railroad branches planned to Oregon and to western Montana verified its potential. The initial copies of the *Ogden Freeman* have been lost or destroyed, but the earliest remaining issues, published in 1876, show that Freeman obtained much of his income from soliciting trips made in Horatio Vattel fashion to outlying western communities. His advertising revenue came from an Ogden–Salt Lake City merchant, a Laramie grocer, a Utah farm implement dealer, Laramie City promoters, and various smaller Ogden merchants. Pages 1 and 4, the "patent outsides," were printed in San Francisco and included a full-width map of Wyoming gold fields on the front page. Freeman printed pages 2 and 3 in Ogden, his advertising space averaging six of the inside fourteen columns.

The widespread solicitation activities brought problems as well as profit. Freeman found that one member of his own profession was more hostile to his efforts to get established than were the Mormons. The vitriolic gentile *Salt Lake Tribune,* which fought Freeman, the Church of Jesus Christ of Latter-day Saints, and the Mormon *Deseret News* without discrimination, reported a visit from Freeman. The editor recounted his conversation with

> this peculiar hermophodite native of the newspaper he represented. I told him I did not think it was either [*sic*] "fish, flesh, foul or good red herring," whereupon he waxed wroth and commenced to abuse the Tribune & Corinne Mail winding up his harangue by asking, "Where will these papers be in six months?["] One of the gentlemen present in the office quietly replied, "Alive and flourishing while the Ogden Freeman will be dead and buried." Not content with abusing the people's paper of Utah, he actually had the audacity to take the part of an apologist for the Mountain Meadows Massacre. I really think that Mr. Freeman had better retire again to his coal mines and leave the editorial department to his estimible [*sic*] lady, taking warning by the fate of his former paper, The Frontier Index.[17]

Inasmuch as no subsidy or support for his newspaper was forthcoming, Freeman ceased to defend the Mountain Meadows Massacre and the Mormons during his first year at Ogden. He now turned on the Mormons in the same manner he had attacked Chinese, Negroes, and Indians in 1868. He found no language too extreme. He claimed that Brigham Young was "fast losing his grip on the people" and that Mormons were not nearly as saintly as they pretended:

> "By hell" is the principal rhyming phrase in Mormon nursery songs, and all the priests pray by hell and swear by hell, and their women use the same words over the washtubs when they find the

clothes washings out of which they make their livings, unusually
dirty, and the same thing with its variations is gotten of when the
old man brings home another polygamous wench—"by hell."[18]

Referring to an advertisement reading, "Dear madam, try Glenn's
Sulphur Soap," Freeman said, "That applies locally. Sulphur soap will
cure itch on a concubine." But it was not only the "concubines" to
whom Freeman objected:

Old Mexico never had so many ignorant, ugly, half-civilized, crazy
fanatics, dwarfs, cripples as Salt Lake has. If it was not for the
half-fare market trains, and the love of lust and the greed of theft
perpetrated in the name of religion, Salt Lake would be a very
poor way station. It however would still be what Brigham's
youngest daughter told him it would. The old scoundrel was up-
braiding the girl for being a little wild on the streets, when she set
upon him in this wise: "Father, I merit no reproof at your hands,
for if Salt Lake City was fenced in and covered over it would be
the biggest bawdy house in the world; and be it upon your head
and upon the heads of your children that you have made it so; and
accused be the dupes who call such villainy the work of the Lord
God Jehovah."[19]

The Mountain Meadows Massacre now offered Freeman an opportunity to attack the Mormons, whereas earlier he had defended
them in this bloody episode:

Now that Johnny W., one of Brigham's bastards, has been
elevated to the second place in the Kingdom, we hear again the
rumors connected with the death of his first born son[,] Joseph.
Joseph it seems had an innate sense akin to nobleness of soul and
incurred the displeasure of Brigham by refusing to accompany
Brigham to a dinner at which Jno. D. Lee, the Mountain Meadows
slaughterer[,] was to be present. "I will not break bread with
murderers[,]" said the young man and he would not go despite the
threats and entreaties of his father. *Soon afterwards Joseph died.*[20]

Lee had been convicted a month earlier by a Mormon jury for his role
in killing 120 Missouri and Arkansas emigrants at Mountain Meadows,
Utah Territory, on September 7, 1857. By 1870 Lee and other Mormons were suspected of the crime. After a hung jury at a trial in 1875,
Lee was convicted in 1876 and was executed at the site of the
massacre in 1877. Mormons kept the massacre quiet to avoid interven-
tion of federal troops.[21]

In a short time Freeman audaciously assigned himself an important
role in the battle against Mormonism. If Brigham Young could truck in
mysticism and revelation, so could Horatio Vattel. He claimed that he
had dreamed at Ogden that his mission in life should be that of a
leader of the "Monogamic white race" against the "polygamic colored

races." Thus "commanded to begin the war," Freeman maintained that the next day the *Ogden Freeman* became a "double-distilled, double and twisted, heels over head, double-shotted, red hot anti-Mahomedan paper."[22] Freeman in later years would more fully document his belief in such revelations, so a spirit command cannot be fully discounted as a motivation here. But it was probably used only as a rationalization for his abrupt hostility to Mormonism.

Freeman was asked why he also attacked Methodists. He replied that the free press assailed the errors of all, and the faults of Methodism were not excepted. He said that he had a "degree of respect" for the old-fashioned Methodist "shouters," their camp meetings, and circuit riders, but he "detested" a Bishop Simpson who "toadied" to the Mormons "he should exert himself to win."[23]

Freeman's willingness to sacrifice consistency while grasping for opportunity precluded him from earning the backing required of a successful newspaper publisher. Although he was a husband, the father of three children, and thirty-three years old, he displayed no evidence of emotional maturity. The *Salt Lake Tribune* publicized with painful clarity his eagerness to find a subsidy. Referring to his initial stance in Ogden, it accused him of attempting to "put money in his purse" by "basely truckling to this Latter-day Monstrosity." To prove his devotion to church interests, it charged, "he went down so low in the mire of sycophany and double dealing as to be almost lost to sight." The *Tribune* charged that he revolted when actual Mormon affiliation was required of him, "and now where shall he resort for his fellowship?"[24]

Illustrating how completely he believed himself to be the anointed leader of the war against the Saints, Freeman heatedly printed a denial that he had ever sought Mormon business:

> Whenever the *Tribune* is lacking in subjects on which to pour out a baptism of contumely, it attempts to touch up The Freeman by averring that we have truckled to Mormons. Our files are open to inspection and the *Tribune* cannot find one line which will serve as a base for such an accusation. . . .[25]

Failing to obtain from the Mormons the subsidy he needed to compete with established newspapers, Freeman sought a political affiliation. He proclaimed himself as the voice of the Liberal party, which had been organized in northern Utah in 1870 as a coalition of gentiles and Mormons who favored separation of the church and politics. Later the Mormons were ejected from its ranks and it became an anti-Mormon party.

In September 1876, Freeman devoted a column and a half to Liberal party meetings and notices of territorial, county, and precinct conventions, but apparently without official sanction or compensation. Instead, the party rewarded the *Ogden Junction* with its advertising. This was a three-year-old newspaper edited by Charles W. Penrose, a

Mormon, who later became a highly regarded editor of the *Deseret News.* Freeman claimed that when he arrived in Ogden he proposed to Penrose that each editor should conduct his paper so that the city would be "built up," thus avoiding personalities in order to attract capital. But when Penrose received the Liberal party patronage, Freeman attacked him, too, as his nearest competitor and greatest economic threat:

> If the plan here is to *pay* the organ of our enemies, and never offer a cent to *The Freeman,* we have done with the so-called Liberals. Those who plead with us for six months to come out as the Liberal organ, take good care that we shall never have any pay for it, but that the enemies of the Liberals shall receive the pay. . . . It is poor encouragement to a publisher to work for a party for nothing and see the enemies of that party paid for the same work. . . . if the Liberals would withdraw all their patronage the Mormon paper [the *Junction*] would not last six months. . . . Then *The Freeman,* with a clear field, would give you the best daily in the Rocky mountains. The Liberals could form a joint stock company, dictate its tone, employ the talent, and we would engineer the finances so as to make it pay handsome dividends. . . .[26]

Freeman denied charges that he was "using" the party. Rather than attaching himself to the Liberal party of Weber County, he claimed that the Liberal party "is attached to us." Referring to his soliciting trips in the Rocky Mountains, he added boastfully, "We have never expected to make our living in Ogden, nor in Utah, and we have not tried to do it." That he had been counting on Liberal party financial support became evident, however, as the 1876 election campaign drew to a close. He chose this time to print a "dun, the first one we have ever made," as he announced a "black list" of those failing to remit $4.[27]

Further evidence that Freeman was short of capital came when he offered to sell a quarter, third, or half interest in the newspaper "to a man who is capable of acting as foreman of the office, who is a job printer, and qualified to localize." Such a partner would be more highly motivated than one working for wages, Freeman contended. His financial difficulties were glossed over in this proposition. As if to entice an investor, he maintained that the office was established on a "healthy paying basis," dependent on no ring, clique, or party for support. He pointed out that he did job work for railroad communities for 500 miles around Ogden. The newspaper's circulation was listed at this time as 2,925. Freeman reported these totals: Utah, 1,100; Wyoming, 550; Montana, 100; Idaho, 175; Nevada, 350; Nebraska, 100; "Other Territories," 250; "Other States," 300.[28]

Apparently no partner was forthcoming, so Freeman attempted another ploy to substitute for the lack of Mormon or Liberal party support. He now professed his sympathy for the cause of Joseph Smith III, leader of the Reorganized Church of Jesus Christ of Latter-day Saints. This group broke off from the main Mormon group following the death of Joseph Smith, Jr., in Illinois in 1844. It remained there after Brigham Young's faction left for Utah. After Smith visited the *Ogden Freeman* office later in 1876, Freeman quoted Smith's denials that his father had ever received revelations about polygamy. Freeman subsequently lauded Smith, hailing "with enthusiastic greetings" the day when Smith and the Reorganized Church would "remain in Zion, and build his grand headquarters here in Ogden."[29]

The decline of Brigham Young's Mormonism was already at hand, Freeman contended, because Young even then was "failing in his spine." Eight months later Young was dead. Freeman's lengthy obituary, although temperate in tone, could not hide his hope that a major turning point of Mormonism was at hand. Included were references to the Mountain Meadows Massacre and to the law suits brought by Young's nineteenth wife, Ann Eliza. The article concluded with these words:

> Whatever of Good Brigham Young may have done, or planned; whatever of his acts may tend to ameliorate the condition of his people; whatever was pure and true in his teachings, we desire such to prosper and flourish, and while that portion of the community known as his people, are wrapped in grief at his demise, we, in respect for the sincerity of their sorrow, will for the time being, let his errors pass to the judgement of that higher tribunal, from whose justice there is no appeal, and whose decrees cannot be evaded.[30]

But the subsequent account of Young's funeral contended that there was little sincerity in the sorrow for the "big Mormon chief." Freeman fell into line among the mourners and passed down the central aisle of the tabernacle to view the remains. His detailed description exceeded his reportorial duties and illustrates his increasing fascination with death. He told his readers of the

> coffin of redwood with two inches surplus space in width and two in length, and the body lying on a cotton bed with the head resting on a pillow, with room enough for the Prophet to turn a little in his coffin if he wished to, as this was in accordance with his written instructions. . . . Mortification was fast setting in as evidenced by the spots on the face. The whiskers had been clipped a little shorter. But little shrinkage had taken place, and upon the whole the corpse might be said to look natural, in the usual acceptation of the term.[31]

Freeman seemed to have an unusual preoccupation with death and the effects of death. Earlier that year he wrote, "George Washington is petrifying. In repairing the tomb at Mount Vernon, an inspection of the sarcophagus discovered the fact that G. W. is now a soft sandstone of a leathery color, perfect in features, lacking eyes and ears which have disappeared. At the next Centennial he is to be set up for his own statue." Later Freeman reported, "A drowned body generates gasses which brings it to the surface in about five or six days subsequent to the loss of life. After floating about three days a collapse takes place and the body sinks and generates other gasses, rising then in about fifteen days, when after floating a short time it sinks to rise no more. The period thus embraced is about twenty-five days at the outside."[32]

Moving to a point directly opposite the corpse, Freeman seated himself and watched the proceedings for five hours. He estimated that fully 20,000 persons passed the bier,

> and without exception every eye was dry, and but few handkerchiefs brought into requisition. . . . Even Mary Ann Angel, the first and—as he swore in court—the only wife of Brigham, barely put her kerchief to her mouth and did not raise it to her eyes. The wife of one of Brigham's sons turned to one side in her seat, after taking her last look, and affected grief, but there were no tears. Two of Brigham's daughters put their handkerchiefs to their eyes as they returned to their seats, but made no appearance of sobbing. . . . As for the thousands of the Prophet's followers, not one exhibited anything more than a morbid curiosity. . . .[33]

Freeman completed his journalistic function by accompanying the mourners to the grave in the family cemetery at the mouth of City Creek canyon. "Brigham Young did not do much good in his lifetime, but during his latter years he resolved to set a good example to humanity; he prohibited the purchase of mourning at his funeral," the account concluded.

Freeman believed that the office of the presidency "unquestionably" now belonged to Joseph Smith III. He wrote to Smith in Illinois and invited him "in this time of ripened harvest to come to Utah and thrust in his sickle and reap." But he met the same discouraging response from Smith that he had from the Mormons and the Liberal party, when Smith replied:

> It is to be hoped that you have correctly diagnosed the case, and that your conclusions are correct, in respect to the feeling in Utah.
> Whatever shall be proper for me to do, as determined by me and the brethren associated with me, that I shall do.
> There are three sides to this question: The Church in Utah, the element called there the outside or Gentile, and the ones we occupy as a Church. What may seem feasible and proper from your standing ground may not be so from ours, all things considered. However, the times are ominous, and changes are imminent.
>   In respect, JOSEPH SMITH.[34]

Freeman had to rely on his travels to generate the suport he could not obtain through local affiliations. But he probably was exaggerating when he claimed in 1877 that the *Ogden Freeman* was the only newspaper in Utah which was "clearing money." He reported an increase of nearly 2,000 subscribers over 1876 among the total circulation of 4,785, with division among these states and territories: Utah, 1,100; Nevada, 350; New Mexico, 150; Colorado, 400; Arizona, 325; Montana, 100; Washington, 240; Dakota, 200; Wyoming, 550; Idaho, 600; Nebraska, 120; British Columbia, 75; Oregon, 275; "other states," 300.[35] However, in a full page advertisement in the *Ogden City Directory, 1878,* Freeman claimed a total circulation of 6,950. Listed were these totals: Utah, 1,765; Nevada, 550; New Mexico, 150; Colorado, 400; Arizona, 325; Montana, 443; Washington, 397; Dakota, 200; Wyoming, 719; Idaho, 981; Nebraska, 120; British Columbia, 75; Oregon, 424; "Other states," 300.[36] A twentieth-century newspaper with a similar circulation charging a similar subscription price could expect a sizable annual gross income. But Freeman obviously did not have 6,950 paying subscribers nor did his advertising ratio provide a normal supplement to subscription income.

No new readers were claimed by the *Ogden Freeman* in Utah Territory itself, although Ogden had grown to 7,000 residents by this time. The city had become a shipping depot for two million persons in the Rocky Mountains and the Pacific Northwest, Freeman said, and it was "the most prosperous place between San Francisco and Omaha." Yet to discourage the arrival of two commercial printers who were rumored to be considering moving to Ogden, Freeman wrote in an ironic vein:

> Ogden is a good place for job printers. Our first week here all that we got to do was $1.50 worth of poetry, printed for an old lady in memory of her son; and after waiting six weeks we took our pay in wormy windfall apples. The job printing in Ogden to-day does not as a rule pay a dollar in money. What little there is goes in barter and truck. . . . If it were not for the custom that we get outside of Utah Territory, in Nevada, Idaho, Oregon, Wyoming, Dakota, Colorado and Montana by personally canvassing for it, we would not remain here a day. No man with simply a job office can get that patronage; in fact, no one but ourselves can get it, for it is personal acquaintance and fitness for our business alone that brings it. . . .[37]

The traveling Vattel undoubtedly had some success in his solicitations, but it is difficult to ascertain Freeman's true financial status at any given time. Across the Wyoming border at Evanston, near the Bear River City site, an unfriendly competing editor conceded that Freeman had realized some gains:

> A short time ago, the bilk who runs the OGDEN FREEMAN, went over into the Sweetwater country to get subscribers for that

contemptible sheet. By talking the people nearly to death, he succeeded in getting quite a number. At Camp Brown . . . the Post
Trader had to order him out of his store. . . . We noticed about 20
copies of the OGDEN FREEMAN on the floor of the Post Office.
. . . addressed to parties here, but they had seen all they wanted of
it . . . [none] wished to take a paper that was run by so low and
contemptible a bilk as the soulless fraud who runs that dirty
sheet.[38]

Even though Freeman antagonized such editors, Ada Freeman
usually won favor, and perhaps sympathy, from those who knew the
couple. The *Utah Evening Mail* at Corinne claimed that the *Ogden
Freeman* came one week on the half shell, "The half we failed to
receive probably contains the reading matter." Apparently either the
"patent outsides" or the Ogden news on pages 2 and 3 had not been
printed. But two weeks later it reported that Mrs. Freeman had visited
the *Mail* office where "this accomplished lady is ever a welcome
visitor."[39]

And Mrs. Freeman attended to her family as well as assisting in
the newspaper office. A fourth son, Smohalla, was born on September
7, 1877, but died two years later.[40] In light of Freeman's anti-Indian
statements, it is strange that he named a son after the Indian
"dreamer" whom he described as a "general disturber of the peace."
However, in 1889, when names for Washington State were being considered, Freeman suggested Smohalla. He claimed then that Smohalla
was "one of the most remarkable of all the aborigines who had lived
on the North American Continent."[41] Freeman's sentiments for
Smohalla may have stemmed from the fact that he himself was interested in "scientific" spiritualism. Smohalla, or Smowhala, was a
member of the Wanapums at Priest Rapids on the Columbia River in
eastern Washington.

Undoubtedly Mrs. Freeman generated much of the goodwill that
brought the newspaper its local income. Early in 1879, Freeman moved
into a new two-story brick building, valued at more than $4,000, which
he termed the first printing office built in Utah by non-Mormon interests. But he never indicated the extent of a mortgage or whether the
structure was in fact built by him. Perhaps the growth of Ogden, for
which he immodestly took primary credit, did give him a greater
volume of business:

> Under the impetus given by the free press, the town which had
> lain dormant for seven years after the great transcontinental
> railroad had formed connections here, began to feel the infusion of
> new life. . . . Ogden is bound to become the greatest entrepot be-
> tween Chicago and San Francisco, with no rival to the north or to
> the south. . . .[42]

Just as he smarted under the "Mormon problem," which precluded the financial base he hoped to establish, Freeman saw most of

his personal problems in Ogden as the result of "Mormon plots" against him. A life-long series of legal battles began for Freeman in Utah Territory. In each case he bore the outcome, whether favorable or not, as the price of being "in the right."

In his first altercation in Ogden, Freeman apparently struck an employee, Joseph Blyman, during an argument. Freeman "used a cudgel so freely as to leave some claret stains about the sanctum, and the head of his late traveling agent," the newspaper at Corinne reported. A justice court judge fined Freeman $25 plus costs after the prosecuting attorney was reported to have stated in summary that "Freeman could not play his insanity dodges" on him.[43] Freeman claimed that he was the one who was attacked and shrilly asked for martial law in Utah to overcome this Mormon conspiracy against the free press:

> Mormon priests commissioned as policemen—rush in and give no chance for a possibility of bail, but drag a man from a bed of pro-tracted sickness at the dead hour of night. Warrant retained by the Mormon sheriff-priest for 18 hours, so as to preclude release on bail. Unmercifully forced through a howling, pelting snow-storm, to the private residence of a Mormon Chief Justice of the Peace, without being allowed a wrapping, a stimulant or to attend to the wants of nature. A bilk, who has committed the highest crime known to the social laws of the Hebrews. A wife deserter, does the dirty assassin's work for the Mormons. The motive is to check the American influence of the Freeman, and to suppress the Press, which the Federal officials wish to make the organ of the Federal Government in Utah.[44]

Before a second year had passed, Freeman became involved in a more serious incident. He began feuding in his columns early in 1877 with Ogden postmaster Neal J. Sharp, reporting alleged mismanagement of postal affairs, shortcomings, and "what seemed criminal action":

> But as it had long been the prayer of the loyal citizens of Utah that a non-Mormon should fill the position, and we supposed that a Republican . . . would conduct the business in systematic and satisfactory manner, we not only refrained from attacking Mr. Sharp . . . but we tried to satisfy the complainants that perhaps their suspicions were ill-founded. . . .[45]

Even this dubious support ended, Freeman reported, when he was forced, because of a smallpox epidemic, to start using the mails for delivery of the *Ogden Freeman* rather than carriers. Because "Sharp was continually on sprees," the newspapers were not delivered or missed train connections, Freeman charged. Finally, the postmaster told Mrs. Freeman that postage for the newspaper mailings was due immediately rather than at the end of the month. Freeman then ac-

cused Sharp of using postal funds for a personal trip to Washington,
D.C., and maintained that the Freeman postage money was needed to
cover the shortage:

> The most highhanded outrage ever perpetrated by a postal
> agent in the history of the Government, has been committed at
> Ogden, and it is the patriotic duty of every one in the land to aid in
> fixing the crime, and seeing the sanctity of the mail service
> restored and preserved.[46]

Freeman apparently asked the United States commissioner at Ogden,
E. A. Street, who had already felt the sting of Freeman's editorial
criticism, for redress. But this "Lickspittle of the Grant ring" ruled
that the postmaster at Ogden held the issues merely for the postage
due, Freeman reported of Street's refusal to intervene.

There the matter seemed to rest while Freeman-as-Vattel went to
central Idaho and Oregon to inspect the route of the "Portland, Dalles
& Ogden railroad." The trip was in no way a retreat from the confrontation with the postmaster. Freeman continued writing and soliciting subscriptions while traveling. But on this trip, news of his trouble
with the Ogden postmaster preceded him. Sharp wrote to the
postmaster at Walla Walla, Washington, claiming, "This man L. R.
Freeman is a dirty, lying, black-mailing bilk, who will visit your town. I
would advise the people to give him a wide berth." A Walla Walla
newspaper, in printing the letter, also quoted a comment from the *Salt
Lake City Daily Tribune* which similarly urged the people of Idaho to
"give this man Freeman a wide berth." With this advice set in type,
the *Walla Walla Union* added its own opinion:

> Whether this is a bilk or not, we do not propose to say, but it
> does seem to us that it looks rather cheeky in the man to get so far
> away from home to canvass for a "patent outside" newspaper. We
> expect to hear of his canvassing San Francisco shortly, where the
> outside is printed. However, there may be something on the inside
> that will interest the people in this country, but we failed to "see"
> it.[47]

While continuing on to Fort Wrangle, Alaska, Freeman sent a dispatch
back to Ogden noting the Walla Walla publication, but terming it a
"viperish" action that failed to harm him.[48]

When he returned, attacks on the postmaster continued in the
Ogden Freeman until the inevitable confrontation occurred. Freeman
went to the Ogden Post Office to pay his postage bill. After the transaction, Marshal Moroni Brown and Postmaster Sharp followed him into
the street where Sharp attacked him, according to Freeman's account,
or a fight ensued, according to the authorities. Freeman and Sharp
were fined $30 and $40 respectively in city court for fighting.

Headlines above the *Ogden Freeman*'s account gave readers a different impression of what had happened:

> ATTEMPTED MURDER. Postmaster Sharp Seeks to Assassinate the Editor of The Freeman with an Iron-Shod Bludgeon . . . Dr. Adams Pronounces that Mr. Freeman is Liable to Die from his Injuries Any Time.[49]

Despite what Freeman would have had his readers believe, his injuries were not serious enough to prevent him from writing his own account of the incident. In unmistakable Freeman rhetoric he cited as evidence of malice Sharp's "long piece of turned wood, in the end of which was a large screw [and] . . . band of iron four inches in width." He dubbed Marshal Brown "Dog Killer Brown" in print, but claimed that Sharp had called Freeman a "son of a b---h" upon his trip to the post office. Freeman said that the pair then followed him into the street,

> and, with murder in his eye . . . Sharp then caught Mr. Freeman by his beard, and with his right arm hurled a most violent blow on the left side of the head, barely grazing the temple. Mr. Freeman fell on the sidewalk, completely stunned, and Sharp, with his great strength and weight jumped on him and plied his blows. Sharp knew that Mr. F. was in the habit of carrying a small pocket Derringer, and he commenced making an outcry, demanding that Mr. F. should "give up that pistol. . . ."[50]

Onlookers broke up the fight and Freeman was taken to a physician's office, where stitches were taken in his scalp wounds. Freeman contended that he wanted to lodge a complaint with the assistant United States attorney against Sharp for assault with intent to commit murder but was temporarily prevented from doing so when Sharp immediately pleaded guilty to the lesser charge.

The following issue of the *Ogden Freeman* called the incident "the most cowardly brutal assassination ever known on the streets of Ogden." Apparently mindful of the reported discrepancies about his condition, Freeman said that despite the *Ogden Junction*'s claim that he was not seriously injured, "Dr. Adams not only pronounced Mr. Freeman's case dangerous, but says that he is liable to develop new and critical phases for several weeks." Initial accounts told how he was "continually retching and vomiting, at times spitting blood."[51]

Freeman swore out the assault complaint against Sharp in federal court. Sharp pleaded innocent, and at the trial Brown testified that the postmaster had said, "Now draw that pistol on me if you dare" when Freeman had put his right hand in his pants pocket before the blow was struck. Sharp was acquitted and Freeman complained bitterly in print, "As no murder was committed none was intended. To prove the intent of committing murder a man must be killed outright."[52]

In his next encounter Freeman was again the victim. The incident stemmed from an article he had printed:

> We understand there is a night operator in town, a recent importation, who has been kept dodging along the line, for some years, as a spy on all the employes. We give this hint to let the boys give him a wide berth. The same fellow is the one who deserted his family down on Laramie plains and wandered about through the mountains for a number of months pretending to be crazy.[53]

A "tall, bony-looking, villainous visaged fellow," saying that his name was Moses, struck Freeman a blow on the head while he was at his office desk. Freeman was again seized by his whiskers and several additional blows were delivered. A printing foreman broke up the assault and the assailant was turned over to the United States commissioner. The accused disappeared while free on bond, but Freeman again printed the story that had prompted the altercation, accepting no responsibility for the incident and stating self-righteously that he had named no one and had identified no agency.[54]

Freeman used his final legal dispute at Ogden as justification for not publishing a special 1879 New Year's edition as he had a year earlier. He contended that to stop publication of the 10,000 extra copies designed to attract gentiles to Ogden, the Mormons engaged two tramps to swear that he had instructed them to burn "fifteen cents' worth of coal from a railway car." For this, he said, he was bound over under $500 bond to appear before a grand jury which "the Mormons packed." He was not specific as to the disposition of the charges against him, but he vaguely prattled on that the ultimate grand jury report was an exposé of the interests that attempted to intimidate "The Free Press of Utah." Although he averred that he would not continue to tolerate such harrassment by Mormons, Freeman also showed that he still smarted from his failure to gain Liberal party support:

> We do not propose to continue to incur and stand the brunt of all such impositions put upon the Gentiles, while nickels are valued by the latter more than the dollars—yea, more than the thousands and hundreds of thousands of dollars that would be gained by united and successful opposition. As we have been left to bear the burden alone, we shall cast off the burden if the present policy of the so-called Liberal element is persisted in. . . .[55]

At the same time he was defining Mormon plots, Freeman's imagination led to a novel journalistic experiment. In an endeavor rivaling anything published in the *Frontier Index,* Freeman established a matrimonial bureau. It was the outgrowth of an offhand published remark that in two years' time five or six of the *Freeman* office girls had married and he had been compelled to look for other help. "We think of opening a matrimonial bureau to furnish spareribs for a consideration. Another matrimonial candidate please come forward."[56] It was only a way of advertising a position, but the idea developed when the *Deadwood Pioneer* of Dakota Territory copied his article proposing to solve this aspect of the "Mormon problem." Freeman's solution called for the Mormon "saintesses" to be married to gentile miners by giving the young women as "premiums" to Freeman's bachelor subscribers:

> If the *Pioneer* doubts that it is feasable [sic] he [sic] should have seen some of the Ogden girls kissing a wooden Indian in front of Dudden's tobacco store the other day. Girls that will kiss wooden Injuns would be very glad to marry flesh and blood white men.[57]

Freeman then received numerous letters asking about the possibility of procuring wives in Utah. He invited the writers to come to do their own courting:

> . . . we have determined to print a few of these missives and invite the attention of the female denomination to them. Marriage is a lottery in most cases, and . . . it takes years of after-marriage acquaintance before a fellow can determine whether he had drawn a prize or not. If there are any unmarried women or girls who feel disposed to profit by the arrangement, we will insert a limited number of advertisements for gentlemen correspondents, or for husbands, free of charge. If gentlemen wish to advertise, they will be treated with the same consideration.[58]

On New Year's Day, 1878, the first printed matrimonial pleas of the miners and maidens were offered. They ranged from the plaintive to the ludicrous:

> Wanted—A wife, under 20; a blond with good figure and a pretty face. Would rather she didn't know too much, so that I could mould [sic] her mind to suit myself. Address "H. H." *Freeman* office.

> A miner with a good claim would like to make the acquaintance of some good woman with about $1,000 capital. My address is, Thompson, care of *Ogden* Freeman.[59]

> I would like to correspond with a couple of well educated young gentlemen. Object fun, and perhaps matrimony. Address, Stella.

> The boys all say I am as pretty as a little red wagon. I have had a good many fellows trying to keep company with me, but I never felt like marrying any of them. I believe when a girl marries

she ought to think more of the man she takes, than of any other person she has ever seen, and I never saw anybody yet that I cared for in particular. I am almost tired of waiting for my mate to come along, and I thought I would advertise for him. Maybe that will bring him. Any respectable single man may answer this. Mary S.

Last night I dreamt that I got a letter wrapped up in your paper, and that a man wrote it and asked me to marry him. I took the dream as a revelation that I am to get a man through your paper, so I concluded to write and tell you my dream, and if there were any men writing to you for wives, you can send me their letters to answer, for I will try that way. Widow.

Put me down for a wife if you have lots of girls in Utah who want to get married. I am like the fellow whose father wanted him to take a wife. "Well dad," said he, "I will, but whose wife will I take." If I take a wife here, I've got to take some other man's and I am a little afraid that would raise a racket in camp. . . . I am a strong, hearty man; not much of a man for drinking or playing cards, and I want a wife who will be true and faithful or I don't want any. Address Rocky Bar John.

I'll be willing to give her all my money and stop sowing my wild oats before I put in a big crop. . . . I am partial to a fair-skinned woman, plump, but not too fat to get around lively of a cold morning, and I wouldn't have the slightest objection to her having an impediment in her speech. . . . I would treat a woman first-rate unless she got to crowding in on to me too much. . . . Handy Andy.[60]

Freeman claimed that the whole western country was in a furor of excitement over his matrimonial bureau and as a result "thousands" of new names had been added to his subscription list, an outcome ensured by his "rules":

In order to reach the desired end, we have arranged to give grand raffles every three months at The Freeman office; and in order that all the bachelors and Mormon lasses within a thousand miles, may have an opportunity to pair off, we have tickets for sale at $1.50 each, bearing numbers represented in the male and female lists, respectively. And any one drawing the mate to his, or her ticket, may on further acquaintance make a match. All purchasers of tickets receive the paper free.

All are requested to write descriptions of themselves, and if possible enclose their photographs.

Extracts from these letters are published in The Freeman and a copy of the paper sent regularly to every one who buys a ticket for the next ensuing raffle. . . .[61]

The new rules prompted even more entries. Among the dozens printed were these:

> . . . there are two young bachelors here, who are dying of loveliness [*sic*], and who would most gladly welcome [from the ladies of Ogden] their correspondence and do their best to merit their approval. "Tall oaks from little acorns grow," and who knows but that we may be able to strike an affinity with some of the lovely fair sex, that will be the open sesame to a life-long happiness. Address all letters to Alpha or Omega.[62]

> I have been left by my husband, to get along the best I could, and make a living for my little boy and me. I have not heard from him for over two years. I think I had better get a divorce, and marry some man, but I don't want to pay out money for a divorce, if I ain't certain of a man. My man will never come back, for he is too shiftless. I am too poor to spend money, but I would have to get my divorce before I would get married. I am a Methodist. A man that wants a wife, can pay for my divorce. Mary Ann

> I am sixteen years old, freckled face, and have red hair. They all tell me I will never get married, because men won't take red-headed girls. Now, if there is any decent man who is not afraid of red hair, he can write to me. Alice[63]

Unfortunately, neither the connubial nor the financial success of this six-month frontier matrimonial bureau is recorded.

Horatio Vattel spent many weeks traveling while Mrs. Freeman ran the newspaper. He looked for stories as well as subscriptions as he wandered throughout the Rocky Mountains. He again became the Indian scout, but the red men he saw during a spring (1879) trip to Fort Washakie, Wyoming, had perhaps changed more than Vattel:

> It was really charming to take in at a glance the military barracks, the Agency buildings, and the lodges of over 2,000 Indians dotting the valley of Little Wind River and its tributaries.
> Black Coal and his northern Arrapahoes [*sic*], numbering about 1,000 souls, had their village pitched along a brook near the famous Hot Springs, while Washakie's lodges, containing 1,200 people were scattered up and down the several beautiful streams, from the Agency to the canyons of the Wind River Mountains. . . . Everywhere that the eye might turn, bands of cattle and ponies were to be seen moving hurriedly in from the hills. The white ranchmen, who had settled on the reservation previous to its being set apart by the Government, were busily engaged in seeding small grain, and the red squaws were employed, some dressing buffalo and deer skins fresh from the winter's hunt east of the Big Horn Mountains, and others packing wood, or ponies, from the creeks to lodges. . . .

Major Upham, from Indian Territory, now is in command of the post and has two companies of cavalry at his service. Twenty odd of the Bannacks captured last Fall are quartered in a building, and they appear perfectly contented. It is the intention to send them to join Chief Joseph at an early date. . . .[64]

Freeman's irrepressible affinity for frontier life is evident in his account. But this was his last recorded trip among Indians. He still depicted them as something less than noble savages, but after his trials at Ogden they did not seem so inferior to the white man as they had in 1868:

> The morning after reaching the Fort a friend kindly loaned a pony and we galloped away to the Hot Springs for a bath. Arriving there we found the water occupied by a number of Arrapahoes, who were going through with such disgusting antics, that after observing for a few moments, we rode away without the bath, preferring the dust from the stage road to the association of the filthy savages. One sinewy old buck was engaged in alternately sucking the breast of his squaw and an old sore on her ankle, and accompanying this with guttural and grunting sounds, and "eh, hi! eh, hi! eh hi!" adding after each manoeuvre a remark to us: "Me heap big medicine!" then he would repeat the nasty antic until at last he drew from the old sore the bloody corruption, which he would spit into his hand and exhibit as proof of his power as a medicine man.
>
> Remembering that this tribe of Arrapahoes are reputed to be rotten with syphilitic diseases, we came to the conclusion that we didn't want any bath in that water. The association was too repulsive. Notwithstanding the depravity witnessed, we will, however, state for the benefit of some brazen gentry who stripped in the bathing trains at Ogden last summer, that not one of those savages was so debased in that degree as to expose his nakedness to the eyes of the spectators. . . .[65]

Freeman continued the account from the Arapaho village itself, in conversation with the war chief, Black Coal, whom he found harnessing a span of ponies:

> Reining up, we ejaculated: "Black Coal, chief!" The finest looking Indian in the group responded by springing forward with open palm, and the utterance: "Yes, me—how! Glad to see you!" He enquired, "Who are you?" and we reminded him of the visits that his tribe had made years ago to our camps on the Yellowstone and other places. He was quite communicative. He is a young man about thirty years of age, fully six feet in stature, with very regular and bold features, as though born to command by his presence. He soon resumed the hitching of his team to a new red wagon, his awkward, skittish movements demonstrating that he was afraid of the two scabby, little bucking and kicking scrubs. Yes, here was a

vaunted chief of a much dreaded tribe exhibiting the fear of an infant. . . .[66]

Riding through the Arrapaho village we noticed a squaw, with face turned downward toward the earth; she was wrapped in a buffalo robe and evidently hiding her features from the observer; enquiring the cause of this we were told that she had been one of the best looking squaws among the tribe, but by receiving the attentions of another than her Hiawatha, she was pursued on to the prairie, knocked down with a club; her head frightfully gashed with a knife so as to spoil her beautiful suit of hair; her face cut to pieces and her upper front teeth entirely cut out, gums and all. Her jealous lord then attempted to stab her to the heart, but was prevented by other Indians who had reached the scene, and who declared that as she was about killed anyway she should be allowed to die without further molestation. She however lived, though her horribly scarred physique is so repulsive that she seeks to hide it. Such is the penalty for unfaithfulness; from being the most admired of the band, this squaw has become the most detestable. The Arrapahoes are reputed to be much less virtuous than the Shoshones. Indeed, the latter say that they always kill an unfaithful squaw.[67]

To the discriminating observer, Freeman displayed a wistfulness for the days of the *Frontier Index* when he reminded the chief of their Yellowstone visits. He clearly was getting restless. It was time for another move, the only remedy for this malady. Perhaps it was only coincidental that upon his return from Fort Washakie, under the headline, "FRONTIER INDEX REDEVIVUS," he announced that a branch of the *Ogden Freeman* would be published in Montana at the terminus of the Utah and Northern Railroad:

The paper will be called The Frontier Index, which all Western men knew as their friend, while running as the "Press on Wheels" at the ten terminal towns of the Union Pacific Railroad and which was destroyed at Bear River City, Nov. 20th, 1868, at the time forty men met their deaths in front of its door.[68]

The Utah and Northern had been purchased by the Union Pacific and was headed for a junction with the Northern Pacific near Butte.

It is significant that in announcing the move, Freeman mentioned a new railroad frontier rather than Montana's mining camps, although he had reported news of Butte, Helena, and the Salmon River country. This time he left his family behind and moved to Montana. By August 1879 he had ordered the *Ogden Freeman* discontinued and had sent for his family to join him.

There is no evidence that news of Freeman's departure from Ogden was received with regret, although even the Mormons obviously held his wife in high regard. The common assessment was later formalized there in print:

In the summer of 1875, Mr. Legh R. Freeman and wife arrived
here, and commenced the publication of a semi-weekly paper bearing their own name, the OGDEN FREEMAN. The first number
was issued by the lady, Mrs. Ada V. Freeman. It was very
conservative in tone and character. Indeed, Mrs. Freeman appeared desirous to conciliate the people of Ogden, and gain their
good will. She succeeded to some extent, by her non-interference
with the religious and social system of the citizens. But when
Freeman arrived here, the policy of the paper was soon changed.
He was a strong anti-Mormon—in fact was a sort of Wild
Ishmaelite. His hand was soon turned against every man that he
could not bulldoze, but he sometimes met with severe retaliation.

Freeman was in continual hot water during the time he remained here, in consequence of his malignity, and abuse of many
of the citizens. In 1879 he collapsed, and the same season he
started with his family for Montana. . . .[69]

While details of Freeman's "collapse" were not provided, it was
undoubtedly prompted in part by his four-year frustration in attempting
to find Ogden resources commensurate with his original expectations.
He had been ignored by the Mormons and the Liberal party and then
had suffered the sting of rebuke from his journalistic competitors. The
Mormon assessment of Freeman's nature was thus at once accurate
and prophetic. A true Ishmael, he would always be a wanderer and at
odds with society. Fortunately for him, the West could still ac-
commodate his now habitual demand for another fresh start.

A "John Brown Republican"

IN EARLY AUGUST 1879 Ada Freeman supervised loading of the Ogden printing equipment into two covered wagons for the trip to Butte, where her husband had revived the *Frontier Index*. She was at the reins of one wagon as the small caravan pulled out of Ogden; a printer drove the second. In the vehicles were Freeman's printing supplies and presses, the family's household goods, and the Freeman youngsters.

By August 16 the wagons had crossed Monida Pass from Idaho and were in the Red Rock country of southwestern Montana, some 150 miles south of Butte. The rough road shook the wagons, dislodging a shotgun hanging in looped straps in the vehicle Mrs. Freeman was driving. It fell into the spokes of a front wheel, discharging a load of bird shot into her hip. The roar, the smoke, and their mother's outcry were never forgotten by the Freeman youngsters.[1] While she was bedded down in the wagon to continue the trip to Butte for medical treatment, word was sent ahead to Freeman, who met the wagons on the road before they reached the town. Freeman charged that the printer accompanying Mrs. Freeman, R. B. Cooley, pillaged a gripsack while she lay wounded in order to obtain a bill of sale for the vehicle and team, sell them, and leave the country. The bill of sale had been in Mrs. Freeman's pocketbook. Freeman said that he had gotten Cooley railroad passes from New England to Ogden and supplied him with a housekeeping outfit. Hired by a rival newspaper in Butte, Cooley sought unsuccessfully to prove in court that the team and wagon were his. He and his family then left for Iowa.

Freeman became a widower at 8:00 A.M. on August 22. The following day's edition of the *Frontier Index* carried the inverted column rules that were the nineteenth-century journalist's black bands of mourning. The editorial Freeman penned for the issue, while taking due cognizance of his wife's attributes as a journalistic helpmate, was not without a passing criticism of the Mormons:

She was one of the noblest women on earth. During the most excruciating suffering she was joyous to the last, and when informed that she must die, said: "Well, I am prepared for death. Tell my children to be good, and meet me in heaven." Even after the soul had taken its flight, her whole face beamed with serenity and pleasure. As joint editor of *The Ogden Freeman,* she performed good work in Utah, and even the Mormons regretted her departure, after opening their eyes to the errors of Mormonism. . . . During life she and her husband pledged each other that which ever one departed this life first, that one would return in the spirit as a proof of a future existence, and this promise was renewed at the hour of dissolution. So that though the flesh be dead, the soul hovers over the living and cheers and comforts him in the performance of earthly duties. Her name will be retained at the head of the editorial columns, and it is believed that the holy diction of this guardian angel will inspire the pen of the surviving editor to pure and noble sentiments.[2]

The fascination with the spirit world expressed in the obituary began some eleven years earlier during a trip to San Francisco, where he observed widespread interest in clairvoyants. He had met one, a Mrs. Helena Dielterlie, who had supposedly told him all about Culpeper County and his western mountain adventures. In fact, the incidents surrounding his wife's fatal accident were foretold to him, he later related, through supernatural revelations. He claimed that when the couple had parted in Ogden, Mrs. Freeman could utter only the words, "Well, father, once more!" Then, on the rainy morning of her accident, he was in a Butte reading room. The proprietor, "who had been pacing the floor," looked up, Freeman said, and exclaimed, "I was just wondering what that d---d thing is, over the door!" Freeman said that he observed a raven perched outside the transom, and later recounted:

This is an incident strikingly similar to the one that suggested "Poe's Raven," wherein Poe[,] in pacing the floor, "Wondered what that was over the door!" And in addressing it for tidings of his beloved "Elanore [sic]," received as a response, a croak which he construed as "Never more!"

Here was Mrs. Freeman's "once more," rhyming to the raven's croak "Never more;" [sic] Exactly at that hour of that day, she received her death wound. . . . After she was apparently dead, at 4 a.m., we said, "She will revive as the sun comes over the mountains;" and the life did come back into her body, the ashen corpse colored up with the circulating blood, and she laughed, talked and joked two hours after she had been pronounced dead by Dr. Holmes.

Following the remains to the grave the singular incident of the raven was referred to, and Mrs. Bowler said: "Why, Mr. Freeman, that was our pet raven raised at our residence where your wife died, and we have not seen it since that fatal hour!"[3]

Legh Freeman with his sons in 1879: (left) Miller, four; (seated) Hoomes, six; (standing) Randolph, nine. (courtesy Western History Research Center, University of Wyoming)

Some of these fantasies may have come as a result of Freeman's remorse over extended absences from his wife, including the one during the latest trip when he had left her with the responsibility of moving the printing plant. But while he may have shunted some burdens upon her, it was not necessarily because of a lack of affection. Horatio Vattel's character made certain demands upon his life that made compliance with family responsibilities very difficult. It was more natural for Freeman to don Vattel's garb than it was to sit by the family hearth or share in the process of community building. This had been true before his wife's death and it would continue to be the case.

It was therefore with some relief that he now placed his sons in school in Utah. The three older sons, Randolph, Hoomes, and Legh Miller, went first to a Catholic school in Salt Lake City and then to Sacred Heart Academy at Ogden. They had been enrolled at Sacred Heart when the family lived in Ogden. A fourth son, undoubtedly Smohalla, is mentioned in Mrs. Freeman's obituary, but there is no further reference to him. Although separated from their father, the educational experience was "not at all unhappy," according to Miller Freeman. Part of the expense of the boys' education was offset by advertisements for the academy Freeman ran in his newspapers.[4]

Butte seemed to be an ideal place for a man of Freeman's nature, for it was a boisterous town whose economy at that time was dependent upon silver quartz mining. Rich placers of gold had been found in the vicinity of Butte in 1864, the first mining district was formed, and the town's population soon reached 500, but the placers gave out and the town nearly died. By 1870 the census recorded only 241 people in town, including 98 Chinese, yet by the mid-1870s a technique was developed to make the mining of black, manganese-stained silver ores profitable. Freeman was thus among those who were drawn to Butte by the hope of a silver boom, but his wanderlust would not let him stay there long. Impatient and fiddle-footed, he had moved on by the time investors such as George Hearst underwrote Butte's spectacular growth and prosperity during the "War of the Copper Kings." In fact, Freeman, chastened by his Wyoming coal speculation, restricted himself in Montana primarily to the newspaper business and apparently shunned mining ventures altogether.

Until this time Freeman had exhibited no real deviation from the strong Democratic allegiance he had first proclaimed in 1868. In joining the anti-Mormon Liberal party in Ogden, Freeman had displayed no Republican sympathy and had seemed preoccupied only with its anti-Mormon tenets. Now, in a radical departure from everything he had ever professed, he claimed to be a Republican of good standing. He showed his willingness, as in Ogden, to change ground for the possibility of the guaranteed financial support most western editors found necessary to survive. His availability to cooperate with a political party, in other words, was typical of the era in American journalism when much of the press, rather than representing the "fourth estate" or the people, spoke for the political body that provided its support.

Not surprisingly, then, Freeman in 1880 backed the Republican candidate for territorial delegate to Congress, Wilbur F. Sanders, who, he told his readers, was the "old war horse." He may have taken this action to get business from local Republicans, to get federal legal advertising from a Republican administration, or, as he later claimed, merely because he came to Butte at the invitation of "leading Republicans." He boasted that during his whole career on the frontier, "a period of 31 years, we have been a John Brown Republican . . . and since the division in Republican ranks, we have been steadfastly stalwart."[5] It was no coincidence, therefore, that Freeman published not only the entire Beaverhead County Republican ticket and platform, but also patent notices for the United States Land Office at Helena. At the government-allowed rate of 50 cents a line and running for sixty days, the income from the legal advertising alone could well have motivated Freeman to become a Republican.

Freeman first took a formal stand for the Republican party in the *Atlantis,* which he published for a short time at Glendale, a Beaverhead County community in the Trapper mining district between Butte and Dillon. He called the publication "a branch" of the *Frontier Index* in Butte and wrote copy and editorials for both newspapers. The defeat of the Democratic candidate, Martin Maginnis, for delegate, Freeman contended,

> will work the emancipation of the democratic party from its slavery to the Helena ring, and secure the free choice of a candidate in 1882 by the masses of the party. . . . With a republican president, who is his intimate personal friend, and a Republican Congress, he cannot fail to be more influential and to give the interests of Montana an impulse that will place her in the front rank of territories. We appeal to the voters of Beaverhead county to ponder upon these considerations to give each its due weight and then to accord their hearty support to Wilbur F. Sanders.[6]

Freeman's support of Sanders notwithstanding, Maginnis—whom Freeman had labeled "Maginnis-sota" for his favoritism toward Minnesota contractors—beat Sanders 173–115 in Beaverhead County and 7,779–6,281 in the territory.[7]

In the same issue of the *Atlantis* (November 17, 1880) in which he announced the county election returns, Freeman accused "the Republican scribbler who writes Democratic slush" for the Butte *Miner* of complicity in a deal for Beaverhead County and Deer Lodge County printing. The *Miner,* a Democratic paper, was well established, having been published since July 1876, initially on a press hauled in from Virginia City. Started as a tri-weekly, the *Miner* became a weekly later in 1876 because only weekly mail service existed and rural subscribers found no need to spend money on unneeded issues. On August 5, 1879, when Freeman was becoming established, the *Miner* became a daily and made available to Butte residents telegraphic news from Western Union wires. But Freeman apparently got at least some of the political plums because he advertised the *Atlantis* as the official newspaper of Beaverhead County.

Competition for political printing became intense. Freeman began publication of the Republican daily *Frontier Index* at the start of 1881 in full competition with the Democratic *Daily Miner*. The rumored start of a third daily newspaper in addition to the *Index* and *Miner* he naturally saw as a threat, especially since it was said to be backed by Republicans:

> The Frontier Index will give the people of Butte all the daily paper that they want to pay for. A third daily paper would simply cripple all the offices so that none of them could publish respectable sheets. . . .
> For the benefit of aspirants to the newspaper business in Montana and Butte especially, we have the following offer to make:
> The proprietor of this paper will give a bond for a deed of the entire news and job office of The Frontier Index, with its business as established, to any party who will give a forfeit bond to run a daily and weekly paper and job office in Butte City, with better success than we have done.
> This is not a piece of levity. We need the forfeit money for a tour around the world, while writing editorial correspondence for The Frontier Index; and we are ready to prove our words by our deed.[8]

No trip around the world materialized, but the third daily newspaper, the *Daily Inter Mountain,* appeared for the first time on March 22, 1881. Within weeks it was making its Republican sentiments known and apparently picked up United States Land Office notices in return. In rhetoric reminiscent of his Ogden days when he lost Liberal party support, Freeman exploded against this "spurious campaign sheet" in his own newly renamed newspaper, the *Inter-Mountains Freeman,* which replaced the *Atlantis* and the *Frontier Index.* This name change was dictated, Freeman said, because the new daily had "attempted to steal the name announced for our paper," and he warned his readers that a solicitor for the competing *Daily Inter Mountain* was heading for Deer Lodge, Missoula, and Helena:

> . . . this man has no more right to solicit for The Inter-Mountains or any paper aping us in the title of our paper, than an angel of the devil has to take his converts into the holy of holies. We applied for a patent for the name of our paper . . . and notice of which was given four months ago in The Atlantis and The Frontier Index; and any infringement on said patent will be promptly prosecuted; and the bogus "wildcat" out fit will soon be closed up by process of law.[9]

Freeman needed no subscription solicitors because his newspaper was distributed without charge.

As if to prove that his newspaper, the *Inter-Mountains Freeman,* was the county's true Republican organ, Freeman in 1881 headlined an off-year "REPUBLICAN VICTORY" in which the "stalwarts" elected every officer in Silver Bow County except treasurer and probate judge. The new county, carved from Deer Lodge County, was "as pure as a virgin," Freeman's headline read. Part of his enthusiasm undoubtedly stemmed from the fact that all Republican printing in the new county was done by Freeman's plant.

> The Central Committee finally saw the nigger in the woodpile [he said], when the fact could no longer be concealed that to get it done through Imitator [*Daily Inter Mountain*] agencies, would be giving it dead away, all the campaign tricks to the morning edition of the Imitator surnamed the Minus [*Miner*].[10]

But Freeman saw a shadowy political conspiracy afoot involving his competitors. He ignored the fact that the *Daily Inter Mountain* had attacked the *Miner* and that the two newspapers had separate corporate officers. He maintained that the former paper was the "Republican edition of the Democratic Minus [*Miner*]" because it was printed at the *Miner* office:

> The whole job was put up by a secret agent of the Minus who not only induced our noble Republican Governor to sign away the public printing of a republican county to a democratic sheet [*Daily Inter Mountain*], before he signed the act, making a law of the Silver Bow county enabling bill; but in addition to this, said secret agent secure to the evening republican edition of the democratic Minus, the land office paper, so far as prospectors and mine owners may prefer to give it to the twilight sheets, instead of the genuine Republican paper—The Inter-Mountains Freeman, which previously had the contract to publish all Federal advertisements. . . .
>
> What do republicans think of such a method of the democracy to freeze out a true republican paper? . . .[11]

Freeman was determined that his publication would not be deprived of these lucrative printing revenues. To confirm his Republican loyalties, he announced a 25-cent-a-week charge for "the genuine Republican paper . . . established 31 years ago by Legh R. Freeman."[12] At the time of this announcement he was only thirty-eight years old.

The continuing dispute between the two newspapers about the confusion in names came to a climax late in 1881. A short time before, Freeman had announced that he had leased the *Daily Inter-Mountains* and weekly *Inter-Mountains Freeman* to two Deer Lodge brothers who planned to publish daily and weekly newspapers to be known as the

Montana News. But the two brothers returned the paper to Freeman less than a month later because he was being sued by the owners of the *Daily Inter Mountain* over his use of the *Inter-Mountains Freeman* nameplate. In Freeman's opinion, the suit was the "cheekiest thing in the history of journalism." As when brought to court in Ogden, Freeman took his case to his readers:

> Such a suit will be worth to us at least $20,000 not only in advertising but in the victory which we are sure to achieve. It is a fact patent to all the people of the inter-mountains region, from Mexico to British America, and from the Missouri to the Pacific, that we have been using the name Inter-Mountains throughout a long term of years, and that the editor of this paper was the originator of the name; that no other living man ever used the term. . . .
>
> From the day that our press began to voice the politics of the Republicans, we have ever been true, consistent, steadfast, zealous and stalwart; and up to the hour that we are carried from the office feet foremost, to be placed beside the partner of our joys, in yonder Masonic cemetery, we shall never deviate, swerve nor hesitate in the pursuit of such a course.
>
> Like Old Davy Crockett, we know we are right, and gallop ahead. . . .[13]

As legal maneuvering in the suit continued, Freeman kept telling his readers that the whole thing was a political plot against him. To be exact, he said, it was an attempt to "filch through the agency of the United States Land Office that which rightly belongs to the administration paper (this one) . . . having published on the frontier for a third of the century. . . ." Freeman mused in print whether "the next thing they undertake will not be to sue us to relinquish our children to them."[14] The case continued for 15 months before being dismissed on March 15, 1883.[15]

Touches of Horatio Vattel had not been entirely absent from Freeman's Montana journalism during the legal skirmishes. In the *Atlantis* he provided a Vattelian critique of a new work of art:

> One of the prettiest pictures in town is hanging in Frank Gilg's Brewery. It is an oil painting of a half nude maiden developed into a form voluptuous and poetical with hair falling naturally down her bosom, as she lies at full length on some mossy rocks beside a rippling stream of limpid water coursing its way through a mountain defile similar to the one in which we live. Byron's poems are spread out before her love-flashing eyes, while trout glide along the stream winking at the nymph, and the black pine squirrels and jack daws leap from bough to bough, chattering among the over hanging trees. . . . The painting is a very refined one, portraying rare and chaste beauty and virtue, and is an excellent specimen of fine art.[16]

In addition to these comments on fine art in a brewery, Freeman also dusted off Vattel's accounts of his experiences with Jim Bridger. He related how the superstitious yarns about ghosts and hobgloblin hosts told by Bridger's partner, Lu Anderson, had stimulated him to explore the Yellowstone country.

Then, in a contrasting vein, one reminiscent of the *Ogden Freeman*'s matrimonial bureau, Freeman announced that he was instituting a women's department:

> In the cities the ladies have their afternoon tea-parties, sewing societies, etc., where house-hold affairs and topics of general information are discussed. But those in Montana and surrounding territories who live on ranches and in little burgs are so far away from everybody else, that they have little opportunity to gossip with their neighbors, and hence are unable to add to their store of household knowledge. Now we propose to give every lady a chance, through our columns, to tell all she knows and ask questions about everything she doesn't know, which she thinks would be of any interest to her neighbors. During the long severe winters many find the days exceedingly dull and lonesome, hence, we thought by forming a ladies Chit-Chat Circle, many dreary winter hours might be spent both pleasantly and usefully by all those who care to become its members. We invite every one, young and old, pretty and plain, rich and poor, to join our circle. . . .[17]

Recipes for cake icing, plum pudding, and egg tonic followed in the "Chit Chat Corner" along with directions for making window curtains. Freeman's logic was unimpeachable. However unlikely this domestic fare might seem in a western territory, eastern metropolitan newspapers, too, were just beginning to devote space to women's news, fashion article, and recipes.

Horatio Vattel could not substitute such women's prattle, however, for the necessity of mountain travel. Because he had no wife or brother to leave in charge of the newspaper, Freeman turned it over to a new editor, George W. Carlton of San Jose, California. The Lightning Scout of the Mountains again sent dispatches back to the newspaper, but now they were signed merely "Legh R. Freeman." The West was being civilized and Horatio Vattel was approaching middle age. Still, the trips seemed to be more an emotional release than mere revenue-soliciting journeys.

During much of 1881 Freeman roamed through Idaho, Montana, and the Yellowstone country, returned to Ogden, and went on to Spokane Falls, Washington Territory. While returning from Wood River, Idaho, on one of these trips, he was hospitalized at Missoula for treatment of "cutaneo-cellular erysipelas" in his right hand.[18] Even though he was temporarily free from publishing responsibilities, his ubiquitous legal difficulties mounted. He was taken before District Court Judge Galbraith by a James A. Murray, who charged him with forcible entry. Freeman was alleged to have taken possession of a parcel of ground, "depriving the plaintiff of the rent issue and profits therefrom, the rental value being $10.00 a month."[19] The judge found in Freeman's favor on March 30, 1882.

During Freeman's absence from the newspaper, Carlton showed that he now controlled the *Inter-Mountains Freeman.* It became a newspaper of moderate tone and of Democratic politics. In fact, the new editor gave readers their first unbiased view of the *Inter-Mountain* legal action:

> It is unfortunate that the names of these papers should be so near alike for it tends to materially complicate the business of the two offices. We have no stock in the legal controversy and shall hail the decision, which ever way it goes, with delight.[20]

Carlton even exhibited cooperation when he announced that the publishers of the three Butte daily newspapers had adopted a uniform scale of prices for advertising. When the 1882 election for territorial delegate to Congress approached, Carlton editorialized in support of the Democratic incumbent, Martin Maginnis, the same candidate Freeman had opposed two years earlier. The full Democratic ticket was reprinted under the newspaper's masthead. Maginnis was reelected by a vote of 12,398 to 10,914.

What Freeman, the galvanized Republican, thought of this switch in editorial policy is not recorded. Nor is it known why he returned to Butte from his travels in the Rocky Mountains and terminated his partnership with Carlton. Perhaps he parted with Carlton in yet another raucous quarrel. By August 1882 he was again editing the *Inter-Mountains Freeman,* and during the next two years he seems to have faced continual financial difficulty. The August 6, 1882, issue of the *Inter-Mountains Freeman* listed total circulation as 7,885. Montana subscribers totaled 2,500; Utah, 1,100; Nevada, 750; Colorado, 400; Arizona, 325; Washington, 240; Dakota, 200; New Mexico, 208; Wyoming, 550; Idaho, 900; Nebraska, 120; British Columbia, 75; Oregon, 275; "other states," 300. Undoubtedly he had by this time lost the Republican printing business he had worked so hard to keep.

When faced by such adversity, Freeman's reactions became predictable. His chameleon-like nature allowed him to become a spokesman for labor interests as readily as he had become an advocate for the Republican party. On April 1, 1883, he announced a new publishing venture, the *Union—Freeman,* a consolidation of his newspaper and the *Daily Labor Union.* Now he claimed that he had always been an ardent friend of labor:

> THIS PAPER is conducted by a Union of Freeman, on bed rock principles of human right. The days of placer mining is [*sic*] past; the quartz era is in full blast, and we propose to go it on the

principle of deep mining below water level; and the reduction and refinement of the novel metals tried by crucial tests; submitted to thorough roasting, milling and smelting. . . .[21]

Freeman listed sixteen stockholders who owned from three to fifty shares apiece. He was not included in the list, but presumably held half the shares based on the real and personal property of the printing plant which he valued at $10,000. It was announced that an "experienced journalist from the mining regions of Pennsylvania" was to be general manager of the new paper.[22]

Labor had been organized in Butte since 1878, the year the Butte Workingmen's Union had struck over wages and had won. Since that time there had been no significant labor problems, so Freeman's confidence in associating with a union venture may have stemmed from the numbers of men working in Butte mining operations. From its 1880 population of 3,364, Butte in 1883 was growing toward a population that would earn monthly wages of $600,000 by 1884 when more than 300 mines were operating and more than 4,000 location notices were posted on surrounding hills. The mines, quartz mills, and four smelters yielded $14 million in copper and silver in 1884. In 1883, when Freeman began his union newspaper, he made his own inflated inventory of these prospects:

> All indications point to the probability that there will be at least 5,000 miners and mill and smelter men, 200 timber men, 1,000 wood haulers and 1,000 coal burners, at work here before the season closes, and that the number of laborers on steady wages, averaging from $3 to $7 per day, will steadily increase until the close of this century.
> The city already looks better in every sense than Virginia [City], Nevada, ever did in the palmy days of the Comstock. . . .
> By the vote last fall, we have proof that there are within a radius of five miles, over 15,000 people. . . .[23]

Once again Freeman was unable to develop a durable base of support. By November 1883 the *Union—Freeman* had evolved into the *Butte City Union,* a new newspaper, but one claiming the heritage of thirty-three years of "the old series." Freeman-as-Vattel was the new publication's "traveling editor." One dispatch reported a rush to the diggings of the Coeur d'Alenes some ninety miles east of Spokane Falls which had been initiated by the discovery of placer deposits in 1882. Within three months the Northern Pacific Railroad published a booklet advertising that every man could expect to make $25 to $100 a day there.[24] The last spike on the railroad's main line had been driven on September 8, 1883, on the north bank of the Deer Lodge River near Garrison, and now it hoped to build up its passenger traffic to the Coeur d'Alene region.

Freeman was not as specific as the railroad about the region's prospects, but what he wrote was enough to help encourage the boom:

> The rush to the placer diggings of the Coeur d'Alenes continues and many doubting Thomases who stayed behind the first stampede have caught the excitement anew from returning prospectors and have either left for the new diggings or are arranging to leave within a few days with the intention of wintering in the new camp. The excitement seems to have extended to every section of the Pacific coast and as far eastward as Dakota and Minnesota. . . .[25]

And the intrepid Lightning Scout of the Mountains himself fell victim to boomtown fever of the Coeur d'Alenes. He might have remained immune to the lure of frontier mining alone, but Horatio Vattel always found it difficult to resist the call of a new railroad town.

Northern Pacific Railroad tracks had reached Thompson Falls, Montana, in November 1882. Merchants in the community 225 miles northwest of Butte near the Idaho border were seeking to monopolize the outfitting trade of the Coeur d'Alene miners. By the spring of 1884 Freeman was established as the publisher of the again revived *Frontier Index* at Thompson Falls. Under the familiar nameplate, Freeman, at age 41, wrote once more with the promotional fervor he had exhibited on the Union Pacific Railroad frontier nearly two decades earlier:

> Spokane Falls merchants are now shipping their goods this way to the mines. And the universal opinion is in favor of Thompson Falls as the base of supplies for the mining region. Thompson Falls is bound to become the Cheyenne of the Northern Pacific. . . . The excitement has not only spread through the United States, but parties from Australia have already outfitted at Thompson Falls, and they say they heard the news in the South Seas islands. The rush is the most unprecedented since that of '49, to the "blue streak" of California. It is predicted by cool headed calculators that Thompson Falls will be as large as Spokane Falls by midsummer. . . . [26]

Freeman was not alone in his optimism. Thompson Falls had drawn more than 2,000 residents, including the "belle of the Black Hills," Calamity Jane. With an enthusiasm he had not exhibited in Butte for either mining or railroad ventures, Freeman reported that "hundreds of anxious people are eagerly awaiting the snow's disappearance from mother earth so that operations may commence at the Coeur d'Alene mines."[27] The zeal with which he entered into his work was recognized as far away as Seattle, where an editor wrote that the *Frontier Index* was

> a newsy and readable paper but likely to make the eastern tenderfoot believe either that Thompson Falls possessed a veritable Annanaias or that God was paying particular attention to a small spot in Montana. . . .[28]

The *Bozeman Chronicle* took note not only of the new paper but also of
Freeman's reputation as a frontier editor:

> The towns [where Freeman published on the frontier] have all
> died but the Index still lives. It is a neatly printed sheet and brim
> full of interesting matter. We hope Mr. Freeman will now take the
> wheels off his press and stay awhile; take out his knitting and set-
> tle down to business.[29]

The *Frontier Index* was again the typical frontier newspaper,
chronicling the mining and business activities of the little community.
But Freeman also gave prominent play to articles on death and spiritualism. Just as he had attributed his attacks on the Mormons to
spiritual instruction, he now revealed that his long-standing anti-
Chinese sentiment was based on a prediction by a spiritual medium.
But he did not attack them as he had in 1868.

To the uninitiated, such columns hinting at a spiritual or philosophical discourse would seem guaranteed to repel western readers.
But as a practitioner in frontier humor and folklore, Freeman knew
what would interest the unoccupied miner, whether he was waiting for
snow to melt or was merely sitting by a campfire at his placer site. He
had acquired the knack from the master himself, Jim Bridger, at Fort
Kearny, Fort Laramie, and on the Bozeman Trail. Besides, as editor,
he had the freedom to fill his columns with one of his favorite subjects.
From his office on Index Avenue, "around the corner" from the Wells,
Fargo & Company express office, he emphasized that he was no
spiritualist "in the common, vulgar, much abused acceptance of the
term." The fact was, he said, that he had had valid "spiritual experiences" which he believed science should study:

> There may be no ghosts in the case, but there is something in it
> —a law of nature never as yet formulated, an occult force, a mode
> of motion, an uncatalogued function of the senses, an impalpable
> medium within which, through their instincts, all living creatures
> are included—some thing there is a natural cause for.[30]

He then recounted the supernatural influences he had been subject
to "all our life." When he was a child of ten, a gypsy fortune teller had
told him he would "go far from home and make our living by writing."
In 1866 he had had a daydream defining the location of the Union
Pacific Railroad via Ogden, when engineers calculated that it would be
built through Salt Lake City. In 1870, in Indianapolis, when a friend
had hailed him on the street with the question, "Who do you think I
met last night?" he had correctly answered, "Tom Smith, the leader of
the riot in which the Credit Mobilier mob had our office burned at
Bear River!" He said he "realized the evil spirit was present" because
he had lain "awake all night, telling [his] wife about the [Bear River]
scenes and incidents."[31]

In 1877, while lying sick in Ogden from "over work in publishing," Freeman continued the account, spiritual mediums came in

> to lay hands on us and one had such a soothing effect that we shut our eyes and said, "the heavens are obscured by black clouds; out of an opening like a full moon, a man descends to the earth dressed in buckskin and cocked hat like the revolutionary forefathers; he approaches a saddled horse grazing, mounts, rides toward a long column of white men marching from the northeast, bearing on their shoulders some metalic substance which they erect into a huge war engine, on a high hill commanding a view of the camp of Asiatics, busy entrenching and fortifying far west of Great Salt Lake."
>
> The telegraph next day brought the information that at the precise hour that we refer to . . . the Chinese barricaded Dupont street, in San Francisco, against the attack of the whites. . . .[32]

Freeman wrote that once while he was on a horseback trip in central Idaho, "something" had whispered, "Go Home." He had followed the mysterious command and the morning after he arrived in Ogden his wife fell and broke both bones of her right wrist "incapacitating her for editorial duties and rendering our presence necessary."[33] A year later, when he was in the Black Hills, he said another whisper had come with the same command. As before, he said, everything was all right the night of his arrival, but the following morning his oldest son had become ill of scarlet fever, as had each of the other three sons in succeeding weeks, and in the fifth week his wife had also become ill.

Freeman recounted the tale of seeing the raven at the time of his wife's fatal accident and then brought his spiritual adventures up to date at Thompson Falls:

> Winter before last, while at Butte, we told Bill Buzzard, whose hat was recently riddled with bullet holes in defending his claim at Eagle City, that we had seen in a dream, a place away over west of Phillipsburg, where in streaks there was more gold than rock, and that some of the pieces were of such singular shapes that they appeared to have been manufactured by men. Some of the specimens already taken out in the Coeur d'Alenes are the shapes of a man's hand, some heart shaped, others wedge shaped, and still others are the size and thickness of silver dollars.
>
> Soon after reciting this dream we had another, in which we visited a beautiful forest, where the Northern Pacific Railway had recently finished its work of construction, and it seemed as if we located a residence site on a towering eminence, rising by a succession of grand terraces facing the most charming river, with a sublime mountain scene beyond.
>
> On the 17th of last March we visited Thompson Falls and recognizing the spot as the one we saw in the vision, . . . we at once located 160 acres of it as a homestead.

In March, 1868, Madame Helena Die[l]terlie, a medium at San Francisco . . . said . . . that in that war [against the Chinese] we would be a leader, and in the end come out a victor and stand under the folds of a flag bearing a cross on its background and that this flag would be held by a beautiful woman whom she described.

The following summer we wrote the first editorial ever penned against the Chinese, and before we left Butte last winter we threw in the following paragraph:

"The war cry of the Coeur d'alene [*sic*] is the same as the watchword of Leadville: 'No Chinaman allowed, except at the end of a larriat [*sic*] thrown over the limb of a tree!' "

This passed the rounds of the press and had the effect of preventing any almond[-]eyed Celestial from ever setting eyes on the gold glittering gorges.

We have found the spot where there is "more gold than rock;" the residence is being erected for the heroine bearing the flag with the cross on it, and we shall anxiously anticipate the rest—which the reader is no doubt by this time ready to take at our miner's three-cornered chimney corner, and partake of our bullion.

We are all dreaming! Some of pleasure; some of fame; some of money! We can't live without dreaming. The mind must first conceive the ideal before the material is born. Everything invisible has a tangibility, and everything tangible has an invisibility.

Shakespeare says: "We are such stuff
As dreams are made of,
And our little lives
Are rounded with a sleep."

Shakespeare was right. We are all bundles of dreams; of thought-projectors; of idealities; without which we could not exist; and then, after all—

"Our little lives are rounded with a sleep."[34]

It was at least coincidental that Freeman ended his Montana publishing ventures in the same tone of mysticism with which he had opened them nearly five years earlier in Butte, where he had written his wife's obituary. More likely, he had continually been preoccupied with the spiritual world and only now had the opportunity to put his experiences into print.

Freeman's spiritual guidance was not potent enough, however, to lead him to the financial and publishing success he craved. Enthusiasm for the Coeur d'Alene strike waned and Freeman and the *Frontier Index* were left high and dry. As the decline set in, his tone became more defensive:

There is still not wanting a certain class of papers who are really gratified to protrude their pompous "I told you so," on any indication that the Coeur d'alene [*sic*] mines are not so fabuously rich as some highly imaginative people have predicted. . . . To quite a large extent the disappointed crowd which has left the mining region in a measure depopulated, have held the newspapers responsible for their failure to strike something that would yield a fortune in a week or two, and they conclude they have no more use for newspapers, nor mines. . . . However mistaken the newspaper may have been in giving publicity to all the rumors of bonanzas in the coeur d'alene [sic], none have [sic] had the brazen hardihood to advise anybody to go into a northern mountain region in mid-winter, with just money enough to get in and yet this is just what many have had the foolhardiness of doing.[35]

By the Fourth of July Freeman admitted that the *Frontier Index* was the only newspaper left in "all this region." After publishing thirteen issues at Thompson Falls, however, he said he was still willing to wager that when the town

> attains the present age of Spokane Falls, this place will be larger and better built than that is now. . . . North of us the country is almost unexplored. South, the richest mineral belt in the world, reaches all the way to Wood River; east and west there is no town between Spokane and Missoula, 300 miles. Such an empire will maintain here a flourishing town.[36]

Thompson Falls today has approximately 1,300 residents. Most major silver-lead mines in the Coeur d'Alene area had been discovered by 1884 and 1885 and were subsequently bought and developed by corporations. But Freeman, who lived the life of Horatio Vattel, did not have the temperament to stay in such a community and work at making his prediction come true, even if it had been accurate. The Northern Pacific was still offering to Freeman and his kind the excitement of boomtowns and a fresh start. As long as this kind of elbowroom lasted, the Lightning Scout of the Mountains could not settle down. Some 500 miles lay between him and the Pacific Ocean; his "Star of Empire" had not fulfilled its course. Besides, he probably had a spiritual revelation ordering him on.

8

"Guerrilla Journalism"

WHILE in Montana, Freeman learned from Northern Pacific officials about their plans for a new community in Washington Territory's Yakima Valley. Property owners in existing Yakima City—which had grown up in haphazard fashion—refused in 1884 to give the railroad necessary depot grounds on the proposed route of its main line to Puget Sound through Stampede Pass in the Cascade Mountains. This route to Tacoma was to replace one leased from the Oregon Railway and Navigation Company along the Columbia River. The Northern Pacific was thus planning a new community, North Yakima, and another classic western battle loomed over rights-of-way between an established but struggling town and a strong railroad.

Freeman considered this information a tip for a potentially profitable venture. But railroad officials may have sought him out with the hope that he would establish a newspaper favorable to them to offset the threat that the *Yakima Record* and the *Yakima Signal* would oppose the railroad's plans. Perhaps the railroad only hoped that Freeman, with his experience in advertising railroad towns, would draw settlers to the new agricultural area and generate revenue from markets on Puget Sound and in the East.

By this time Freeman had demonstrated that wherever he went he became enmeshed in controversy. Thus, when he moved into a community already inflamed by the railroad issue, it was predictable that he would find himself at the center of bitter discord. By now, also, it was equally evident that he would readily change his journalistic coloration to capitalize on the advantages of a new setting. As a result, in the Yakima Valley he would not only become an agricultural authority but also would plunge first into one side then into the other of the town-moving controversy. If Freeman was now irrevocably an opportunist, it was also only a matter of time until the influence of the transient Horatio Vattel would predominate. In short, he would again forfeit the opportunity to become a part of a new community, grow with it, and become a substantial citizen.

A Northern Pacific train in 1884 carried Freeman and his three sons from Montana down into the summer heat of eastern Washington's Columbia River basin area. Here was a sagebrush-covered land, later described by Owen Wister as a barren, dismal, sorrowful region reminding him of a line from Robert Louis Stevenson which told of "The most distressful country that ever yet was seen."[1] The printing equipment accompanying the family was unloaded at Ainsworth, near the confluence of the Snake and Columbia rivers where Lewis and Clark had camped some eighty years before. There the proposed railroad route through the Yakima Valley branched from the temporary main line. The type and presses were hauled northward by wagon toward Yakima City and Freeman and his family traveled the dusty roads in a buggy.

They stopped the vehicle for a midday meal at the lower Yakima Valley ranch of noted cattleman Jock Morgan, whose twenty-foot dining table was lined with his sons and cowboys. Legh Miller Freeman, then nine years old, later remembered the table conversation had included Morgan's opinion that the day of range cattle was ending with the advent of the railroad. It was an accurate prediction; Northern Pacific tracks later bisected a part of Morgan's 400,000-acre range.[2]

When the Freeman family registered at David Guilland's hotel at Yakima City, after crossing the eastern edge of the Yakima Indian Reservation, the main topic of conversation they heard centered on speculation as to what would happen to the town when tracks approached later in the year. But no one disputed the agricultural potential of the brown earthern valley floor. For more than a decade private irrigation canals had been taking water from the Yakima River and its tributaries to prove the land's productivity.

Freeman made arrangements for his youngest son to live with the Elisha Tanner family on an irrigated farm on Ahtanum Creek, west of Yakima City. Indian hero Kamiakin had introduced irrigation into central Washington in 1853 on this tributary of the Yakima River. Freeman than began to lay the groundwork for his newspaper. Because Yakima City had only some 600 residents, he was probably hesitant to compete with the town's two established newspapers despite the promise of the railroad boom ahead. He again found himself in the position of having to compete as a latecomer without guaranteed support. The five-year-old *Yakima Record* was published by a Republican, Charles M. Holton, and the *Yakima Signal* had been published since January 6, 1883, by James Madison Adams, a former United States Land Office receiver. But by late summer Freeman had worked out with Holton a joint operating agreement similar to one he had first envisioned in Ogden and the one he had tried in the labor publication at Butte. He now thought he had found the solid business arrangement he deemed essential.

The immediate result of these negotiations was publication of the *Washington Farmer*. This newspaper was a combination community-agricultural sheet whose name has been continued on various periodicals to the present. Today, as an agricultural magazine, it accurately lists on its Spokane masthead that year in Yakima City, 1884, as its founding date.[3] In establishing this wide-ranging publication, Freeman displayed not only his amazing versatility, but business acumen as well. The *Washington Farmer* was one of only some dozen and a half farm publications printed in the developing agricultural land beyond the Midwest, although 215 were being published in the United States.[4]

During the first year in Yakima City, all activity seemed to be tied to the issue of the new town rather than to agriculture. Few residents were neutral on either this question or partisan politics. Even though the railroad had offered free lots to all who would move to North Yakima, there were those who saw such an offer as a bribe and found it difficult in any case to envision a future metropolis where only a restaurant, a livery stable, and two saloons stood amid the sagebrush. And heated public meetings reflected the division.

Local editors were judged in light of their stand in the controversy. Reflecting the interest in the burning question, the first issue of the *Washington Farmer* discussed the division of community sentiment:

> The opening of the Cascade branch will give to the towns of Eastern Washington a direct route to Sound ports . . . market for grain, cattle, and one here for Coastal goods. . . . A few talkative people in Seattle, and a few more in the Yakima valley, eager to make out a cause of complaint against the Northern Pacific Company and to start an anti-monopoly hue and cry, have been arguing of late that the company has never intended to build the Cascade branch. They are now forced to acknowledge their error. There never was any reasonable show of foundation for their charge.[5]

Freeman's newspaper thus took its first editorial stand with the railroad, perhaps in hopes of subsequent financial support.

Editor Adams of the *Yakima Signal* was the leader of the "anti-monopoly" party composed of Democrats and antirailroad Republicans. This coalition backed the nomination of Charles Voorhees as territorial delegate to Congress on a platform demanding cancellation of the Northern Pacific's "unearned" land grant. The railroad's opponents still believed that it would not build on across the Cascade Mountains after opening Yakima Valley farmland for speculative purposes. The *Klickitat Sentinel* at Goldendale predicted that the railroad would build to the foothills of the Cascades, "gobble the agricultural land and then take to the brush."[6] Voorhees was sent to Congress, aided in his election by a Yakima County majority.

For the first time since the days at Bear River City, Freeman found himself on a brand-new railroad frontier and made no attempt to hide his enthusiasm. Certainly it appeared that Wyoming had been transplanted when cowhands from the nearby Moxee area would tear into town "at full gallop, draw up in front of the Alfalfa [North Yakima] saloon, throw their reins over the horses' heads and march into the bar with a great swagger." And Freeman saw his role again as a professional town and real estate promoter. In fact, a Seattle editor contended that Freeman would tell the world more about the Yakima country than could three "ordinary" newspapermen.[7]

But Yakima City itself had not been created by the arrival of hungry railroad speculators and there was no "Hell on Wheels." This was a tame agricultural setting, but Freeman never grasped the distinction. His methods of intimidation and confrontation would not work here, either. The two communities bearing the name of Yakima prided themselves, even in this period before statehood, on their numerous contacts with metropolitan centers.[8] They thought of themselves, as did many other territorial communities, as the "equals in essentials, and especially in potential," of any comparable towns in the United States.[9]

Freeman promised to publish a newspaper befitting such a demanding readership. The agreement he worked out with Holton should have provided a solid foundation for a successful publishing venture. Both publishers consented to place the assets of their respective printing plants in a new corporation and obtain working capital in a stock subscription drive among Yakima City residents. The two men pledged to work harmoniously in their new arrangement, but it was a relationship that probably never could have succeeded. Although of different backgrounds, the fact that both were seeking success in a western territory attested to their aggressiveness and, perhaps, even their ultimate incompatibility. Besides, the history of Freeman's broken publishing partnerships insured discord.

Holton, only four years older than Freeman, was a native of New York State who had attained the rank of captain in the Union army during the Civil War. A Republican appointed in 1892 by President Benjamin Harrison as consul at Swansea, Wales, he had come to Washington Territory in 1880 as one of three Indian commissioners appointed by President James A. Garfield. It was shortly after his arrival that he purchased the Yakima Valley's first newspaper, the *Yakima Record,* from its founder, Richard V. Chadd.

Articles of incorporation of the new Capital Publishing Company were filed in the Yakima County Auditor's Office on August 27, 1884.[10] A stock issue of 20,000 shares at $1 each was approved, with Freeman holding 7,500 paid up, unassessable shares and Holton 1,500 shares. Illustrating community acceptance of the venture, the list of the remaining stockholders, who were to pay 20 percent of their subscription pledges by October 15, read like an inventory of Yakima's founding fathers. Among the supporters was Ben Snipes, well-known lower Yakima Valley cattleman. Also subscribing to the stock drive were the original owners of the North Yakima and Yakima City town sites, two probate judges, three of the first North Yakima city councilmen, a county commissioner, the county sheep commissioner, the county treasurer, a former county treasurer, a railroad commissioner, two Yakima County settlers, two Kittitas County settlers, several businessmen and merchants, and a stage driver.

Each of the principals in the corporation published notices to his readers when the first four-page edition of the *Washington Farmer* was issued on September 20, 1884. Freeman, who was listed as both the managing editor and the business manager, promised that the newspaper would be neutral in politics and "devoted to the advancement of the material interests of the people."[11] His two older sons, ages eleven and fourteen, were employed at the printing office. Holton was technically Freeman's employee, but he took his salary in stock.

Holton told his subscribers that the *Yakima Record* had ceased publication and he gave as his main reason for entering into the venture the realization that his newspaper "was wholly inadequate in size and resources to meet the wants of this growing country of varied interests." He also saw Freeman as holding "the power of a journal backed by experience and capital." For such reasons, Holton said, he was ready to "willingly sacrifice an independent, growing business, for the public good."[12]

Even before this initial edition had gone to press, Freeman, Holton, and Edward Pruyn as officers of the corporation had issued a call for a stockholders' meeting on November 22 to increase the capital stock of the corporation from $20,000 to $30,000. The increase undoubtedly reflected the arrival of additional steam-printing equipment which Freeman personally transferred from Montana and Idaho. The newspaper's future seemed bright, but there was trouble ahead.

As the Northern Pacific laid its rails up the Yakima Valley, aggravating the Yakima City–North Yakima conflict, personal controversy once again swirled around Freeman. Only three months after he arrived at Yakima City, he "let out" Holton as a newspaper employee, claiming that his services were "worse than worthless."[13] Two incidents may have helped to precipitate the action. When Freeman returned from his Idaho and Montana trip, subscribers to the stock refused to pay freight charges on the additional printing equipment as Freeman requested. Also, his attempt upon his return to collect from the stock subscribers the 20 percent assessment levied in September was disputed.[14]

And so, the issue was joined. Holton and a majority of those who had subscribed to the stock held a series of meetings to discuss the fate of the Capital Publishing Company while Freeman continued publication of the *Washington Farmer* and operation of the business. He collected sums due not only the newspaper but also due the *Yakima Record* while it had been published under Holton. Freeman did not attend, or was barred from attending, the meetings.

On November 15, "by a unanimous vote," again in Freeman's

absence, the group decided to suspend work of the firm, to discharge all employees including Freeman, to halt all expenses, to issue no further papers, and to turn all assets over to the trustees.[15] Holton, apparently as one of these trustees, removed from the *Washington Farmer* office the equipment and files of the old *Yakima Record,* an action Freeman later said he allowed only "because it was deemed the easiest way to get rid of him as a nuisance, incompetent and dishonest." Holton then used his equipment to start the publication of the new *Yakima Republican* in which, Freeman charged, he seemed "intent on trying the case in the papers."[16] It was obvious by this time that the dispute would ultimately reach the courts.

Freeman then launched a counterattack. The long-scheduled meeting, called to increase the corporation's stock from $20,000 to $30,000, was held on November 22 with Freeman presiding. Holton, of course, was absent, and Freeman could not secure a vote favorable to the proposal. He contended that a mere head count majority of the stock subscribers could not dissolve the business, that only those who had paid-up shares could participate and these at a rate of one vote per $25 share. This meant, he said, that there were only 100 and ⅓ votes for Holton's dissolution motion while he held 400 votes against the proposal. No matter what action was taken, he claimed, the November 15 meeting was not legal inasmuch as the required eight-week notice had never been published and he, as the "proper officer," had not presided.[17]

In Freeman's view, there was no dispute over who should control the company's business affairs since he held a majority of all the stock:

> Of course no publisher would move a printing office 600 miles and put in the services of himself and family under any conditions that would pass the control out of his hands. . . .[18]

This, then, was the very point to which Holton's group, which apparently included most if not all of the original stock subscribers, objected. Freeman had moved into their community, established a company drawing upon their resources, and placed himself in a position of such complete control that he could fire the second major stockholder and continue receiving both prior and current income due the firm.

The essence of Freeman's position was that since he was making the major contributions of equipment, manpower, and experience to the venture, he was entitled to control. He said that Holton's faction, voting without regard to amounts of paid-up stock, could not in his absence strip him of what had been legally placed in the new business and return it to Holton. He was continuing the operation for those reasons.

Freeman's involvement in this feud with Holton obviously reduced his vaunted effectiveness as a railroad town boomer. The first train reached Yakima City on Christmas Eve, 1884, but instead of giving the historic event predominant play, Freeman devoted all of the *Washington Farmer's* front page on January 3, 1885, to his side of the Capital Publishing Company controversy. Calling Holton a "Benedict Arnold" and his opponents "double dealers," he had to reach beyond the English language to find the right words to express his contempt:

> *Dechalander* is the French word that expresses the whole sentence: "to entice or get customers away from," and it is just the term that applies to the ways that are dark and tricks that are vain, resorted to by a certain soi-disant [self-styled] paper man in his vain effort to raise a few subscribers for a jim-crow sheet that he undertook to force on the people a few weeks ago, and in which he has made a successful failure. He is simply a tool to involve certain persons in a damage suit of no small dimension, while covertly and with sinister and base motives he undertakes to excite their sympathy which is already rebounding as contempt, unaccompanied by pity. . . .

Holton's "auditing committee," Freeman further said, had not paid him or his sons any wages, his six months' house rent, or any bills "as they were instructed to do." The committee's attempt to levy a 10 percent assessment on the Holton and Freeman equipment, he contended, was a "full legal admission" that the material was still the property of the corporation and that the deed that Holton made back to himself was not "worth the paper it was written on." He promised that the stock of the corporation would shortly be paying a dividend.

Freeman purposely attempted to intertwine the railroad and newspaper controversies, perhaps because Holton was in the pro–North Yakima camp. Although the *Washington Farmer* had supported the Northern Pacific in its first issue on September 20, 1884, by December Freeman named himself as spokesman for the antirailroad faction, simply ignoring that Adams of the *Signal* had led the antimoving forces. (The supporting editorial may have been written by Holton if Freeman was in Montana at that time collecting printing equipment.) The Yakima City faction may have seemed stronger to Freeman so he promised the residents there that his newspaper would "not go off on a tangent as against the wishes and interests of the mass of this community. We shall watch developments and do the square thing."[19] He was forced to take this action because he was again without support and he desperately needed backing.

Freeman claimed that the railroad company never would have undertaken an opposition town but for the "ruction" created in the publishing company. He identified the prime mover as Holton, who had "deeded half of his homestead to the railroad pool," and who was "in the pay of the new town syndicate." If the citizens of the old town would rally "to the paper that has been true to them," Freeman blatantly promised to save the people from bankruptcy "and the town from obliteration and total annihilation." After all, he boasted extravagantly, "we have published in 17 towns, and have all the methods."[20]

Although he had just charged that Holton was "in the pay of the new town syndicate," Freeman within only three weeks just as enthusiastically hailed the new community. Apparently no one had given him proper recognition as the self-proclaimed spokesman for "old town" interests. The railroad had not yet filed a plat of its new community, but Freeman later in January predicted that "New Yakima" would be the "Metropolis of Eastern Washington."[21] Perhaps his judgment was swayed by the three-column Northern Pacific advertisement carried in the same issue of his paper. Here was the type of support he sought.

The advertisement assured readers that the new town would not only be the state capital but would attract colleges and "manufactories" which "the syndicate of capitalists leagued with the company, have determined to build here at the central spot in Washington." Land was offered by the railway's land office at from 40 cents to $7 per acre with warranty deeds, the average being $2.[22]

Just at the time Freeman thought he glimpsed opportunity in the railroad community, Holton, in behalf of the Capital Publishing Company, filed suit against him. The action alleged that Freeman had been discharged as business manager at a meeting of Holton's faction. Holton asked the court for a temporary restraining order enjoining Freeman from using the names of the Capital Publishing Company and the *Washington Farmer* and from collecting debts of the corporation.[23]

Neither party to the suit realized satisfaction in the short time Freeman had earlier predicted. A final judgment in the case was not handed down until twenty-one months after the suit was filed. Then Freeman was credited with $806.90 from the company's operation and was ordered to pay $541.30 of the business debts, leaving a balance of $292.60 that Holton and his supporters owed him.[24]

Meanwhile, Freeman had fallen victim to the boomtown fever. A plat of North Yakima was filed on February 4, 1885, and although Yakima City itself was not to be relocated, many residents planned to move. In his issue of February 14, Freeman advertised that persons owing the *Washington Farmer* money could wipe out their debts by hauling his twenty tons of printing material to the new town. Yet he promised, "We shall have no mud to throw at the old." The editor of the *Spokane Falls Review* commented that Freeman "must have a tremendous outfit or a big stock of gall" to claim that he had twenty tons of equipment to move. But it was granted that the newspaper "will whoop up the new town when it gets settled as it is a whooper from whooperville."[25] Freeman announced his plans to begin publication of the *Daily Capital* "in a few weeks," but he published only the *Washington Farmer* at North Yakima.[26]

With the enthusiasm of Horatio Vattel, Freeman devoted the entire front page of his first issue there (February 28, 1885) to details of the new community of forty buildings under the headline, "THE BOOM TOWN." He observed nostalgically that a camp of tents on the west side of the tracks "reminds one of the good old days when the Union Pacific was sending its forces across the continent on wheels, and the military moved side by side as a protection against the savage tribes of the frontier." Part of the infectious excitement came from the daily arrival of buildings from the old town and beyond, reminiscent of the instant cities of the Union Pacific frontier. A roundhouse arrived from Ainsworth and the main portion of the Guilland Hotel made the trip "in good shape" from Yakima City.[27] Some stores continued to remain open for business while being pulled "on rollers." It was a common sight to see customers hitch teams to the end of a moving building, transact business, load their moving wagons, and untie the animals for the trip home.[28]

The veteran of the *Frontier Index,* who in 1868 was an avowed opponent of the Union Pacific's real estate division, now asserted that he was "the agent" for the 2,000 lots in North Yakima held in the name of Northern Pacific officials:

> REAL ESTATE BROKER. Persons desiring to buy, sell or lease city or farm property, will consult their own interest in placing their wants with the undersigned [Freeman], who will ADVERTISE THE SAME FREE! And make no charge except the ten per cent on amount of sales.[29]

The Northern Pacific, of course, maintained its own land office.

Freeman asked everyone interested in farming, stock raising, poultry, dairying, orchards, and gardening to work among their neighbors to increase the circulation of his newspaper. But he also promised full coverage of local news; comic caricatures similar to those of the *New York Graphic;* and illustrations such as "Men and Women of the Hour," blooded stock and poultry, and "the country seats of gentlemen." He gave assurances that the contents of the *Washington Farmer* would be kept "clean enough for the hearthstone of any family of girls." He said that no objectionable quack advertisements or items conveying double meanings "from which lewd inferences may be drawn," would be published.[30]

With Freeman thus dropping Yakima City interests for the Northern Pacific's new town, the railroad's opponents started their own newspaper. They published a single edition of the one-page *Yakima Sun* on February 17, 1885. Its backers said that it was not a weekly or monthly newspaper, but would appear at any time the people saw fit to "vindicate and defend their city and property from any and all persons who are working by false representation to crush them and render their houses and property worthless."[31]

*Legh Freeman, in the mid-1880s.
(courtesy Western History Research
Center, University of Wyoming)*

A committee of three representatives, including Adams of the *Yakima Signal,* was elected to lay the grievances of Yakima City before Northern Pacific directors in New York. But before Adams departed he apparently gave instructions to place his newspaper office on jacks in preparation for a move to North Yakima. On April 18, 1885, two days after he left, a dynamite explosion rocked his office. It was apparently detonated by someone who saw a double-cross in Adams' preparations to move and leave Yakima City without a newspaper. The explosion, which was felt throughout the community, tore the sides of the building open, made holes in the roof and floor, destroyed the marble imposing slabs, and scattered type beyond retrieval. There was little damage to the press, however, and with the contribution of equipment by Freeman, *Signal* associate editor E. M. Reed was able to move to a new building in North Yakima and print the next issue of the newspaper on time.[32] Adams returned with a promise from Northern Pacific directors that moving costs of Yakima City residents would be met by the railroad, an outcome, ironically, further reducing the influence of the Yakima City faction.

Despite Freeman's gesture of cooperation following the dynamiting incident, he soon found himself in a bitter fight with Reed, who called the *Washington Farmer* "a sheet which all speak of as the most unreliable of the unreliables, and which never makes a statement without coloring it beyond the semblance of truth." Reed said that Freeman called the *Signal's* contents "Guerrilla Journalism" because of its continual "scoops." He contended that Freeman

> is a nice man, a very nice man, and evidently intends to do what is right, but the fact is that there is either a soft spot under his hat which grew in extent with his town-booming proclivities or else he is a natural damphool, a failing which has a tendency to warp a man's judgement. We will be charitable and conclude that it is the former and allow as one of his witnesses testified in the Capitol Publishing case that he is worth so much as an editor, (very small); so much as a manager (a little more); and so much as a BOOMER (in-calculably great.)[33]

Freeman's lengthy response a week later is significant not only for clarification of what had transpired following the dynamiting the previous year, but because the story itself became the justification for a libel suit Reed filed against him:

> The Walla Walla Union says: "The Yakima Signal is praising the Northern Pacific. What mean things has the company done that calls for this punishment?" The Washington Farmer answers: The company gave the Signal two car loads of lumber as an inducement to keep its mouth shut; then, when the office was damaged about $75 worth by a stick of giant powder [dynamite], Paul Schulze [Northern Pacific land agent] took up a collection of

$240 on the streets of North Yakima as a "relief fund", and then he had one of his strikers take up another collection of about an equal amount to pay the expenses of the editor to New York and back while out to interview President Harris on the scheme of how best to finish ruining the homes at Yakima City, and besides this the same editor was traveling on a round trip pass. . . . when the Capital Publishing Company's case was on hand, Reed went into court and tried to swear down the earnings of our employes to the lowest possible figures and swore that the press [work] on one side of the Signal was only charged for by us of a nominal figure, and therefore press work was worth no more than that sum because we were doing press work of that figure as an accommodation. . . . If there is anything on the earth that will make a printer testify strongest it is in favor of a fellow workman, but what can be expected of a fellow whose own brother would not trust him and who prior to coming here couldn't earn his board at the business, and who testified that he is not allowed to receive over $15 a week on the Signal and scarcely ever gets that and yet he has full charge of the finances of the Signal and takes all the money that comes in above the ordinary expenses. . . . Moreover, he swore that he received no other consideration for his services than that stated and then walked directly to the door and said: Why I have already received an appointment as deputy U.S. marshal as a part of the consideration for conducting the Signal as a Voorhees paper.[34]

Reed filed suit on September 18, 1886, claiming that the story was false and defamatory and injurious to his reputation. He asked $3,000 from Freeman plus costs, saying that he was now unable to earn a livelihood as editor and deputy United States marshal because of the allegations that he was "not worthy [of] public confidence."[35] Freeman in answer countercharged that Reed had abused him in the "Guerrilla Journalism" article. In the end Freeman won the case, perhaps because he testified in court that Reed had been discharged by the publisher of the *Walla Walla Statesman,* was thrown into the street from the "lowest saloon in Walla Walla" because of misconduct, and was discharged as "unworthy of the trust" from the *Walla Walla Journal* where his brother was editor.[36] Although he had ample grounds, Freeman never sued Reed for libel. But for years thereafter, readers of the state's press judged Freeman by the vindictive opinions Reed published and which were in turn reprinted by Washington editors.

The Capital Publishing Company case was indirectly brought into a second legal action Freeman faced. Hotel owner David Guilland filed suit for $160 allegedly unpaid on a board and lodging bill of $212 which the Freeman family had supposedly incurred between October 4, 1884, and February 8, 1885.[37]

The case may have merely been Guilland's attempt to collect an unpaid bill because he was hard pressed financially after losing his herd of cattle at Yakima in the winter of 1882. But the dispute was undoubtedly inflamed, if not motivated, by the publishing suit. Guilland had subscribed $300 to the newspaper venture, but, according to Freeman, had never made any payment toward the stock. As one of those on record supporting Holton in the dispute, he was undoubtedly among those participating in the controversial November 15 vote to remove Freeman from the business. Freeman, at least, thought the affairs of the Capital Publishing Company were directly involved in Guilland's claim. Unlike that suit, however, Guilland's case was resolved in the relatively brief time of seven months. Freeman was ordered to pay Guilland $136. Among the six witnesses testifying were five of the original Capital Publishing Company stock subscribers. The sixth was fifteen-year-old Randolph Freeman.[38]

Although Holton had backers in the disputes against Freeman, the *Washington Farmer* was not without support. Freeman bid for the new city's printing contract and on March 8, 1886, two months after North Yakima was incorporated, the *Washington Farmer* became the city's official newspaper.[39]

Freeman was preoccupied by necessity with details of the continuing legal maneuvering, but his mind turned frequently to his native South. He corresponded with his sister, Maria Allison Freeman, who was a teacher in a boys' school at Cuthbert, Georgia. She had written to Freeman about a close friend, Janie Nicholas Ward, a native of Georgia, who was a mathematics teacher at Andrews College at Cuthbert, the second oldest women's college in Georgia. Freeman initiated a correspondence with "Miss Janie" and, apparently in 1886, he went to Cuthbert, some eighty miles south of Atlanta, to propose marriage. Freeman was forty-three years old and his bride thirty when they were married on June 10, 1886, in the Cuthbert home of Sam Freeman, Legh's brother.[40] In a circuitous way, Mary Kemper Freeman's emphasis on education for her daughters had brought Freeman and his bride together.

The couple moved into the family quarters at the rear of the North Yakima printing shop and Freeman's newspaper again became a family affair, as it had been in Ogden. Residing with them were Freeman's three sons. Miller, at age ten, had moved from the Ahtanum ranch and had completed his formal education. On the farm he had herded cattle on the hills leading down to the Yakima Indian Reservation. In town he found his work less exciting:

> My day began at 6 in the morning when I built a fire in the woodburning stove, and then swept out the printing office before breakfast[;] from 7 in the morning until 6 at night I was setting type, doing job printing, making up type forms, running the presses and doing all the varied and multiple tasks. . . .[41]

Janie Ward Freeman, as had been Freeman's first wife, was also employed in the printing office.

Freeman in his three years in North Yakima was successful not only in courtship but also in his legal entanglements. He had won a net
judgment of $292.60 over Holton; he had, upon appeal, reduced a $160
claim by Guilland to $136; and he had been the victor in the libel suit
brought by Reed. To Horatio Vattel, such harrassments of civilization
were merely endurable forms of the same problems he had faced at the
hands of Indians, frontier mobs, and, in his imagination at least, Mormons. In publishing a combination community newspaper and
agricultural journal, he was free to some degree to assert his independence from community factions and seek his support not only
from rural subscribers but from advertisers throughout the Northwest
who wanted to reach agricultural consumers. In seeking income
beyond North Yakima, he was merely following the strategy he had
employed when he traveled as Vattel beyond the meager population
base on the Union Pacific frontier and the Mormon-dominated economy at Ogden.

Freeman showed his tactics in an edition published in April 1888.
The nameplate of the *Washington Farmer* boasted that the newspaper
had the "largest circulation in the new Northwest." He boldly urged
exchange editors to "give us a nice notice on this grand edition and we
will reciprocate." The issue contained twenty-four pages. Although it
claimed to be a weekly livestock and farm journal, it fulfilled its goal of
carrying local news as well. North Yakima's growth to 1,500 residents
was reported and an inventory of the town's businesses was printed
which included everything from the community's eight general merchandise stores to its brass band.

The Northern Pacific was clearly responsible for opening the
Yakima Valley and initiating this community development. The town
had passed from a pioneer stock-raising period into an era of modern
agricultural business methods. Land values were rising, speculation
was heavy, and settlers were being attracted from the East.

But if Freeman's emphasis was on North Yakima, he also devoted
space to feature stories about the Washington communities of Colfax,
Garfield, Dayton, Pomeroy, Pullman, Conconully, and Tieton, and
Moscow, Idaho. He published articles as varied as a biographical
sketch of the first white woman at Walla Walla to methods of crossing
the Cascade Mountains. Pictures of cattle, plants, and camping on the
Tieton River illustrated the pages. He reported that placer mining had
been profitable for twenty-five years on the headwaters of the Yakima
River and that he had inspected a $760 gold nugget the size of a man's
fist.

Freeman and his wife also entered into several modest real estate
ventures, perhaps with money she had saved while teaching. These investments were factors, although not then recognized, in determining
that Freeman would spend most of his remaining life in North Yakima.
His earliest real estate transaction there was the acquisition of his

printing office site for $1 from the Northern Pacific, which originally owned all North Yakima property. This transaction was not officially recorded until 1887, although he had moved to the city two years earlier. The following year his wife, "from her own separate funds and estate," purchased for $100 one acre of property at the outskirts of North Yakima. A month later she paid $225 to the Northern Pacific for a lot adjacent to the printing office. Early in 1889 Freeman completed the purchase of six lots—located two blocks north of his office—from the railroad for $1,200. That summer he bought a $900 lot which was across the street from the *Washington Farmer* office.[42]

It appeared from the acquisition of the numerous parcels of property that Freeman was finally about to settle down to become a community builder, joining the many North Yakima founders who were the early *Washington Farmer* stockholders. Certainly this group aggressively promoted the town's potential as statehood was achieved in 1889, and so did Freeman in his own way, although documentation is difficult because of the scarcity of extant copies of the *Washington Farmer*. He urged that a state mental institution be built at North Yakima, but his suggestion was not appreciated in all quarters. Reed, a co-founder of the new *Yakima Herald,* clearly displayed his continuing pique as a loser in the libel suit:

> Will some one please tell that egregious ass who runs the Farmer to take out that standing tom-foolery which heads the local columns in which so many wonderful things are projected for Yakima. If we could only get that "permanent $275,000 state insane asylum" which the Farmer has projected for us, the Herald would suggest that it be built around the . . . [*Farmer* office].[43]

But the town was no longer a railroad frontier to Freeman and neither was it the boomtown he had envisioned. Its growth, based on the valley's developing agricultural economy, proved to be steady but unspectacular. Within the 200 miles between Freeman and the Pacific Ocean was another railroad frontier and boomtown to tempt him. With completion of both the Northern Pacific and Canadian Pacific railroads, Puget Sound port communities were heralding a boom as they competed to construct tracks to tap transcontinental trade. For Freeman, a prospect finally loomed offering not only the elusive subsidy, but a monopoly publishing situation as well. To one like him, who had not forgotten the "good old days" on the Union Pacific frontier, the possibilities were irresistible.

9

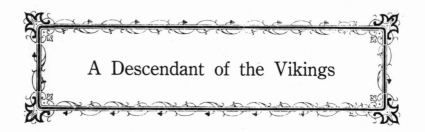

A Descendant of the Vikings

AS FREEMAN left North Yakima in 1889, an era was drawing to a close for him. His twenty-five-year westward quest ended on Puget Sound when he obtained the subsidy that had always gone to his competitors. In a way, he had personified the American westward movement, and now he felt assured that after his 3,000-mile trek, success was finally guaranteed.

It was reported that Freeman had agreed to move the *Washington Farmer* to Fidalgo Island, thirty miles south of Bellingham, in return for deeds to a total of 367 acres of property valued at between $10,000 and $20,000. The deeds of from 3- to 80-acre parcels of land were to be turned over to him by nineteen donors when he published his first issue at the site.[1] These speculators no doubt turned to him in order to benefit financially from his town-booming talents. Freeman must have found the arrangement extremely satisfying. He was called upon to practice his specialty, town booming. In return he was assured of the coveted publishing monopoly. The land was to be his without further obligation once he was settled. And he was to be in the center of another railroad boom as port communities sought to be terminal cities. Competition was intense among the prospective cities on Fidalgo Island, which was equidistant between the Northern Pacific at Tacoma and the Canadian Pacific at Vancouver, British Columbia.

Ever since he had arrived in the Yakima Valley, Freeman had been a perceptive observer of maritime problems. From his publishing site among the sagebrush, he had noted that with the completion of the Canadian Pacific, "the Union Jack will fly from thousands of masts, while the senile convoys of the stars and stripes will be contrasted a thousand per cent. below par."[2] He had called upon the Cleveland administration to foster trade in American bottoms, an obvious advantage to the revenue-hungry Northern Pacific then building to Puget Sound.

To dramatize his point, Freeman had showed that Horatio Vattel still lived. On a voyage in 1885 from Portland to San Francisco aboard the *Queen of the Pacific,* he supposedly donned a robe made from a polar bear skin and a helmet representing the head of a walrus, but with eagle wings. He marshaled the cabin passengers and marched them to the upper deck of the vessel and saluted the captain on the bridge.

"Captain Alexander, where are we now sir?" Freeman asked.

"Seven miles off Furtunas [*sic*], northern arm Cape Mendocino, coast of California, United States of America," was the answer.

> Captain Alexander, I am now about to perform the most momentous act ever recorded in human history. My name is General Horatio Vattel. I am a direct descendent [*sic*] of the Vikings on both paternal and maternal sides and as such I here set up my claim to three-quarters of the earth's surface, all of the high seas and shall proceed in the presence of your ship's company and the cabin passengers at this place one hour before sunset, March 17, 1885, to throw off an anchor and buoy to mark here the initial point of the Republic of all the High Seas, the capital of which I now locate on the crest of Erie Peak, Fidalgo Island, Skagit County, Washington. The revenues to support my government will be derived from two sources, import duties on all vessels and royalties collected from all precious substances taken from the mighty deep. For executive and judicial purposes all of my territory shall be annexed to the government of the United States.[3]

The prime object of his act, Freeman said, was to attract the attention of the people of the country to the necessity for restoring the American merchant marine to prominence on the high seas.

The Freeman family moved to Puget Sound and almost simultaneously disposed of the North Yakima printing office. The last issue of the *Washington Farmer* under a North Yakima dateline was published during the third week of August 1889, and the printing equipment was apparently loaded on a Northern Pacific train on the main line just a block from the printing plant. Once at Puget Sound, the equipment was placed aboard the steamer *State of Washington*—probably at Tacoma—and was unloaded in a driving rainstorm onto a new wharf at the south end of Fidalgo Island on August 30. After three days the equipment was moved by raft to a new building on the property he had been deeded—at a site called Gibralter.[4] It was not until later in September that sale of the three business lots the Freemans owned in North Yakima was recorded. One G. W. Jones agreed to buy the printing office property, the adjacent lot which had been in Mrs. Freeman's name, and the lot across the street for $5,700. He agreed to pay $300 down for the property the Freemans had purchased for $1,126 and he recognized in the legal documents that "time is of the essence of this contract."[5]

The new home of the *Washington Farmer* was several miles from the envisioned "giant city" at Anacortes, a "city that will equal if not exceed in size either Seattle or Tacoma." The key to this growth was the anticipated completion of the Seattle and Northern Railroad. Work on wharves and coal bunkers at Anacortes had already begun and the railroad, the *Seattle Post-Intelligencer* (August 21, 1889) said,

> will no doubt use every effort to turn the trade of the entire Northwest portion of Puget Sound in that direction. . . . Real estate values have been more than doubled by the railroad boom on Fidalgo [Island] and land on Guemes [Island] is held nearly as high as in the vicinity of the future great city.

The Seattle area was not yet the western terminus for a transcontinental railroad, but the Ship Harbor Townsite Company of Anacortes opened an office in Seattle and offered Anacortes lots for $150 to $350 "where the Canadian and Union Pacific Railroads are fast building."[6] The truth was somewhat less spectacular, but the Seattle, Lake Shore and Eastern Railroad had resumed construction in July of its Seattle-to-Canada route after a year's cessation of work. Crews were working simultaneously south from the Canadian border and north from Snohomish, where regular train service to Seattle had been instituted a year earlier. At the same time, 1,000 men were employed on the Seattle and Northern Railway Company's twenty miles of grade and bridges from Anacortes to Skagit Valley coal mines. When this construction was halted and employees were paid in due bills of the Oregon Improvement Company, M. Coltenbaugh, merchant and postmaster at Bayview—east of Anacortes—was asked by a reporter whether any of the great transcontinental railroad lines were responsible for the layoff. "Oh, yes," Coltenbaugh replied. "There are many who figure it out to be a [result of the] serious competition between the Union Pacific and Northern Pacific Railroad Companies."[7]

In this intoxicating atmosphere, Freeman immediately set about fulfilling the conditions of the transaction that had put the private land grants in his hands. In the initial issue he promised to supply his customers with a newspaper in which the advantages of Fidalgo, Guemes, and neighboring islands would be set forth to the world "in the best possible manner." He said that he would not "talk up" any one locality in preference to another, "but all shall receive uniform, fair treatment." He asked that settlers act on that "broad gauge basis" which he deemed necessary:

> Let us have no narrow-contracted policy. Let us impress the world that we are capable of grasping the situation and making developments on true business principles. Let us not be misled by the whims of any one, but go forward as true Americans and develop a plan and work to it, and in so doing build on this island the great commercial metropolis of the Northwest. . . .[8]

But Freeman's task in attracting settlers was not automatically assured by the geographic advantages he depicted. As well as seeking the attention of the transcontinental railroads, investors in the competing railroad ventures had also devised their own promotional schemes and were now vying for attention. Freeman was thus once again a newcomer, but his subsidy and the frantic railroad activity made Fidalgo Island different from Ogden, Butte, and North Yakima. A boom linking rail and maritime trade facilities was building there. A fertile opportunity thus seemed to loom for Freeman's town-booming talents. It was true that the first Anacortes settler, Amos Bowman, an amateur publisher, had established a newspaper there more than a decade earlier. While that publishing effort had been somewhat premature, Freeman felt his time had now come.

As early as 1876 Bowman and his wife had bought 168 acres at the future site of Anacortes. They had built a wharf and store and established a post office and newspaper. They had acted as a result of information on a Northern Pacific map showing 1873 surveys for a rail line from Fidalgo Island to the big bend of the Columbia River by way of Skagit Pass and the Wenatchee River. Bowman claimed that Anacortes would have been the Northern Pacific terminus instead of Tacoma if the Jay Cooke financial empire had not failed and Northern Pacific construction, as a result, had not been halted. He further maintained that the map, which he reproduced repeatedly from 1882 to 1886 in his newspaper, the *Anacortes Enterprise,* was responsible for interesting former Northern Pacific president Henry Villard in Anacortes.[9] As a result, Villard's associates in 1888 supposedly organized the Seattle and Northern Railway Company to build from Anacortes, where it had 5,000 acres, to Spokane via the Skagit River and from Seattle to the Canadian border. Completion of the Northern Pacific over the Cascades negated the Skagit-Spokane proposal, but the Seattle-Canada plan now attracted interest at Anacortes.

Charles Prosch of Seattle, historian of the Washington Press Association, in 1889 termed Bowman's *Anacortes Enterprise* the "oddest newspaper venture ever conceived by sanguine or ambitious journalists." It was issued where no town existed, he pointed out. One lone building was visible at the Anacortes steamer landing, "yet here was where the paper came from." He said he could only conclude that the object of the publisher was to boom a city in embryo which existed only on paper.[10] The name, Anacortes, derived from the maiden name of Bowman's wife, Anna Curtis Bowman, became permanent and the town did boom. But the *Enterprise* was gone by the time Freeman arrived.

The same potential seemed to exist farther south on Fidalgo Island, where Freeman envisioned a land boom no less extensive than the one Bowman had expected. Present asking prices for property stood in sharp contrast to early Fidalgo Island land values. Perhaps one of the reasons that property owners were so generous to Freeman was that they had obtained their acreages without substantial cost. In 1886 a considerable portion of Fidalgo Island was still government owned. Even land with title was sold usually at no more than $2 to $10 per acre. By the early part of 1889 a price of $90, $100, or $150 per acre was common. When Freeman arrived, prices began to soar to $300, $400, or $500, or almost anything that the owners had the nerve to ask.

Although he had the land subsidy and a genuine boom to encourage him, at Gibralter Freeman faced hostile competing editors as he had all across the continent. These competitors cannot be given the sole responsibility for Freeman's failure on Puget Sound, but neither can they be dismissed as an insignificant factor in creating an unfavorable climate of opinion against him among speculators who might have otherwise followed his advice. Even before he moved from North Yakima, he began to face their wrath. The *Puget Sound Mail*, published at LaConner, fumed:

> In view of the fact that the Washington Farmer is an agricultural journal and can therefore be published as conveniently on the island as anywhere else, this is an enormous bonus for the simple removal of the plant from one point to another. It amounts to far more than the original cost of the entire outfit. . . . We presume if a combination of circumstances should make a large city at Ship Harbor [Anacortes], which is among the possibilities, Mr. Freeman will claim the entire credit for it as he has in the case of North Yakima which was in reality built by the Northern Pacific. Now this looks to us like the wildest kind of a wild cat speculation. . . .[11]

The *Skagit News*, published at Mount Vernon, questioned how the land donors, "most of whom must reside miles from the proposed location," would get a return from their investment even if Freeman did remain to publish a newspaper.[12]

Although "Viking" Freeman had removed himself to his "sea domain" on Fidalgo Island, he still sought the development of North Yakima. Washington was to become a state within months and Freeman felt that the state capital should be built at North Yakima rather than at Olympia or Ellensburg. His stand was so vehement that one competing editor claimed that the *Washington Farmer* "should be relegated to the waste basket or fire, as unworthy of the perusal of decent people." Its words were a "disgrace to American journalism," the editor contended. He conscientiously informed his readers of Freeman's property holdings in North Yakima, adding sarcastically that Freeman's conflict of interest in the issue "should cause our citizens to break their necks in their headlong haste to vote for that city for capital. Our town owes him a debt of gratitude for his wonderful (?) journalistic productions." It was therefore with ill-concealed glee that the *Skagit News* reported a week later that as evidence of the *Washington Farmer's* influence, the island precinct cast only three votes for North Yakima in the capital vote "and these were probably cast by employees of the Farmer office."[13]

Freeman did not entirely ignore his Fidalgo Island responsibilities, however. He proposed a ship canal across Fidalgo and asked the Washington legislature to locate all state schools on the island. He questioned whether residents of Skagit County really wanted a $50,000 bridge over the Skagit River rather than improved roads throughout the county. The *Skagit News* retorted that the "carpetbagger sheet" displayed its "dense ignorance" of affairs in the county. "If the [county] commissioners were cast in the same narrow caliber as the editor of the Farmer, Skagit County would be without roads today."[14] It was an ironic charge against Freeman, who would later claim to be the "father of good roads." Freeman had equally poor success in his effort to change the name of Deception Pass to Gibralter Pass. In this regard, the *Puget Sound Mail* (October 3, 1889) asserted, Freeman had the "queer propensity" for changing the names of all American institutions to coincide with similar institutions in the old world.

While Freeman was unable to initiate a move to rename Deception Pass, he affixed the Gibralter name officially to his 130-block town site plat which he filed at Mount Vernon on December 10, 1889.[15] At the opening sale he disposed of 47 lots, but speculators elsewhere on the island were more successful. After Fidalgo City was platted, the initial sale there disposed of 252 lots. Anacortes became the official name of the Ship Harbor site early in January 1890 when a five-acre plat of Anacortes was filed. The railroad's Anacortes plat of 200 blocks, held in the name of individuals rather than of the Seattle and Northern or Northern Pacific itself, was filed on January 21, 1890. Fueling the boom was the knowledge that men such as Governor Elisha P. Ferry, Seattle developer Arthur Denny, and James McNaught of the Northern Pacific were interested in Anacortes real estate.

Freeman's judgment about Fidalgo Island generally, if not Gibralter specifically, thus seemed vindicated early in 1890. Anacortes had a population of only 40 persons as the platting activity commenced in January, but by February the number had jumped to 500; it reached 2,000 in March and was estimated to be 3,000 by March 15. But this activity at Anacortes forced Freeman to once again face a perennial problem. He found himself several miles away from the actual boom. Two Anacortes newspapers, the *Daily Progress* and the *Anacortes American,* were at the center of the activity that saw steamboats, often loaded beyond lawful capacity, carrying passengers in by the hundreds. At one point there were nearly as many tents as houses. Twenty-seven real estate firms were in competition. An estimated $1,500,000 had been invested in land clearance, street improvements, new buildings, water works, street railways, railroad terminals, and wharves.

Although the *Skagit News* warned in April that the boom was about to collapse, negotiations were under way to induce the Northern Pacific itself to build in that direction and locate terminal buildings there. The railroad, it was said, asked for a subsidy of 500 acres. The *Daily Progress* reported that the Northern Pacific had concluded a contract for the acquisition of the Seattle and Northern, and through the lines of the Seattle, Lake Shore and Eastern at nearby Woolley it could enter Anacortes and establish it as the northern Puget Sound terminus of the railroad. On July 21 the railroad announced that it had secured controlling interest in the Seattle, Lake Shore and Eastern. Its stated objective was to keep James J. Hill and the Great Northern Railroad from gaining control and shutting the Northern Pacific out of the territory north of Seattle. Just being the northern terminus was enough for Anacortes. The first through train from Seattle and Tacoma reached the town on November 25, 1890, amid a cannon salute, festooned streets, a banquet, speeches, and songs.

The success of Anacortes meant that competing town sites such as Gibralter could not realize similar success. But an irrepressible quality in Freeman's personality inevitably surfaced during times of adversity. As he watched the likelihood of his financial success evaporate, he sought psychological compensation. Just as the editor of the *Puget Sound Mail* had predicted, Freeman claimed the entire credit for everything that had happened at Anacortes:

> Yes, the people could well afford to hold an annual celebration and before they commence it they should improve their city park and erect therein a statue of Legh R. Freeman and on every anniversary day take their children to the foot of the statue and have them bow their heads and clasp their hands and in reverent supplication invoke the Deity to endow them with some of the enterprise, foresight and patriotism of the man in whose honor the statue is erected.[16]

Yet an Ellensburg editor envisioned a different type of appeal to the Deity regarding Freeman,

> the anniversary of whose removal the good people of . . . [North Yakima] celebrate with much enthusiasm semi-annually. Since he shook the alfalfa from his flowing locks and the sands of Yakima from his feet, he has wandered to the classic shades of Fidalgo Island. . . . Poor Freeman. It is with reluctance that we print the following item received from a correspondent at Deception Pass. "A novel prayer meeting took place last Friday night at Gibraltar [sic], those present asking Almighty God to remove one L. R. Freeman, a public nuisance, from their midst." If the prayer is answered and the divine powers intervene in behalf of a long suffering public, the good people of Gibraltar and Yakima can fall on each others' neck [sic] and weep for joy at their deliverance.[17]

At North Yakima Reed, too, reminded readers that Freeman had been given a land bonus for moving his newspaper: "It is more than intimated that the people . . . [at Gibralter] stand ready to double the bonus if he will move away."[18]

Yet not all editors were so consistently vindictive. The *Skagit News* admitted that one issue of the *Washington Farmer* contained a "splendid" description of Skagit County and its resources, but added that "Brother Freeman" should have abandoned his "silly" attempts to change established place names for advertising purposes. The newspaper said that it planned to reprint the *Washington Farmer's* four-column history of the Skagit Valley and Mount Vernon and added that the *Farmer* had done much to draw population to Fidalgo Island. What Freeman had predicted eighteen months earlier regarding a railroad boom had become fact, the *Skagit News* admitted. But when it was rumored that the *Farmer* might be moved to Port Gardner, the *News* wondered whether there were any "suckers" there.[19]

Freeman did move the *Farmer,* but only to Anacortes. Belatedly he sought to share in some of the profits of the boom. His family, enlarged by the birth of a son, Richmond, in 1890, accompanied him from the inactive Gibralter townsite in 1892. They were joined in Anacortes by Frederick Freeman, who resumed a partnership with his brother after twenty-four years. Characteristically, Frederick Freeman established a real estate office in addition to helping publish the newspaper. Financial problems continued, however, and Legh Freeman made repeated but futile trips to meet with the county commissioners at Mount Vernon to seek reductions in his Gibralter tax assessments from $5 per lot to $6 per acre.

In the aftermath of the Anacortes boom, Freeman fared better than the *Anacortes Progress,* which was forced to suspend publication early in 1892. The *Washington Farmer's* agricultural emphasis and circulation beyond the publishing site again enabled Freeman to remain in business. He attracted advertising from the Northern Pacific, Union Pacific, Wisconsin Central, Great Northern, and Seattle, Lake Shore and Eastern railroads. Additional advertising revenue came from hotels, new communities such as faraway Kettle Falls and Pullman, the Puget Sound Brewery, ubiquitous Royal Baking Powder, and producers of medicinal products. In accepting advertising from a San Francisco firm, which offered to diagnose the "true condition of men suffering from the errors of their youth," Freeman apparently thought more of revenue than his earlier pledge to keep the *Washington Farmer* "clean enough for the hearthstone of any family of girls." He divided the editorial columns of the newspaper into sections on turf, cattle, swine, sheep, poultry, apiary, aviary, orchard, flowers, garden, forestry, agriculture, dairy, irrigation, veterinary, and "home circle." The turf section included racing news from Kent, Spokane, and Moscow, Idaho, and he reported graduation ceremonies at the State Agricultural College at Pullman. The *Washington Farmer* carried a Spokane, as well as an Anacortes, logotype dateline, apparently through an arrangement with a correspondent there.

The agricultural orientation of the *Washington Farmer* was one factor that led Freeman to take an early Populist stance in politics. Following the February 22, 1892, convention at St. Louis of the Knights of Labor, Farmers' Alliance, and affiliated organizations, Freeman devoted nearly two columns to the official directory of the National Farmers' Alliance and Industrial Union and an additional column to the recently adopted People's party platform. There was no indication, however, that the *Washington Farmer* was a member of the National Reform Press Association, the organization of newspapers of the Populist movement.

Freeman was also active in the Skagit County Taxpayers League Convention in Mount Vernon during the spring of 1894, but his persistent critic at the *Skagit News* thought he detected an ulterior motive in Freeman's actions:

> The resolutions introduced by Legh R. Freeman contained a goodly sized coon in a wood pile. Many convention members were unaware that Mr. Freeman has large holdings in North Yakima and that his real object in opposing the building of the capitol [at Olympia] is to try to submit the capitol question to the people for another vote. Freeman's resolutions conveyed the impression that the capitol was to be built by direct taxation instead of by the sale of granted lands received from the government when the territory became a state.[20]

When the *Washington Farmer* finally suspended publication in 1894, the *Skagit News* claimed that the demise had probably been hastened by the collapse of the taxpayers league itself, but there is no evidence that Freeman enjoyed any formal support from the league.

Other, more substantial factors, however, contributed to the end of the *Washington Farmer* at Anacortes. The railroad boom had subsided and the economy of the town was inadequate to wrest significant rail traffic from the ports of Seattle and Tacoma. The financial panic of 1893 erased any hope of profit in Freeman's Fidalgo Island land venture.[21] A paper transfusion of $5,000 from the Washington Farmer Publishing Company to Freeman and his wife in exchange for the company's assumption of title to the nine lots the Freemans owned in North Yakima was apparently insufficient to bring solvency.[22]

Miller Freeman suggested to his father that the family move to Seattle and commence publication of a daily newspaper, with the three oldest boys reporting the news and operating a printing office. The father rejected the plan as being too ambitious, deciding instead to return to North Yakima. A factor in this decision was the property, although perhaps mortgaged, that Freeman still held there. His wife had sold the acre she owned for a $500 profit. The business property had reverted to Freeman in a foreclosure action. He had repurchased the property for $521.91 at a sheriff's sale after realizing less than $400 from the original contract before the purchasers defaulted.[23]

Freeman, at age 52, his family increased in 1894 by the birth of a daughter, Varinia Allison,[24] returned to North Yakima that year to continue the *Washington Farmer* without funds. For a twelve-month period his total cash business collections were less than $100. The family subsisted on the butter, vegetables, and fruit traded by farmers for subscriptions. Cordwood was obtained in the same way. Clothing and flour were exchanged by merchants for advertising.[25]

Freeman's return to North Yakima marked the first time in nearly thirty years that he moved eastward. Like the farmers about whom he wrote, he found that problems could no longer be solved, actually or hypothetically, by yet another westward move. But this was not only a geographical problem. A new philosophy about the nature of opportunity in America was about to be formulated.

10

The "Red Horse Candidate"

In the twenty years of his life remaining after he returned to North Yakima in 1894, Freeman failed to find the financial success that had been one of the forces drawing him across the North American continent. The frontier had truly turned back upon itself, and Freeman now joined the Populists in seeking from political action what they could no longer find in the land.[1] But Populism proved no panacea for him, personally or politically. Freeman's problems seemed to multiply in his last years as he faced numerous additional legal actions, the death of his second wife, the total alienation of his sons, and three political campaigns that bordered on the ludicrous. Yet befitting Horatio Vattel, he met most of these problems with a flair and lived out his life with disregard for the orthodox.

The Populist ground swell drew much of Freeman's attention during his first years back in North Yakima. In 1894 the party displaced the Democrats as the major opposition party in Washington. The Populists gained 39 percent of the popular vote in the state, the second highest in the eleven western states. They controlled several county commissions and elected three state senators and twenty state representatives. Freeman was the editor of a farm paper, but there is no reason to believe that he became a Populist merely to profit from the political ground swell. He had followed the expedient course before, but as early as 1885 Freeman had enunciated an incipient Populist stance long before editors of the state labeled him the "Whiskered Pop":

> It is *underconsumption* and not *over-production* that causes the hard times in our country. The products of the farm are virtually taxed an average of fifty per cent on revenues that benefit only certain classes and do not raise market prices of agricultural staples, and all the while foreign pauper labor is being imported to fill the

places of millions of mechanics, coal miners, etc., and the Chinese coolies are swarming the Pacific Coast, and millions of white men and women are either idle or working their lives out at wages that will not buy the necessities of life. . . . We must find means to increase the *consumption* of our poor laborers; this will settle the question of *over-production.*

The policy pursued after the [Civil] war, to wit: contraction of the currency funding [three words illegible] and the squeezing process necessary to restore the gold standard, while it piled up wealth in the vaults of the money kings, crippled production, paralyzed enterprise and impoverished the people. The result is, the huge mountains of corporate wealth, overshadowing the awful depths of poverty and the barren plains of idleness, want and death. . . .[2]

Freeman's critic at the *Yakima Herald,* E. M. Reed, thought he detected inconsistencies in Freeman's current Populist philosophy. Early in 1895 Freeman advocated driving the Chinese from North Yakima because they were supposedly usurping the places of "deserving" Americans, the "defrauded white laborers." Reed contended that Freeman took this editorial position only because a blackmail scheme had failed. He told readers of the *Yakima Herald* that Freeman had tried to force North Yakima Chinese to advertise with him and that if they refused, he would drive them from town:

> That blatant old fraud Freeman is still running about the streets hollering "Chinese". . . . He seems to forget that it was only through the force of the law that one of his own employes recently secured the wages justly due him. The legislature should provide an asylum for such nuisances.[3]

High on the state Populist platform in 1896 was a prohibition of free railroad passes and the reduction of freight and passenger rail rates. Newspapermen were commonly among recipients of railroad passes. Late in 1895 Freeman attacked the Northern Pacific, but Reed said that he had a hidden motive for doing this, too. He identified Freeman as the unnamed North Yakima newspaperman who had sold the use of his railroad pass "after signing an agreement not to so transfer it." As a result, Reed claimed, Freeman lost Northern Pacific advertising and his passenger pass; thus Freeman's editorial criticism was due to his "discomfiture in this respect."[4]

Buoyed by the gains of 1894, Populists at both the national and state levels were optimistic in 1896, although state leaders remained divided about the wisdom of fusion with Democrats and Silver Republicans. That the state conventions of the three groups were scheduled concurrently for August, in Ellensburg, itself was a victory for the fusionists. The Yakima County Populist convention in June demonstrated its approval of fusion by reaffirming a platform plank with which Freeman agreed. It favored "a union of all reform forces at the coming national convention at St. Louis, provided the union can be accomplished without the sacrifice of principles."⁵

Freeman was among seventy-five delegates to the county convention held at the courthouse. He sought to be the delegate from Klickitat, Kittitas, and Yakima counties to the National Populist Convention at St. Louis in July, but he received only one vote. Further demonstrating his stand on fusion, Freeman was on hand early in August when North Yakima's Silver Republicans ratified the nomination of William Jennings Bryan and Arthur Sewall at Mason's Opera House. He appeared on a panel, apparently as the Populist representative, to discuss fusion. The other participants were State Attorney General Wesley L. Jones of North Yakima, a Republican, and a Judge Reavis, who apparently represented the Democrats. Although the *Yakima Herald* and Freeman agreed on the Bryan-Sewall ticket, the *Herald* reporter told his readers that Jones and Reavis "acquitted themselves with much credit," but because of Freeman's "harangue" the reporter was forced to "quit in disgust."⁶

Free silver became the consuming issue as the 1896 elections approached, but in the state, interest in fusion was even higher. After Bryan was nominated by the Populists in St. Louis, Washington Populists still could not agree with Democrats on fusion. Freeman's political expertise as displayed throughout the course of this dilemma was not as limited as the *Yakima Herald*'s biased reporting claimed. As the state conventions opened the following week in Ellensburg, Freeman was named chairman of the conference committee composed of representatives of the three parties which was instructed to prepare a fusion slate of candidates for state elective offices.

On August 13 Freeman brought to the Populists a committee report rejecting the Democratic and Silver Republican proposition for a fusion slate. Freeman was sent back to the committee "without instructions."⁷ At the same time, he was the Populist representative on the three-member Yakima County conference committee upon which H. J. Snively, an attorney who had represented Freeman in court, was the Democratic appointee.

Freeman reported to the Populist convention on August 14 that the state conference committee "reports progress and asks for further time." Populist convention delegates saw the lack of a substantive report as merely gaining time for a coalition of Democrats and Silver Republicans to defeat fusion. He attempted to make a short explanation, but the slate as it stood at that point was read. In it the Populists were allotted the positions of governor, lieutenant governor, secretary of state, auditor, land commissioner, two presidential electors, and one congressman. The Populists approved this report of the committee and gave the Silver Republicans and Democrats each one congressional candidate. The effect of the action, and the Populist domination of seven of twelve other available positions, was reported by a Seattle Republican newsman:

> The Populists, by sheer bull-headed obstinacy, not only held their own against the adroit and trained politicians among the Democrats and Silverites, but carried off the great bulk of the offices, from governor down. Of the three, it is the dominant party, which has in practical effect absorbed both the others. . . .[8]

However closely Freeman had associated himself with the victorious Populists, he was not successful in having himself nominated to one of the party's positions. He reportedly had sought to be a Populist candidate for Congress. Yet his political activity accelerated, spurred on by fusionist success that fall which saw a sweep of state offices, control of the legislature, and the election of two congressmen. Early in December Freeman issued a call for a citizens' meeting in North Yakima to name a "People's Party" municipal ticket. He was chosen chairman of the session and attacked the city's water, light, and power company. Freeman's speech made him a "dangerous factor in any community," the *Yakima Herald* reported, but it did not quote him in detail.[9] Some of the nominees refused to serve and not one was elected.

Undaunted, Freeman went to western Washington in January 1897 in an attempt to convince state legislators to name him to the United States Senate. The *Seattle Times* reported that he had spent a week in Seattle and dutifully combed his whiskers every day in the lobby of his hotel. He established no headquarters, but distributed a circular printed in red which was headed: "The Red Horse Candidate" and which depicted him with "populist whiskers," clothed in frontier garb, and mounted on a "magnificent steed." The text set forth his plea to legislators for support:

> Why not ballot on Legh Richmond Freeman, the Veteran and Venerable Editor of the Washington Farmer?
>
> Is not your duty to the State greater than to party, geographical position or personal friends?
>
> Elect the old pioneer Editor, Explorer and Farmer. He is an indomitable worker and will reflect unbounded credit on the people of the great state of Washington.
>
> His home is 172 miles from the Pacific ocean and 172 miles from the Idaho line. He knows well the wants of every portion of the state; and no man is capable of rendering better service to the commonwealth.
>
> He has been tried by every test and proven to possess the highest order of manhood.
>
> He has read law and is a superior Parliamentarian, Orator and Statesman.[10]

The *Seattle Times* merely reported that Freeman was one of the candidates. Clark Davis and John P. Fay were "black-horse candidates," a score of others were "dark-horses," but Freeman was the great and only "red-horse candidate," the newspaper said. The *Yakima Herald* characteristically added that members of the legislature said that the only fault they found with the picture of the horse "was that a certain part of the animal's anatomy was astride of him."[11]

The novelty of Freeman's campaign had no real effect, and he was not among the numerous nominees for the United States Senate in the 1897 Populist-controlled Washington legislature. Legislators after several days of balloting turned to another man who had been prominent at the Ellensburg convention—Spokane attorney George Turner. But Freeman continued to seek satisfaction in politics. Years later he turned to the people to seek the position he could not obtain from the legislature.

Yet Freeman's Populist participation was not without indirect effect. He found one measure of Populist-inspired legislation a mixed blessing. Congress in the fall of 1892, as a result of pressure by the Grange, Farmers' Alliance, and Populists, permitted the postmaster general to use $10,000 to experiment in carrying mail to farmhouses. Between 1896 and 1897, eighty-two pioneer routes were established, including one in the North Yakima area. What this meant was that nearly everyone now had his mail delivered. The *Washington Farmer* could thus reach the subscriber immediately upon publication, but of course competing daily newspapers also could be delivered as rapidly.

Freeman was a Populist, but there is no indication he entertained Socialist sympathies, even though he wrote to Eugene V. Debs in 1897 asking him to establish on the Yakima Indian Reservation a colony that he was proposing. Freeman's motivation seems to have been more economic than political. And his proposal again drew the criticism of the *Yakima Herald.* "If Freeman could be located on a small sized reservation somewhere the people never would want it opened," Reed wrote. "He is a pestiferous nuisance."[12]

Within days of his unsuccessful senatorial quest in Olympia, Freeman suffered a loss that would have greater personal ramifications for him than his political rebuff by the legislature. He was confronted by his son, Legh Miller, who, at age 21, asked his father for wages, a commission, or an interest in the printing business. Both of Freeman's older sons had already left home. In being unable to come to terms with his father, Miller now found as had his brothers before him that Freeman felt that his children were, in effect, his property and that only he could decide what they should do. On this subject, as on all others, Freeman tolerated no dissent, his son later remembered:

> I can never recall a *conversation* with my Father. When he was talking to one of his family he did the talking. He neither expected any response nor tolerated one, regardless of how courteous and

Legh Freeman, the "red horse candidate,"
probably about 1887. (courtesy Yakima
[*Washington*] Herald-Republic*)*

intelligent it may have been. When he talked to any of us it was strictly a one-sided affair. We were expected to listen and no more.

I don't think my Father ever understood the failure of his fatherhood. I do not think he ever understood why his brood broke up and we all went our ways almost as soon as we were able. . . .

Legh Freeman made a fetish of self-discipline. He had no room in his life for soft things. This went to the point where he would tolerate no cushions on our chairs.[13]

The public learned of the family's trouble through the columns of the *Yakima Herald:*

Perfect harmony has not prevailed for some time past between Legh Freeman Sr. and Legh Freeman Jr. of the Farmer newspaper and as a result the brains and balance wheel of the concern has left and the Red Horse candidate is compelled to pay wages for an assistant. They [wages] must indeed be . . . [irritating] to one who most heartily dislikes to pay for anything.[14]

Miller Freeman's next steps led to ironic and distasteful consequences for Legh Freeman in subsequent years. The young man, who had only $3 in cash and a bicycle, decided to publish a farm paper in competition with his father. However, he planned a publication covering the technical aspects of agriculture as opposed to the emphasis he felt his father misplaced on the politics of Populism. He selected the name *Ranch and Range* and in an act of faith spent all of his cash on a week's meal ticket at a North Yakima restaurant. He then made arrangements to use the *Yakima Republic* printing plant—which had passed out of Holton's ownership—when it was idle.

Within two months he had sold 250 subscriptions and collected $80 in advance on advertising. After writing all the articles, setting type and advertisements, running the press, and preparing his press run of 1,000 copies for mailing, the young Freeman made a net profit of $100 on his first issue. He hired a printer for the second issue and, after traveling to Spokane and Seattle to solicit business, he decided to move permanently to Seattle. Starting only blocks from his father's establishment, Miller Freeman had laid the foundation for a career in which he would realize within a decade the financial reward his father was unable to compile in a lifetime. The lesson was not lost on Legh Freeman.

In addition, legal entanglements faced Freeman again, and in one instance he appeared at first to have struck a new low. A businessman, C. V. Bissell, had Freeman arrested for using "vile, offensive, and threatening language." The *Yakima Herald* asserted that Freeman had ordered some screen doors and when Bissell would not deliver them until a previous bill was paid,

Freeman then opened his sewer of filth and notwithstanding the presence of Mr. Bissell's daughter, who is so sick that her recovery is doubted[,] he continued his threats and vile speech until the young woman was taken with a spasm.[15]

Freeman was acquitted, but Reed—at the *Herald*—was still reluctant to clear Freeman's name before the public. "Through one of those very uncertain bodies, a jury, a conviction was not obtained," he wrote.[16] Although legally innocent, Freeman ironically was treated in the pages of the *Yakima Herald* in the same manner that he had treated the Ogden postmaster, his competitor in Butte, Holton, and others who had somehow challenged him. Freeman may have used strong language in his disagreement with Bissell. It was generally known that he frequently displayed irritation and was capable of going on a "rampage." But it is unlikely that he used a "sewer of filth" before a girl. "Vile speech" was not consistent with the character of being a Southern gentleman which he sported. He professed to view with disgust untoward language in the presence of any lady. Also in court at this time was a suit with a printing firm which took four years to settle. This dispute grew out of an unpaid 1894 account of $47.49. In 1898 Freeman was ordered to pay the sum, which he had undoubtedly failed to do out of principle rather than poverty.[17]

Freeman's difficulties continued, and that is perhaps why he sought a psychological outlet in something that had given him success and satisfaction. He readily reminisced in conversation with others about the days on the Union Pacific frontier, and in this, too, he painted the picture larger than life. There is no hint of law suits or bills in letters he sent to C. G. Coutant, who inquired about Freeman's activity in Wyoming for preparation of a history he was writing of that state. Ignoring his brother's role, Freeman claimed that he had published the *Frontier Index* at all eleven towns between Fort Kearny and Ogden. Then he further embellished his past:

> With the Washington Farmer steam printing plant I founded the seaport city of Anacortes.
> I was born Dec. 4, 1842, in Arlington Heights overlooking the national capital and was thoroughly imbued from childhood with the high moral standard of the founders of this government whose sons and daughters were [my] playmates and companions. . . .
> I was a prominent candidate before the Ellensburg convention for Congress; and only missed being made United States Senator by the last legislature by a scratch. I am known as the "Red Horse Senator" because all my explorations in the West have been on the backs of spirited red horses and I never go about anything as a dark horse candidate. . . .
> Do me up in good shape, colonel, and I will deed you a block in the Seaport City of Anacortes.[18]

But Freeman's misfortunes continued in 1897. The Freeman home, which had been built at least a block north of the printing plant, burned that year. The family was forced to move back to the quarters at the rear of the printing office. Late that year Mrs. Freeman contracted a serious case of "typhoid malaria" and died shortly after midnight on November 2, a month before she would have reached the age of forty-two. The *Yakima Herald*, now under new ownership after Reed's departure, editorialized at the time of the funeral at North Yakima's Presbyterian church, "In his hour of trouble Mr. Freeman has the sympathy of the entire community."[19] At the end of a week, Freeman presented several hundred volumes of books, perhaps his wife's, to the city library.

Left for the second time with a family of youngsters, Freeman sent his son Richmond to be with Miller Freeman in Seattle. Varinia, who was three, stayed with a North Yakima family when she, too, became ill. Freeman later sent the children to live with their maternal grandparents in Georgia.

Freeman, at age fifty-five, devoted his full time to his work, broadening the scope of his publication. By the first of 1898 it carried the title of *Washington Farmer and Freeman's National Farmer and Turfman*, "established 1847." Above a full front page drawing of a Seattle street scene, the *Farmer* listed its places of publication as "North Yakima and Seattle, Wash., and Washington, D.C." The regular subscription price was $2 per year, but subscribers could obtain it for $1 by paying "cash in advance."[20] For $1.25, a joint subscription to the *Farmer* and the *Seattle Weekly Times* was offered. But the newspaper itself continued to be an unlikely mixture of agricultural articles and North Yakima community news. Reports of the North Yakima City Council were published amid such agricultural notices as a letter from President E. A. Bryan of the Washington Agricultural College announcing the fourth annual winter school for farmers at Pullman.

In April 1898 the United States declared war on Spain and by June armed forces recruiters were active in North Yakima. Freeman went to the recruiting office to report the activity, but, according to one account, asked the extrareportorial question of how many "suckers" had enlisted. When the recruiting officer suggested that Freeman vacate the premises immediately, Freeman supposedly ignored the implied command. A sergeant assisted him from the office "amid the smiles of a number of spectators."[21] Whether Freeman's question reflected his opinion of the terms of enlistment or of the war itself was not reported. Such belligerence may have precluded Freeman once again from being an effective community publisher. His experience in the next few years illustrates his continuing frustration.

He divested himself of the *Washington Farmer* in 1899, but it was only coincidental that this action occurred at the same time as the arrival in North Yakima of Wilbur Wade Robertson. This newcomer became the dominant and most respected newspaper publisher in North Yakima, where eighteen newspapers had sought success at various times. After he purchased the *Yakima Republic,* Robertson continued in business there, in contrast to Freeman's practice of constantly moving. After adding the *Yakima Herald* to his holdings in 1913, Robertson lived on to become the city's sole publisher.

It had been rumored in the fall of 1898 that Freeman, now free from family obligations, would move to Tacoma. He remained in North Yakima, but he did turn the newspaper over to a North Yakima free-lance writer, Joel Shoemaker. By early March 1899 this arrangement was terminated when it was announced that Freeman had consolidated the paper with his son's publication, the *Ranch,* in Seattle. Freeman opportunistically hoped to take advantage of the financial success his son was beginning to realize. That Miller Freeman and his father could agree on a partnership arrangement was deemed newsworthy. The *Yakima Epigram* (March 4, 1899) reported, "It is understood that both father and son will hereafter work harmoniously together." For the first time the "Press on Wheels" did not accompany Freeman to a new publishing site. He disposed of most of his type and equipment to the publisher of the *Yakima Democrat.* Closure of the plant cleared up a county treasurer's attachment for $19.43 for unpaid 1896 personal property taxes. A public sale of unspecified goods to raise the sum took place on March 24.

As his first assignment from his son, Freeman traveled to Pendleton, Oregon, for the Northwest Wool Growers convention and to Portland for the Oregon State Dairymen's convention. The modes of transportation had changed and the conventions did not compare with frontier life, but an aging Horatio Vattel had found another arrangment by which he could roam the countryside. In the summer of 1899 he went to Virginia by way of St. Paul, Minnesota, and it was perhaps on this trip that he was robbed in Chicago of "everything except his pass and his honor."[22] Apparently the former Populist was no longer concerned about the effect of accepting gratuities from railroads. Ironically, Freeman left the scene of the robbery with the gift of a gold nugget, although he lost $200 in cash. After exposing his roll of bills, he had been invited by the robber to view a collection of nuggets, and one was presented to him as a gift before he was asked for his money.[23]

Although his new job offered him the opportunity to travel, Freeman and his son were not working "harmoniously together" in Seattle. It became public knowledge in mid-August that Freeman had served written notice on advertising patrons of the *Ranch* warning them not to pay any money to his son until certain "financial differences" were adjusted.[24] Freeman then filed a King County Superior Court complaint against his son, asking for $3,500 and charging that Miller Freeman had breached their partnership agreement by not printing Legh Freeman's name as editor, paying his expenses, or printing articles he wrote and running advertising he secured. He maintained that his son had written to patrons advising them not to deal with him and to do no business with the newspaper except through mail from the Seattle office. He asked that a receiver be appointed to conduct the business.[25]

In an answer and cross-complaint, Miller Freeman denied that he had breached any terms of their agreement, but declared that his father had been derelict by keeping subscription and advertising money for his own purposes. He asked that his father be restrained from interfering with the business and from "hindering and embarrassing" him in collecting money due the partnership.[26]

The case was heard on November 2 and the court decided that the partnership should be dissolved by a sale of assets. Later that month the assets were sold for $1,010 to Miller as the highest bidder. The final decree was filed over Legh Freeman's protest. He complained that his son was not forced to pay cash for the assets.

Father and son were back in court within a month when Miller asked for an injunction restraining his father from publishing a magazine, the *New Northwest Farm & Dairyman,* which Miller purported to be the outgrowth of the partnership. The court granted Miller his requested injunction and restrained Freeman from publishing any journal with a name similar to the *Ranch* and from implying that he had anything to do with the publication, its successors, or predecessors.[27] Although otherwise candid about his relationship with his father, Miller Freeman failed to mention the law suits in his *Memoirs.*

Freeman never achieved a reconciliation with Miller or his other sons after this incident. In a will, which he had drawn up seven years later, he displayed his continuing bitterness:

> Give my sons Randolph, Hoomes, Legh Miller, and Richmond $1 each. This is done in consideration of the fact that after they contracted with me that if I would educate them to a knowledge of the printing and publishing business, they would pursue permanently that vocation; and in violation of that contract they one and all deserted me and the business which I had established and threw upon me in my old age the burden of paying off the mortgages that I had placed on my property to procure money with which to school the above named sons.[28]

But the schooling had indeed been brief. Miller ended his education at the age of ten. Richmond, Freeman's son by his second marriage, ran away from home at age fifteen.

The harsh terms of the will were also dictated by Freeman's pique at his son's success, which had been publicly reported the previous year. In a story about Miller Freeman's marriage to the daughter of Judge W. H. Bogle of Seattle, it was stated that the bridegroom had made not only his publication a success but:

> He saved his money and branched out into other investments. In these he was successful. Last spring he is reputed to have cleared

up in the neighborhood of $75,000 on his tide land investments, and it is said that he is worth more than $100,000.[29]

The pair's wedding trip would have made Horatio Vattel envious. It included stops in California, Mexico, Texas, "the Southern states," Washington, D.C., New York, Boston, and a trip home on the Canadian Pacific "in time for the Christmas dinner" in Seattle. The newspaper account made no reference to the bridegroom's parentage. The "successful investments" had been realized only nine years after Miller Freeman had left his father's North Yakima printing plant. It was the foundation of a career which would make Miller Freeman wealthy. In contrast, Legh Freeman faced two additional court actions for nonpayment of debts before he left Seattle. A lumber company filed suit to collect $19.89 from him and a second complainant went to court to collect $58.60.[30]

Freeman returned to North Yakima and began yet another publication, the *Northwest Farm and Home.* But the "long felt want" which the *Yakima Epigram* said existed at the Freeman printing office remained unfilled: "Who will be the lucky girl [filling] the need for a lady editor[?]" the newspaper asked.[31] Freeman had met a prospect for this role while on a business trip to St. Paul, probably the one during which he was robbed. He had been in correspondence with Mary Rose Genevieve Whitaker of St. Paul, who was employed in a wholesale produce commission firm, John B. Hoxie & Company. She was a graduate of the commercial department of the University of Minnesota and supposedly held the highest grade-teacher's certificate issued in that state. On July 11, 1900, Freeman, at age fifty-seven, took Miss Whitaker, a Roman Catholic in her midthirties, as his third wife.[32] Her wedding ring was made from the nugget obtained in the Chicago robbery. A year later Freeman went to Georgia to bring his two young children back to North Yakima.

Mrs. Freeman was officially installed as the associate editor of the *Farm and Home,* which allowed Freeman to spend two months in 1902 on Puget Sound and in British Columbia "in the interests of his paper."[33] Such absences indicated to some observers that Mrs. Freeman's life with her husband may have been unpleasant at times. For example, a friend of Mrs. Freeman's—a fellow member of the St. Joseph Catholic parish in North Yakima—once asked for a blotter at the printing office. As Mrs. Freeman was about to give her one as a gift, the woman remembers that Freeman slapped his wife across the face. When the customer expressed dismay, Freeman asked whether her husband had never done that to her. She replied that he had not, "because he is a gentleman," and she left without the blotter.[34]

But Varinia Freeman, who was reared by her stepmother, remembers in contrast to her older stepbrothers that life in the Freeman home had its moments of levity. Her stepmother enjoyed working in the printing office "tremendously," Miss Freeman recalls, and she enjoyed talking to the people who frequented the newspaper plant. She claims that Freeman and his wife "did a great deal of joking," and, unlike her stepbrothers, she remembers that "pleasant and uplifting conversation at the dining table was the rule."[35]

Freeman was concerned about the food served at his table; he liked to have his meals served promptly and without additives or preservatives if possible. But if a meal were late, he would jokingly chide his wife by spreading his fingers toward his chin, saying there were ten hungry tapeworms reaching up through his throat. He preferred beef round steak for breakfast, fish for noon dinner, and eggs for supper. He concocted his own bread of yellow cornmeal, whole wheat flour, buttermilk, and soda which he named "Freeman bread." He taught his young children to chew all their food thoroughly, which, he admonished, was necessary for good digestion.[36]

If at home Freeman was pampered, he received no special consideration in the community. Early in 1905 he was taken to court by a plaintiff who complained that Freeman had agreed to sell the printing office property but then refused to convey a deed. The suit was dismissed by agreement two years later.[37] But even before that case was settled, Freeman was sued by an attorney for $176 in legal fees. These had accumulated when the lawyer had won $1,800 for Freeman in 1906 in a claim against the United States Department of the Interior for destruction of unspecified property in Montana by Indians. Perhaps this claim involved real estate that Freeman had claimed in 1866 or 1867. This suit was also dismissed by agreement.[38] Freeman was unsuccessful, however, when he attempted to collect a $225 bill for an advertisement he had published for three years in the *Northwest Farm and Home*. The court held that he could not collect because the advertising contract was only for twelve months and that Freeman had continued the publication for two years on his own authority without approval from the advertisers.[39]

Emphasis upon Freeman's legal skirmishes, however, could be misleading. He continued not only his interest but participation in public issues during the last fifteen years of his life. For one of the few times, he joined other publishers and members of the North Yakima business community when he advocated that the federal government undertake development of irrigation in the Yakima Valley following passage of the Reclamation Act of 1902. In fact he is given credit for playing a major role in encouraging passage of subsequent state enabling legislation as he denounced the private "wildcat" irrigation schemes designed to sell unirrigable lands to gullible investors.[40]

These vested interests offered the strongest opposition to federal reclamation. Small land owners, who feared private monopoly of water sources, fought for measures permitting federal participation. When citizens petitioned the federal government to develop storage reservoirs on the upper Yakima River, the private companies planned their own reservoir dams. As a result of this activity and opposition, the Reclamation Service decided not to intervene in the Yakima Valley.

But the secretary of the interior in March 1903 approved a canal on the Yakima Indian Reservation.

W. W. Robertson of the *Yakima Republic* became the spokesman for supporters of the national irrigation plan. His influence was among the factors causing government officials to change their minds. In 1904 federal spokesmen announced that the Reclamation Act did authorize the Reclamation Service to undertake work in regions that were already settled. But they demanded a new code of state irrigation laws permitting settlement of contested water rights and construction of a reservoir dam. A state irrigation commission was appointed to prepare such a code, but its recommendation was discarded by legislators in Olympia under pressure from private irrigation concerns.

On February 28, 1905, the state House of Representatives passed an irrigation code. The state Senate approved it on March 1 and the governor signed it on March 4. The bill authorized the federal government to use the right of eminent domain in acquiring reservoir sites and canals and to appropriate all available water in the state. It was only a matter of time until the secretary of the interior formally approved the Sunnyside and Tieton projects in the valley.

Freeman sneered at rival claims by the *Seattle Post-Intelligencer* and *Seattle Times* as to which did the most to advance the cause of national irrigation. Neither newspaper had taken a significant stand on the issue, Freeman said, until he "went to Olympia and secured the passage of the government irrigation law, and defeated the private corporation irrigation acts."[41]

His lobbying efforts were probably not decisive, but they undoubtedly did have some effect. Robertson, and the *Yakima Herald* as well, allowed western Washington interests little credit for help in passing the legislation. The Puget Sound concerns could only see water potential for generating electricity. The research of Calvin B. Coulter, an authority on Yakima Valley irrigation, confirms this assessment.[42] As a result of his role at Olympia, Freeman, with characteristic flair, gave himself the title of "father of irrigation" when he attended an irrigation congress at Spokane. He told reporters there that he had also introduced irrigation methods into Wyoming forty-three years earlier.[43]

Freeman also called himself the "father of good roads." In this endeavor, too, he was an early proponent of governmental aid for development of a state highway system, but he could not work with community forces long enough to be effective. A state Good Roads Association was organized to combat opposition, primarily from rural interests, to a statewide road building and maintenance program financed by a one-mill road tax. But at a meeting of the Good Roads Association in North Yakima, Freeman made a speech intimating that the "big six" of North Yakima, later described as "grafters," were

always trying to push themselves forward, gobble up the positions on committees of trust and vital importance to the community, and

especially where "honor or money" were concerned could always
be found in the front ready and willing to dictate affairs.[44]

He said that others than these six, apparently including himself,
were capable of holding responsible committee positions. The incident
received statewide news coverage, and at a second association meeting,
Alex Miller, a prominent North Yakima businessman, asked Freeman
to explain his charge. T. A. Noble, an engineer who had undertaken irrigation survey work for the federal government, made a similar request which was formalized as an approved motion.

Freeman arose to his feet, but it was reported that he

> talked around the point. He was called down[,] then he arose again
> and began to talk. He talked all round the point. Again he was
> called out of order. Finally Chairman Steinweg took the floor and
> amended the motion before the house which called for an explana-
> tion from Mr. Freeman. He moved that Freeman be asked to
> either name the six grafters or leave the meeting. The amendment
> carried. Then Mr. Freeman was given an opportunity to defend
> himself. He had nothing to say, but rising suddenly to his seat and
> glaring wildly around him, seized his hat and left the room. When
> he had gone the business of the meeting proceeded and much good
> was accomplished.[45]

Although he obviously did not have the support of community
leaders, Freeman hoped to use his activity in behalf of federal irrigation and good roads to succeed United States Senator Samuel H. Piles,
who announced that he would retire when his term expired in 1911.
The Washington legislature still named senators, but a preferential
primary was scheduled for September 1910. As early as September
1909 Freeman, at age sixty-six, addressed the announcement of his
Republican candidacy to the "Freemen" of the state in a blatant
display of self-esteem. It read like Horatio Vattel's autobiography:

> I was born on a farm in Culpeper County, Virginia, and as a bare-
> footed boy attended the long school house in the corner of the
> woods, afterwards taking a course at Kemper's college,
> preparatory to the university. I went to college only to learn how
> to learn and the 50 years schooling that I have received by coming
> in contact with the rugged frontier and vigorous inhabitants has
> brought me to the graduating exercises in which I shall receive my
> diploma in 1910. . . .
>   It was mainly through my efforts that the good roads and ir-
> rigation departments have been installed at the University of
> Washington and that the first good roads building in the world is
> maintained there. When 17 years of age I came west and began
> the publication of the Northwest Farm and Home. I have therefore
> spent half a century describing and illustrating the west and
> teaching modern farming. I am proud of the appellation that is ac-

corded to me as "The Father of Good Roads and Irrigation." I was the originator and organizer of the State Taxpayers' League which greatly improved the tax laws of the state. I have studied law and pursued a course that would qualify me for the office that the people are now asking me to accept. . . . I am a republican because that party is the party of progress and prosperity and represents the true spirit and genius of the age. My constituents will recognize the fact that no democrat can wield an influence at the national capital sufficient to obtain for this state the appropriations that the commonwealth ought to receive at the hands of the dominating party.

I have taken active part in the creation of the states of Nebraska, Utah, Colorado, Wyoming, Idaho, Montana, and Washington . . . as I blazed the trail for the vanguard of civilization across the western two-thirds of America and I named Wyoming. My life-long career in the west as a strong factor in the building of states and an empire is sufficient evidence to my constituents that I am capable of the best service in the upper house of Congress.

. . . I have organized and promoted most of the agricultural societies of the state. All who am [sic] acquainted with me know that like Henry Clay[,] "I would rather be right than president.[']"

. . . Note—as the oldest journalist in the west I ask all members of the press to render me all the aid they can consistent under the primary campaign. . . .[46]

Freeman appealed to each county central committee in the state for its "heartiest" support. He said he would personally visit each committee and "meanwhile friends should be organizing 'Freeman Clubs.' "[47]

He distributed to the press copies of the handbill announcing his 1869 Culpeper lecture. He also recalled his 1885 appearance in polar bear skin and walrus head helmet to emphasize the plank in his platform calling for "restoration of the American merchant marine and the development of shipbuilding" in the state:

> [Freeman] disagrees with the president in regard to a ship subsidy and he does not favor the purchase of vessels built in other countries. He thinks that no matter what it costs to build vessels in the United States or how high the wages of the sailors may be, if we can carry between this country and other countries the products of our farms and factories on our own vessels.[48]

He proposed reenactment of a pre–War of 1812 law providing that vessels should be built domestically, owned by American citizens, and protected by a tariff of only 10 percent on goods imported in American ships. Under this law, he said, British vessels "disappeared as if by magic" from American ports in 1812 and as a result "England declared war." Freeman claimed that the 864 Japanese vessels afloat in 1910 would likewise "disappear like an icicle before a chinook breeze" and

Puget Sound and Grays Harbor "would be alive" with active shipyards:

> It does not seem possible for Japan, a nation just evolved from barbarism, to practically monopolize the business of the Pacific ocean while the United States has but one vessel, Jim Hill's Minnesota, manned by Chinese, crossing the ocean and flying the stars and stripes.[49]

Freeman asked residents of the state to make his election "as nearly unanimous as possible," predicting that he would be elected by a large majority. He claimed that he would have been in the United States Senate years earlier if the state's primary law had been in effect. But to many he seemed to be only a figure from a bygone era. Editors reminded readers that Freeman's "wealth of whiskers" covering tie and shirt front was left over from the days of Populism when he sought to receive the senatorial appointment in the legislature.[50]

One week before the senatorial primary, Freeman, claiming Seattle as his home, sent a telegram to President William Howard Taft:

> Eliminate other west side candidates. Freeman of Seattle made 13 months' campaign, is editor of Northwest Farm and Home, straight old line republican, member of Grange and supported by Farmer's union and all plain common people. Only statesman and orator of the nine candidates for United States senator. Only man who can beat [Miles] Poindexter. Will popularize your administration. Answer North Yakima.[51]

One editor who reprinted the telegram dryly observed that as he went to press, no emergency "flash" had come over the wire from Taft.[52]

In an election in which 117,633 votes were cast for eight Republican candidates and 7,456 votes for two Democratic candidates, Freeman polled 1,975 votes. He ran fifth among the Republican contenders, far behind Poindexter, who got 67,714 votes and was ultimately named senator by the 1911 Washington legislature. Freeman received 1.57 percent of the total state vote and 1.67 percent of the Republican votes cast. He polled only 179 votes in Yakima County, which was 4.16 percent of the total county vote. In King County he received 193 votes, but only 3 in Garfield County.[53] In politics, as in business, Freeman continued to live in the shadow of his son. Miller Freeman was elected to the Washington legislature in 1912 as a Republican.

As might be expected, Freeman did not make it through the campaign without becoming involved in a law suit. American Color Type Company of New Jersey sued him for $539 which it claimed was due on election calendars picturing him on horseback. Freeman answered that his picture was too small, not reproduced from a photograph that had been furnished, and the color work was not "first class," among other faults. He asked for $1,500 damages in a counterclaim. Freeman, did not obtain the damages he sought, but when the civil trial was completed a jury found in his favor and awarded him his legal costs from the type company.[54]

The senatorial race was not Freeman's final campaign for office. Early in 1914, shortly before his seventy-second birthday, he announced his candidacy for the position of mayor of North Yakima. Echoing the rhetoric of contemporary Progressives and muckrakers, he directed his campaign against incumbent Jack Splawn:

> Since you came into office as Mayor three years ago have you not joined forces with those who have established a meat trust, a laundry trust, a power trust, a water trust, a gas trust, a heating trust, an electric light trust, a newspaper trust, a saloon trust, a blind-pig trust and a gambling trust? . . .
>
> Did you not close up the Hotel Blair and the redlight district and scatter the sporting women all over town? . . .
>
> Is it not a fact that many women and gamblers pay monthly dues for police protection, and the money does not find its way into the city treasury? . . .
>
> Do you not pay the paper which is controlled by the Pacific Power and Light Company's trust, six times as much for advertising as Freeman offered to do it for in his weekly paper? . . .
>
> Is it not a fact that ever since Feb. 22, 1911 when Freeman complained to the "Public Service Commission" in regard to the methods of the Pacific Power and Light Co., pertaining to the supply of water, lights, and power, you have used every subterfuge at your command to prevent any betterment for the people? . . .[55]

Mayor Splawn did lose the election, but not at the hands of Freeman. Splawn placed third in a field of four candidates, with 30 percent of the total vote, and still did substantially better than Freeman. The old Red Horse Candidate polled only 158 votes, 4 percent of those voting. In some precincts he failed to win any support at all. In only one did he get as many as 18 votes.

In eleven weeks Freeman was dead. He had suffered from kidney disease and bronchitis for many years. At times he would have to stop on the street to get his breath before walking on. On February 1, 1915, he was hospitalized in "extremely critical" condition for treatment of what had been diagnosed as Bright's disease, but he conversed with his wife until a few minutes before he died on February 7.[56] In lieu of the customary lily, a red rose was placed in his hand.

Because Freeman had no church affiliation, having preferred to worship God "in his own way," his wife and daughter decided to have funeral services at a mortuary. Despite his lack of religious affiliation, Freeman enjoyed philosophical discussions with Jesuit priests in his office. H. V. Snively, the attorney who had represented Freeman and had served on the county committee with him in Ellensburg in 1896, delivered a memorial address from the steps of the mortuary.[57] A crowd assembled in the street to hear his words.

Freeman's body was buried in North Yakima's Tahoma Cemetery next to that of his second wife. Engraving on a six-foot obelisk on her grave already identified him from 1897 as her husband. A similar marker was shortly placed on his grave.[58] Mary Freeman and her step-daughter inherited the farm paper. Probate of Freeman's will showed the total value of his estate to be $11,586.33, including $4,525 in real estate, $7,061.33 in personal property—primarily the printing equipment—and $515.33 cash on hand in a bank.[59] Three of his four sons, including Miller, acknowledged receipt of the $1 checks issued from the estate. A month after his father's death Miller renamed the *Ranch* the *Washington Farmer*. At the end of that year he sold the publication to the W. H. Cowles family of Spokane, where its publication continues.

Mrs. Freeman's farm publication, the *Northwest Farm and Home*, was discontinued shortly after she died unexpectedly of pneumonia in 1917. Varinia Freeman sold the printing equipment for $4,750 to a group of Toppenish and Sunnyside, Washington, businessmen.[60] She moved to Seattle, where she was employed by Miller Freeman.

No marker today designates Legh Freeman's grave, although his wife's stone remains intact on the adjacent grave. It is as though Horatio Vattel, even in death, could not be tied down and restrained from his legendary journeys.

11

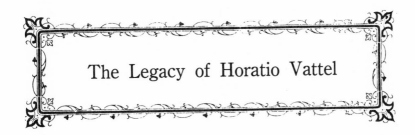

The Legacy of Horatio Vattel

THE ASSESSMENT of the life of Legh Freeman began before his body was buried. Appropriately, the words of H. V. Snively's memorial address were as full of exaggeration as any tale ever spun by Horatio Vattel:

> Early in his life, Mr. Freeman, as he often has personally told me, contracted a dislike for slavery, and this more than anything else caused him at the early age of seventeen, to leave a comfortable home and the opportunities afforded by a well-to-do family, to try his fortunes in the west, with but little to assist him other than his magnificent energy. To my mind, no episode in Mr. Freeman's long life is more indicative of his strong and independent mind or his self-reliance and self-confidence than this act in leaving his home on account of his convictions. We rarely find a youth, nowadays at least, who at the age of seventeen has reached a mental development which would lead to such an initiative as the act of Mr. Freeman in cutting his bridges behind him on account of his convictions on slavery and starting life on his own responsibility in a new and unknown country. . . .
>
> . . . no doubt many thousands of homesteaders of the central west and their descendants owe their prosperity to Mr. Freeman's engaging and convincing exploitation of the opportunities that awaited sturdy and energetic easterners upon the western prairies. . . .
>
> Mr. Freeman has often told me that one of the mistakes in his life was in not remaining at Ogden, which offered the finest sort of a field for newspaper development, but Ogden was destined, as he foresaw, soon to be no longer the front, and the restless spirit of Mr. Freeman coupled with the love of excitement which had been developed in him through his progress always at the front from the Missouri river to the Rocky mountains, could not tolerate in a prosaic settled community. . . .
>
> I personally am of the opinion that our departed friend has done more toward attracting people to the Yakima valley, and

directing and encouraging their efforts and energies after they got here than any other man who now lives or who has ever lived in this valley. . . .

Our friend was inherently a man of deep convictions and he was always honest and fearless in the expression of them. He hated public duplicity and abhorred demagogism and, while he made many enemies in his uncompromising attacks upon these inequities, which at times was more or less a personal drawback to him, yet the public owes him much because it is only by righteous denunciation that the villainies of the demagogue and the corruption of public officials can be curbed. Our friend and neighbor was feared by those who had cause to fear justice, but he was loved by those who admire courage. May he rest in peace.[1]

Freeman would have been pleased to know that the life of Horatio Vattel of Culpeper, which he had nurtured through his lifetime, had endured to the end.

It is true Freeman was unafraid to act on his convictions, thus he usually unabashedly adopted an attack-the-Establishment stance. He was therefore precluded from identifying with the ruling elite of a community as he might have done had he truly come from a "comfortable home" and experienced "the opportunities afforded by a well-to-do family. . . ." Ironically, he had the potential of carrying out a prime function of a journalist—getting outside of the community power structure and examining it objectively. But his objectivity was often motivated by personal opportunism, and he frequently seemed more of a malcontent than the objective critic whom Snively portrayed.

The assessment of Freeman's journalism is not dependent upon the one who delivered the eulogy and who accepted uncritically the myth of the genesis in Southern aristocracy. The literature of frontier journalism, while dispersed among numerous regional studies, affords generalizations that illuminate the seminal frontier phase of the "Press on Wheels."

"MYTH" OF THE RUGGED INDIVIDUALIST

Freeman's frontier life reflects a robustness in the tradition of "gunshot wounds, broken bones, duels, coats of tar and feathers, imprisonments, conflicts and quarrels."[2] Freeman-as-Vattel offers no documentation for the contention that the frontier publisher-printer as a rugged individualist and adventurer was only a myth fabricated by professional writers. Freeman displayed no "banality matched only by a lack of individuality," and he was not a passive leader in society, lacking in crusading spirit except in political matters, and allowing society to force change on him.[3]

POLITICAL ACTIVITY

Legh Freeman and his brother were active at each of the three levels of political journalism discernible in the frontier press. Most editors, including the brothers, took little time to analyze that their endeavors "played a primary role in establishing and transplanting laws and customs to the West in building new governments."[4] However, neither editors nor readers had difficulty in recognizing the second level of political activity, the frontier newspapers' partisan role. The anti-Grant editorials the Freeman brothers wrote in 1868 were among twenty-five editorials on national political affairs, which accounted for 29.41 percent of the eighty-five editorials identifiable in the extant issues. No other subject prompted as many editorials as national political affairs, although nearly all of the sixty other editorials (68.23 percent) reacted to local or regional problems. No more than two editorials (2.35 percent) were devoted to national nonpolitical subjects.

The Freemans were able to turn their published party loyalty into the ultimate step of becoming civic or political leaders. Illustrating this were Frederick's roles as member of the Council of the Nebraska Territorial Legislature and delegate to the 1868 Democratic National Convention and Legh's election to the Territorial Council, his Wyoming mayoralty candidacy, and postmaster appointment.

SOCIAL ROLE

The Freeman brothers and their fellow frontier editors demonstrably performed a vital role in their community's social and governmental development. The political support the brothers won stemmed from efforts to organize Democrats in two territories. Legh's activity in the vigilante cause illustrates the press's role in effecting civic organization, however extralegal. In their townsite promotions they gave a widespread identity to instantly created communities.

However, certain generalizations about the social function of the frontier press fail to account for the pecuniary interests of the Freemans and the temporary nature of the railroad frontier. To attribute an altruistic motivation to Legh Freeman by claiming he was "aware of his responsibility to society" would contribute a questionable latter-day interpretation.[5] Freeman undoubtedly rationalized a responsibility, but to say that the presence of the *Frontier Index* was necessarily a catalyst for social change would ignore the riot at Bear River City (although social change was certainly precipitated there). It would also overlook the divisive qualities Legh Freeman exhibited in usually fighting a complacent "sense of community."[6]

While literary features served an entertainment function, frontier newspapers by their mere existence are said to have raised the educational level of society, civilized the West, and been an agent of literacy.[7] Frontiersmen were avid readers, but whether racist anti-Grant editorials or land promotion schemes achieved such enlightenment is questionable. Legh Freeman hardly helped to civilize the West if his inflammatory vigilante or political editorials prompted the riot at Bear River City.

The Freeman brothers undoubtedly devoted more editorials to booming their communities than to any other subject. Promotion of Freeman townsites or railroad cities prompted twenty-one editorials (24.7 percent of the total in extant copies); local nonpolitical affairs, fourteen (16.47 percent); local politics, thirteen (15.29 percent); Indian affairs, six (7.05 percent); and the *Frontier Index* itself, four (4.71 percent). The Freeman brothers are thus among the frontier editors who expressed strong-minded opinion rather than those who were known for their lack of comment. This task of attempting to attract a population was one which their eastern counterparts had to perform only infrequently. In their promotional proclivities the Freemans were typical of nearly all frontier editors, but further generalizations would probably be inaccurate. On the transitory railroad frontier they could not become the type of promoters who were content to be long-range community builders, hoping to profit from the eventual prosperity community development would bring. Nor in such a setting did they fulfill only a passive economic function of recording property sales, new businesses, or similar important but innocuous items.

The *Frontier Index* seems to have escaped being a myopic promotional publication. The Freemans' desire to portray their communities as ideal did not preclude them from talking frankly about problems such as crime and the need for vigilante action. The editorials on national political affairs were as self-serving as the promotional editorials, but they saved the newspaper from being provincial as did Legh's literary allusions, reports of his travels throughout the West, and the attention to the economic potential of the transcontinental railroad throughout the West. Daniel J. Boorstin, in *The Americans: The National Experience* (p. 134) presents a view that such boosterism is the secret strength of American journalism.

INDIVIDUALISM

In defining the unusual aspects of the *Frontier Index* as "the most interesting in the history of American journalism," and the most "fascinating story," James Melvin Lee and Douglas C. McMurtrie recognized the individualism demonstrated by the Freeman brothers, and Legh Freeman especially.[8] Individualism is a recognized frontier characteristic, and to the extent that it is observable among editors, it will compromise the validity of generalizations that attempt to stereotype frontier journalism.[9] One of the primary conclusions thus called into question by the "Press on Wheels" is whether a frontier newspaper can serve as a mirror of frontier society.[10]

As the projection of two complex and imaginative personalities, the *Frontier Index* could be both the "emblem of American Liberty" and a "filthy rebel sheet." The "Press on Wheels" was perceived by the two Southern brothers without inconsistencies as the height of political and social responsibility in the aftermath of the Civil War, even as it demonstrated to unsympathetic readers the excesses of the Ku Klux Klan. With the *Frontier Index* more accurately reflecting its editors than the communities it served, it can be deemed representative or typical only in illustrating the highly personalized content possible in frontier journalism.

The personal nature of the Freeman newspaper was fostered by the impermanence of the railroad frontier. Conclusions about the frontier press that do not differentiate among types of frontiers and their effect on the freedom of editors may prove to be equally oversimplified. Their individualism may therefore compound the problems in the development of a synthesis of characteristics of the frontier press.

THE POSTFRONTIER LEGACY

The relatively brief frontier publishing experience of Legh Freeman colored his journalism for life. The restlessness of the frontier became permanently ingrained, and there is evidence that he attempted to replicate the heady and unfettered atmosphere of the frontier in all of his subsequent publishing ventures. Certainly the frontier had a yet unmeasured personal and psychological impact on the subsequent lives of other editors as well. Horatio Vattel did not pass away with the frontier; a legacy of tall tales, boosterism, and even racism seems to make inaccurate the statement that the frontier press bequeathed nothing that the West of the immediately succeeding era wanted to keep.[11]

Freeman-as-Vattel could not share in the prosperity of the settlers who spent years developing their claims, helping to weave a deep social fabric in their communities. As his bank account attested at his death, Freeman, unwilling or unable to share in this role, was a victim of a restlessness born in the freedom Horatio Vattel found first in Jim Bridger's country. He had sought financial security, but unlike many frontier editors, he was temperamentally unsuited to pay the price necessary for founding a community publishing enterprise of influence. He may not even have recognized the substitute reward: freedom from the routine and monotony necessary for such community success. The name of Horatio Vattel was not familiar in Washington State, but the Lightning Scout lived in Freeman's every move, political campaign, and defiant outburst.

Although Freeman initiated his agricultural publication in North Yakima in one of several urges for personal success, his columns did tie together a statewide community of farmers and ranchers, affording them information about their varied interests. The ultimate success of the *Washington Farmer* through its successive owners attests to the need Freeman recognized and which his publication first fulfilled. His experiment disproved the claim that since the pioneer editor was not himself a farmer, he could only clip items from eastern journals and farmers' publications.[12] Starting with a weekly newspaper, Freeman did the reporting necessary for the *Washington Farmer's* authentic information, undoubtedly aided by his boyhood on the Greenfield property in Virginia.

Thus it was in this agricultural capacity that Freeman made his major contribution, however veiled it was in lawsuits, political failures, family squabbles, and continued restlessness. It was possible only after he escaped from the lure of the less stable railroad frontiers in Nebraska, Wyoming, Utah, and Montana, and ironically sought still other railroad vistas in Washington. He could not have been judged successful by his contemporaries, who were determined to demonstrate the civility they had achieved. The "deep convictions" and Horatio Vattel's uncompromising fearlessness in expression, which Snively recognized, might have found a more receptive readership only in competition with the faceless corporate journalism of the late twentieth century.

NOTES

PREFACE

1. James Melvin Lee to Grace Raymond Hebard, Librarian, University of Wyoming, June 27, 1916, Western History Research Center, University of Wyoming, Laramie. Lee was director of the Department of Journalism, New York University, and president of the American Association of Teachers of Journalism; his brief published commentary on Freeman is in his *History of American Journalism*, rev. ed., pp. 322–23.

2. Legh R. Freeman, *The History of the Frontier-Index (The "Press on Wheels"), The Ogden Freeman, The Inter-Mountains Freeman and the Union Freeman*, ed. by Douglas C. McMurtrie, p. 1. Freeman's "history" was published as a newspaper article in the *Union-Freeman*, June 24, 1883.

3. Robert B. Heilman, "The Western Theme: Exploiters and Explorers," p. 5.

CHAPTER 1

1. Varinia Allison Freeman to the author, March 10, 1969. Miss Freeman was Legh Freeman's daughter. Pronounced "Lee," Legh is frequently misspelled "Leigh" in print.

2. Ibid.

3. *Virginia, A Guide to the Old Dominion*, p. 392.

4. DeWitt Gilbert, ed., *The Memoirs of Miller Freeman, 1875–1955*, p. 2. Miller Freeman, of Seattle, Washington, was Legh Freeman's son.

5. Ibid., p. 4.

6. Cf. Edwin Morris Betts, ed., *Thomas Jefferson's Farm Book*, p. 510; Gilbert, Memoirs, p. 4; Elizabeth Wright, *Independence in All Things, Neutrality in Nothing: The Story of a Pioneer Journalist in the American West*, p. 18; and Betts, ed., *Thomas Jefferson's Garden Book*, pp. 299, 309.

7. Betts, *Farm Book*, p. 517.

8. Ibid., p. 23; Betts, *Garden Book*, p. 326.

9. Betts, *Farm Book*, pp. 445, 517. See Betts, *Garden Book*, pp. 326–27, for Jefferson's defense of Freeman as a man of "honest character" when slaves accused Freeman of taking property, and pp. 314–15, for a letter to Freeman about work not done.

10. Gilbert, *Memoirs*, pp. 3–4.

11. George W. Glass to the author, March 20, 1967. Glass has prepared a genealogy of the Freeman family.

12. Gilbert, *Memoirs*, pp. 3–4.

13. Robert R. Jones, "Forgotten Virginian: The Early Life and Career of James Lawson Kemper, 1823–1865," p. 27.

14. Deeds recorded May 3, 1825, filed in Deed Book RR, pp. 509–10; September 10, 1832, filed in Deed Book 2, p. 64; April 10, 1835, filed in Deed Book 2, p. 566, Culpeper, Virginia.

15. *Population Schedules of the Seventh Census of the United States, 1850, Virginia: Culpeper, Cumberland, and Dinwiddie Counties*, Schedule 1, Free Inhabitants, Microfilm 432, p. 227.

16. *Population Schedules of the Sixth Census of the United States, 1840, Virginia*, vol. 3, Microfilm 179, pp. 249–50, 273.

17. *Population Schedules of the Seventh Census*, Schedule 1, Free Inhabitants, Microfilm 941, p. 241, and Slave Schedule, Microfilm 985, p. 905; *Population Schedules of the Eighth Census of the United States, 1860, Virginia*, vol. 6, Schedule 1, Free Inhabitants, Microfilm 293, p. 47, and vol. 2, Slave Schedule, Microfilm 303, p. 339.

18. Legh Richmond Freeman to C. C. Coutant, April 26, 1897, Hebard Collection.

19. *Population Schedules of the Seventh Census*, Schedule 1, Free Inhabitants, Microfilm 941, p. 261.

147

20. Deed recorded June 15, 1839, filed in Deed Book 5, pp. 160–63, Culpeper, Virginia.
21. Ibid., p. 162.
22. Ibid., p. 163; *Population Schedules of the Sixth Census*, vol. 3, Microfilm 179, p. 249; Varinia Freeman, quoting "In Memoriam Legh Richmond Freeman" (brochure), to the author, March 10, 1969.
23. Deed recorded January 1, 1850, filed in Deed Book 10, pp. 405–8, Culpeper, Virginia.
24. Ibid., p. 406; *Population Schedules of the Seventh Census*, vol. 3, Slave Schedule, Microfilm 985, pp. 941–92.
25. Wright, *Independence in All Things*, p. 16. Elizabeth Wright states that she does not know what the Greenfield estate looked like, "but it is obvious that it was large to house a family of twelve children. Also as Arthur Freeman was a farmer he kept slaves. It was not hard to construct the probable setup which followed the southern establishment pattern." (Elizabeth Wright Freeman to the author, November 5, 1974).
26. Robert R. Jones, ed., "The Mexican War Diary of James Lawson Kemper," p. 388.
27. Maria Kemper to James Lawson Kemper, November 23, 1853, James Lawson Kemper file.
28. Mary Freeman to James Lawson Kemper, March 20, 1858, James Lawson Kemper file. Photographs of Legh Freeman's parents are reproduced in Wright, *Independence in All Things*, pp. 20–21.
29. Mary Freeman to James Lawson Kemper, June 20, 1853.
30. Ibid.
31. Wright, *Independence in All Things*, p. 21.
32. Cf. Robert C. Black III, *The Railroads of the Confederacy*, pp. 26–27; Mary Freeman to James Lawson Kemper, April 3, 1854; March 22, 1871; September 22, 1871; and November 21, 1875.
33. Wright, *Independence in All Things*, p. 20.
34. Mary Freeman to James Lawson Kemper, August 12, 1856; Jones, "Forgotten Virginian," p. 78.
35. Mary Freeman to James Lawson Kemper, December 24, 1854.
36. Ibid., August 12, 1856.
37. Ibid., April 21, 1860; January 30, 1861.
38. Ibid., April [1854?]; April 23, 1856; April 21, 1860.
39. Wright, *Independence in All Things*, p. 22. There is no evidence that this book deliberately alters facts to portray a favorable family image.

CHAPTER 2

1. Robert R. Jones, "Forgotten Virginian: The Early Life and Career of James Lawson Kemper, 1823–1865," p. 229.
2. Grady McWhiney, "Controversy in Kentucky: Braxton Bragg's Campaign of 1862," p. 23.
3. All facts in this chapter pertaining to Freeman's military service were obtained from the Legh Freeman military service file, National Archives and Records Service, Washington, D.C.
4. See the *Ogden Freeman*, May 30, 1879.
5. Frederick Freeman's statement in 1916, quoted in DeWitt Gilbert, ed., *The Memoirs of Miller Freeman, 1875–1955*, p. 24, that Legh Freeman was captured when Morgan was killed, is obviously in error. Morgan died on September 4, 1864, in Greeneville, Tennessee.
6. "Rock Island Prison Barracks," p. 13. (Lithographed.)
7. Dee Alexander Brown, *The Galvanized Yankees*, p. 65.
8. Ibid., pp. 14–15.
9. Ibid., p. 4.
10. Lillian M. Willman, "The History of Fort Kearny," p. 291.
11. Myrtle D. Berry, "Fort Kearny," pp. 9–10; Brown, *Galvanized Yankees*, p. 31.
12. *Union—Freeman*, June 24, 1883.
13. Letter of Moses H. Sydenham to the Lincoln, Nebraska, *State Journal*, printed March 6, 1906, and quoted in H. S. Robinson, "Leigh Richmond Freeman and the Frontier Index."

14. J. Sterling Morton, *Illustrated History of Nebraska*, vol. 2, pp. 369–70.

15. Douglas C. McMurtrie, "The Sweetwater Mines, A Pioneer Wyoming Newspaper," p. 164.

16. The date of Freeman's discharge from the army is not recorded in his military service file.

17. Gay Wilson Allen, *The Solitary Singer*, p. 312.

18. Maria Kemper to James Lawson Kemper, October 17, 1865, James Lawson Kemper file.

19. Susan Elizabeth Matthews to James Lawson Kemper, undated, James Lawson Kemper file.

CHAPTER 3

1. Benjamin Pfeiffer, "The Role of Joseph E. Johnson and His Pioneer Newspapers in the Development of Territorial Nebraska," p. 132. Further discussion of Johnson appears in John Myers Myers, *Print in a Wild Land*, pp. 28, 31.

2. *Nebraska Republican*, January 4, 1866.

3. James B. Carrington, "Across the Plains with Bridger as Guide," p. 66.

4. Ibid.

5. Ibid.

6. Ibid.

7. Ibid.

8. James C. Olson, *Red Cloud and the Sioux Problem*, p. 33.

9. DeWitt Gilbert, ed., *The Memoirs of Miller Freeman, 1875–1955*, p. 24.

10. *Union—Freeman*, June 24, 1883.

11. Remi Nadeau, *Fort Laramie and the Sioux Indians*, p. 210.

12. Legh R. Freeman, "A Graphic Sketch of Frontier Life," p. 12.

13. Nadeau, *Fort Laramie*, p. 210; Grace Raymond Hebard and E. H. Brininstool, *The Bozeman Trail*, vol. 2, p. 178; George E. Hyde, *Red Cloud's Folk, A History of the Oglala Sioux Indians*, p. 139; and Olson, *Red Cloud*, pp. 35–36, all contend that Red Cloud left because of Colonel Carrington's untimely arrival. Dee Alexander Brown, *Fort Phil Kearny*, pp. 39–40, 42, 45, states that Carrington arrived at Fort Laramie on June 14 and met with the chiefs and that Red Cloud left during the night of June 16.

14. Freeman, "A Graphic Sketch of Frontier Life," p. 12.

15. Ibid.

16. Ibid.

17. William S. Greever, *The Bonanza West: The Story of the Western Mining Rushes, 1848–1900*, p. 219.

18. E. S. Topping, *The Chronicles of the Yellowstone*, p. 45.

19. Orrin H. Bonney and Lorraine Bonney, *Battle Drums and Geysers: The Life and Journals of Lt. Gustavus Cheyney Doane*, pp. 215–388.

20. Hebard and Brininstool, *Bozeman Trail*, vol. 1, p. 221.

21. Oliver Knight, *Following the Indian Wars*, p. 4.

22. *Frontier Index* (Laramie City, Dakota Territory), May 5, 1868.

23. Maria Kemper to James Lawson Kemper, November 2, 1868.

24. William F. Schmidt to the author, June 18, 1965.

25. Robert West Howard, *The Great Iron Trail: The Story of the First Transcontinental Railroad*, p. 214.

26. Microfilm estimates, miscellaneous issues, *Frontier Index*, July 26, 1867–November 17, 1868. The issues ranged from a low of 55.3 percent advertising on October 30, 1868, to a high of 76.3 percent on May 26, 1868.

CHAPTER 4

1. *Frontier Index* (Green River City, Wyoming Territory), August 24, 1868.

2. Vattel is used here to designate Freeman's imaginative writing irrespective of the actual byline used.

3. Quoted in Robert Edson Lee, *From West to East: Studies in the Literature of the American West*, pp. 151, 152.

4. *Frontier Index* (Fort Sanders, Dakota Territory), March 6, 1868.

5. Mark Twain, *Roughing It,* pp. 34-38; James R. Dow, "Folklore of the Wyoming Territory from Printed Sources," p. 25.

6. Dale L. Morgan, *Jedediah Smith and the Opening of the West,* p. 85.

7. Gene Caesar, *King of the Mountain Men: The Life of Jim Bridger,* p. 166.

8. C. Grant Loomis, "A Tall Tale Miscellany, 1830-1866," pp. 38-39; B. A. Botkin, ed., *A Treasury of American Folklore: Stories, Ballads, and Traditions of the People,* p. 595.

9. Walter Blair, *Native American Humor,* p. 119.

10. *Frontier Index* (Laramie City, Dakota Territory), June 9, 1868. Cf. James Fenimore Cooper, *The Prairie,* pp. 73-77.

11. *Frontier Index* (Laramie City, Dakota Territory), June 1, 1868.

12. Ibid.

13. Ibid., June 9, 1868.

14. Cf. Morgan, *Jedediah Smith,* p. 91.

15. *Frontier Index* (Laramie City, Dakota Territory), June 16, 1868.

16. Ibid., May 22, 1868. Freeman or the typesetters inexplicably used single quotation marks.

17. H. L. Mencken, *The American Language: An Inquiry into the Development of English in the United States,* 4th ed., pp. 567-68.

18. Blair, *Native American Humor,* p. 122.

19. *Frontier Index* (Fort Sanders, Dakota Territory), March 24, 1868.

20. Ibid.

21. Ibid. (Bear River City, Wyoming Territory), October 30, 1868; Henry Nash Smith, *Virgin Land: The American West as Symbol and Myth,* p. 9.

22. *Frontier Index* (Green River City, Dakota Territory), August 11, 1868; Ibid. (Laramie City, Dakota Territory), July 7, 1868, quoting the *Manchester* (New Hampshire) *Daily Union* (undated).

23. *Frontier Index* (Laramie City, Dakota Territory), May 29, 1868. "Brick" Pomeroy was Marcus M. Pomeroy, a popular nineteenth-century humorist.

24. Ibid., May 19, 1868.

25. Edwin Fussell, *Frontier: American Literature and the American West,* p. 231.

CHAPTER 5

1. *Frontier Index* (Green River City, Wyoming Territory), August 25, 1868.

2. Ibid. (Laramie City, Dakota Territory), May 29, 1868; June 16, 1868.

3. *Union—Freeman,* June 24, 1883. Powell discounted claims of even better documented voyages such as the one by James White, a trapper. See Wallace Stegner, *Beyond the Hundredth Meridian: John Wesley Powell and the Second Opening of the West,* p. 33, for a version of Powell's interview with White. Freeman printed an account of White's adventure, without comment, in the *Frontier Index* (Green River City, Wyoming Territory), September 22, 1868.

4. F. K. Freeman, "The Press on Wheels," in DeWitt Gilbert, ed., *The Memoirs of Miller Freeman, 1875-1955,* pp. 21-22.

5. *Frontier Index* (Laramie City, Dakota Territory), May 19, 1868.

6. "The Frontier Newspaper: A Guide to Society and Culture," p. 727.

7. *Frontier Index* (Green River City, Dakota Territory), August 11, 1868; (Laramie City, Dakota Territory), June 9, 1868.

8. Ibid. (Green River City, Dakota Territory), August 18, 1868. Horatio Seymour of New York and Frank P. Blair of Missouri were the 1868 Democratic presidential and vice-presidential candidates

9. Ibid. (Green River City, Wyoming Territory), September 18, 1868.

10. Ibid. (Laramie City, Dakota Territory), May 19, 1868.

11. Ibid. (Green River City, Dakota Territory), August 18, 1868.

12. Ibid. (Bear River City, Wyoming Territory), October 30, 1868. See Horace E. Scudder, ed., *The Complete Poetical Works of Oliver Wendell Holmes,* pp. 200-201, for the complete poem.

13. *Frontier Index* (Bear River City, Wyoming Territory), October 30, 1868.

14. Ibid. (Laramie City, Dakota Territory), May 19, 1868; June 12, 1868.

15. Ibid., June 16, 1868.

16. Ibid., June 19, 1868.

17. Ibid., May 29, 1868.

18. Ibid., June 16, 1868.

19. Lloyd Lewis, *Captain Sam Grant,* pp. 326–29; Bruce Catton, *U. S. Grant and the American Military Tradition,* pp. 50–51.

20. *Frontier Index* (Green River City, Dakota Territory), August 18, 1868.

21. Robert Howard West, *The Great Iron Trail: The Story of the First Transcontinental Railroad,* pp. 294–95.

22. *Frontier Index* (Green River City, Wyoming Territory), October 2, 1868.

23. Ibid. (Bear River City, Wyoming Territory), November 13, 1868.

24. Ibid. (Laramie City, Dakota Territory), May 29, 1868.

25. *Ogden Freeman,* August 20, 1878.

26. *Frontier Index* (Bear River City, Wyoming Territory), November 3, 1868.

27. Ibid., November 6, 1868.

28. Ibid., November 10, 1868; November 13, 1868.

29. Ibid., November 13, 1868. The justification is nearly identical to that by Thomas J. Dimsdale for Montana vigilante action only three years earlier. See Dimsdale, *The Vigilantes of Montana,* pp. 13–15.

30. *Frontier Index* (Bear River City, Wyoming Territory), November 13, 1868.

31. Lola M. Homsher, ed., *South Pass, 1868: James Chisholm's Journal of the Wyoming Gold Rush,* p. 16.

32. J. Cecil Alter, *Early Utah Journalism: A Half Century of Forensic Warfare, Waged by the West's Most Militant Press,* p. 159, quoting the *Salt Lake Telegraph,* November 23, 1868.

33. Elizabeth Arnold Stone, *Unita County: It's Place in History,* p. 83.

34. Ibid.; *Ogden Freeman,* August 20, 1878. Troops at Fort Bridger were also requested early in May 1869 to free Thomas C. Durant, Union Pacific vice-president and general manager, who was being held captive to be exchanged for payment of back wages due construction workers. The telegraphed request for troops never reached the fort, but the railroad company paid the back wages before the Golden Spike ceremony at Promontory, Utah Territory, on May 10, 1869 (Howard, *The Great Iron Trail,* pp. 329–30).

35. Alter, *Early Utah Journalism,* pp. 158–59, quoting the *Salt Lake Telegraph,* November 20, 23, 1868; *Ogden Freeman,* August 20, 1878; C. C. Coutant, *The History of Wyoming,* vol. 1, p. 683; Stone, *Unita County,* p. 83; James McCague, *Moguls and Iron Men: The Story of the First Transcontinental Railroad,* p. 259, quoting the *Salt Lake Tribune,* June [?], 1961; Larson, *History of Wyoming,* p. 61.

36. *Union—Freeman,* June 24, 1883. For a discussion of the Credit Mobilier scandal, see Howard, *The Great Iron Trail,* pp. 286–87, 346–47.

37. *History of Wyoming,* pp. 621–22.

38. Freeman, "The Press on Wheels," p. 23.

39. *Frontier Index* (Laramie City, Dakota Territory), April 21, 1868.

40. Alter, *Early Utah Journalism,* p. 159, quoting the *Salt Lake Telegraph,* November 23, December 9, 16, 1868.

CHAPTER 6

1. Reprinted in the *Yakima Morning Herald,* January 5, 1910.

2. Clarence A. Miller, "Recollections of the Life of Ada Virginia Miller," in DeWitt Gilbert, ed., *The Memoirs of Miller Freeman, 1875–1955,* pp. 12–13.

3. Robert Howard West, *The Great Iron Trail: The Story of the First Transcontinental Railroad,* p. 317, illustrates how some authors have relied on inaccurate material about Freeman. Howard claims that Freeman covered the Golden Spike ceremony at Promontory, Utah, on May 10, 1869, for the *Frontier Phoenix.* He also states that after the 1868 Bear River City riot, "Legh and Ada Freeman went back to Bryan [Wyoming] and announced plans for publication of the *Frontier Phoenix.*"

4. Miller, "The Life of Ada Virginia Miller," p. 15.

5. Gilbert, *Memoirs,* pp. 4–5.

6. *Frontier Index* (Laramie City, Dakota Territory), May 19, 1868.

7. Ibid. (Green River City, Wyoming Territory), September 18, 1868.

8. Ibid. (Laramie City, Dakota Territory), May 26, 1868.

9. Nels Anderson, *Desert Saints: The Mormon Frontier in Utah*, p. 272; *Frontier Index* (Fort Sanders, Dakota Territory), March 6, 1868.

10. *Frontier Index* (Laramie City, Dakota Territory), June 23, 1868.

11. F. K. Freeman, "The Press on Wheels," in Gilbert, *Memoirs*, pp. 22-23.

12. J. Cecil Alter, *Early Utah Journalism: A Half Century of Forensic Warfare, Waged by the West's Most Militant Press*, p. 158, quoting the *Deseret News*, June 8, 1868.

13. Ibid., p. 160, quoting the *Deseret News*, June 3, 1875.

14. *Ogden Freeman*, January 16, 1877.

15. Freeman, "The Press on Wheels," p. 20.

16. Alter, *Early Utah Journalism*, pp. 160-61, quoting the *Deseret News*, September 1, 1875, and E. W. Tullidge, *Tullidge's Histories*.

17. *Salt Lake Tribune*, August 8, 1875.

18. *Ogden Freeman*, September 5, 1876.

19. Ibid., September 8, 1876; September 29, 1876.

20. Ibid., October 13, 1876.

21. Howard Roberts Lamar, *The Far Southwest, 1846-1912, A Territorial History*, pp. 344-45, 384. See also Juanita Brooks, *The Mountain Meadows Massacre*.

22. *Ogden Freeman*, November 10, 1876.

23. Ibid., August 23, 1878.

24. *Salt Lake Tribune*, October 5, 1876.

25. *Ogden Freeman*, October 6, 1876.

26. Ibid., September 8, 1876.

27. Ibid., September 12, 1876; October 31, 1876.

28. Ibid., November 3, 1876.

29. Ibid., December 12, 1876.

30. Ibid., August 31, 1877.

31. Ibid., September 4, 1877.

32. Ibid., March 6, 1877; June 8, 1877.

33. Ibid., September 4, 1877.

34. Ibid., September 18, 1877.

35. Ibid., December 14, 1877.

36. Alter, *Early Utah Journalism*, p. 166.

37. *Ogden Freeman*, June 18, 1878.

38. Alter, *Early Utah Journalism*, p. 162, quoting the *Evanston* (Wyoming) *Age*, November 4, 1876.

39. Ibid., quoting the *Utah Evening Mail*, May 17, 31, 1876.

40. Varinia Freeman to the author, November 14, 1964.

41. *Ogden Freeman*, October 15, 1878; Jane R. Stewart, "The Name for the New State," *Spokesman-Review Magazine*, September 4, 1966, p. 8.

42. *Ogden Freeman*, May 30, 1879.

43. Alter, *Early Utah Journalism*, p. 161, quoting the *Utah Evening Mail*, March 31, April 19, 1876; John Myers Myers, *Print in a Wild Land*, pp. 121-22.

44. Alter, *Early Utah Journalism*, p. 161, quoting the *Ogden Freeman*, April 13, 1876.

45. *Ogden Freeman*, January 5, 1877.

46. Ibid., January 9, 1877.

47. *Walla Walla Union*, February 17, 1877.

48. *Ogden Freeman*, March 6, 1877.

49. Ibid., April 3, 1877.

50. Ibid.

51. Ibid., April 6, 1877; April 3, 1877.

52. Ibid., April 6, 1877.

53. Ibid., October 9, 1877.

54. Ibid.

55. Ibid., January 3, 1879.

56. Ibid., June 12, 1877.

57. Ibid., November 6, 1877.

58. January 1, 1878.

59. Ibid.

60. Ibid., January 8, 1878.

61. Ibid., January 11, 1878.
62. Ibid., January 18, 1878.
63. Ibid., January 25, 1878.
64. Ibid., May 2, 1879.
65. Ibid.
66. Ibid.
67. Ibid., May 9, 1879.
68. Ibid., May 23, 1879.
69. Alter, *Early Utah Journalism*, p. 166, quoting the 1883 Ogden City–Weber County directory.

CHAPTER 7

1. DeWitt Gilbert, ed., *The Memoirs of Miller Freeman, 1875–1955*, p. 1.
2. *Frontier Index* (Butte, Montana Territory), August 23, 1879.
3. Ibid. (Thompson Falls, Montana Territory), May 31, 1884.
4. Gilbert, *Memoirs*, p. 27.
5. *Inter-Mountains Freeman*, December 11, 1881.
6. *Atlantis*, October 27, 1880.
7. Ellis I. Waldron, *Montana Politics Since 1864: An Atlas of Elections*, p. 39.
8. *Frontier Index* (Butte City, Montana Territory), January 7, 1881.
9. *Inter-Mountains Freeman*, April 10, 1881.
10. Ibid.
11. Ibid.
12. Ibid., July 10, 1881.
13. Ibid., November 20, 1881.
14. Ibid., December 18, 1881.
15. Frank J. Gabse to the author, July 8, 1964. William Goodheart Breitenstein, "A History of Early Journalism in Montana, 1863–1890," p. 26, states that Freeman was enjoined from the use of the name "Intermountain." The source for this claim may have been Michael A. Leeson, ed., *History of Montana, 1739–1885*, p. 335, which goes no further than stating that "law proceedings were taken against the owner to estop the use of the name."
16. John Myers Myers, *Print in a Wild Land*, p. 200.
17. *Inter-Mountains Freeman*, December 25, 1881.
18. Ibid., September 5, 1882.
19. Frank J. Gabse to the author, July 8, 1964.
20. *Inter-Mountains Freeman*, March 5, 1882.
21. *Union—Freeman*, April 1, 1883. The *Union—Freeman* was unrelated to a later progressive-labor newspaper, the *Butte Daily Bulletin*, which was published for six years starting in 1917 following a mine fire and resulting strike (Guy Halverson and William E. Ames, "The Butte Bulletin: Beginnings of a Labor Daily," pp. 262–63). Coincidentally, a *Daily Bulletin* was published free of charge at the *Union—Freeman* office in 1883, but it was primarily an advertising sheet for the mercantile firm of Sands & Boyce (*Union—Freeman*, May 6, 1883).
22. *Union—Freeman*, April 1, 1883.
23. Ibid.
24. William S. Greever, *The Bonanza West: The Story of the Western Mining Rushes, 1848–1900*, p. 274.
25. *Butte City Union*, November 4, 1883.
26. *Frontier Index* (Thompson Falls, Montana Territory), April 12, 1884.
27. Ibid., April 19, 1884.
28. *Washington Farmer* (North Yakima, Washington Territory), April 18, 1885, quoting an unspecified issue of the *Seattle Chronicle*.
29. *Frontier Index* (Thompson Falls, Montana Territory), quoting the *Bozeman Chronicle*, May 17, 1884.
30. Ibid., May 31, 1884.
31. Ibid.
32. Ibid.
33. Ibid.

34. Ibid.
35. Ibid., June 14, 1884.
36. Ibid., July 5, 1884.

CHAPTER 8

1. W. Storrs Lee, ed., *Washington State: A Literary Chronicle*, p. 373.
2. DeWitt Gilbert, ed., *The Memoirs of Miller Freeman, 1875–1955*, p. 28.
3. The *Washington Farmer* today is published by William H. Cowles III, who is also an owner of the *Spokane Daily Chronicle, Spokane Spokesman-Review,* and Spokane radio and television stations.
4. James S. Evans and Rodolfo N. Salcedo, *Communications in Agriculture: The American Farm Press*, pp. 3–5, 170.
5. *Washington Farmer* (Yakima City, Washington Territory), September 20, 1884.
6. Ibid.
7. Gilbert, *Memoirs,* p. 29; *Washington Farmer* (North Yakima, Washington Territory), April 18, 1885, quoting an unspecified issue of the *Seattle Chronicle.*
8. The original Yakima City townsite was platted at Yakima City, but the post office was merely "Yakima." The town the railroad founded, North Yakima, was renamed Yakima, and Yakima City was renamed Union Gap by an act of the 1917 Washington legislature. No newspaper carried the word "North" as part of its logotype.
9. Charles Marvin Gates, ed., *Readings in Pacific Northwest History: Washington, 1790–1895,* p. 301.
10. Articles of Incorporation, Capital Publishing Company, August 27, 1884, District Court of the Fourth Judicial District of Washington Territory, Yakima County Auditor's Office, Yakima County Courthouse, Yakima, Washington. The spelling of "Capital" is varied as "Capitol" in records pertaining to the corporation.
11. *Washington Farmer* (Yakima City, Washington Territory), September 20, 1884.
12. Ibid.
13. Ibid., January 24, 1885.
14. Civil Complaint, Capital Publishing Company v. Leigh [sic] R. Freeman, January 22, 1885, District Court of the Fourth Judicial District of Washington Territory.
15. Ibid.
16. *Washington Farmer* (Yakima City, Washington Territory), January 3, 1885.
17. Ibid., January 22, 1885.
18. Ibid.
19. Ibid., December 13, 1884.
20. Ibid., January 3, 1885.
21. Ibid., January 24, 1885.
22. Ibid.
23. Civil Complaint, Capital Publishing Company v. Leigh [sic] R. Freeman, January 22, 1885, District Court of the Fourth District of Washington Territory.
24. Statement of Accounting, Capital Publishing Compay v. Leigh [sic] R. Freeman, October 10, 1887, District Court of the Fourth District of Washington Territory.
25. *Spokane Falls Review,* February 25, 1885.
26. *Washington Farmer* (Yakima city, Washington Territory), February 14, 1885.
27. Ibid., (North Yakima, Washington Territory), February 28, 1885.
28. William Dennison Lyman, *History of the Yakima Valley Washington Comprising Yakima, Kittitas and Benton Counties,* vol. 1, p. 402.
29. *Washington Farmer* (North Yakima, Washington Territory), February 28, 1885.
30. Ibid.
31. *Yakima Morning Herald,* December 18, 1907.
32. *Dalles Times-Moutaineer,* April 25, 1885. Copies of stories in this newspaper and others subsequently noted were obtained from the files of the late Click Relander, city editor of the *Yakima Daily Republic,* Yakima, Washington; hereafter cited as Relander Collection. The bulk of this collection of newspapers and manuscripts is now in the Yakima Valley Regional Library, Yakima, Washington.
33. *Yakima Signal,* September 4, 1886, Relander Collection.
34. *Washington Farmer* (North Yakima, Washington Territory), September 11, 1886.

Randolph Freeman received $7.50 a week as wages at the time of the suit and Hoomes received $2.50.

35. Complaint, E. M. Reed v. L. R. Freeman, September 18, 1886, and Amended Complaint, April 12, 1887, District Court of the Fourth District of Washington Territory.

36. Statement, Legh R. Freeman, October 11, 1888, E. M. Reed v. L. R. Freeman, District Court of the Fourth District of Washington Territory.

37. Civil Complaint, David Guilland v. Legh Richmond Freeman, May 13, 1885, Yakima Justice Court, County Clerk's Office.

38. Judgment, David Guilland v. Legh Richmond Freeman, October 27, 1885, District Court of the Fourth District of Washington Territory.

39. Minutes, North Yakima City Council, March 8, 1886, City Clerk's Office, City Hall, Yakima, Washington.

40. Varinia Allison Freeman to the author, August 3, 1964, October 25, 1969.

41. Gilbert, *Memoirs,* p. 30.

42. The Freeman real estate transactions are filed chronologically in Book E, p. 488; Book F, p. 470; Book G, pp. 138, 301; Book H, pp. 325, 329; Book I, pp. 409, 494; and Book J, p. 261, of Real Estate Transactions, County Auditor's Office, Yakima County Courthouse. The extent to which these parcels of land were mortgaged is not indicated.

43. *Yakima Herald,* May 2, 1889.

CHAPTER 9

1. *Puget Sound Mail,* November 15, 1888.

2. *Washington Farmer* (North Yakima, Washington Territory), February 28, 1885.

3. *Yakima Morning Herald,* January 5, 1910.

4. *Washington Farmer* (Gibralter, Washington Territory), September 6, 1889. Although Freeman spelled the townsite "Gibralter" in his initial issue, it is spelled "Gibraltar" in some other references.

5. Book J, p. 484, Real Estate Transactions, County Auditor's Office, Yakima County Courthouse, Yakima, Washington.

6. *Seattle Post-Intelligencer,* July 17, 1889.

7. Ibid., September 6, 7, 1889.

8. *Washington Farmer* (Gibralter, Washington Territory), September 6, 1889.

9. *An Illustrated History of Skagit and Snohomish Counties,* p. 209, quoting the *Anacortes Progress,* August 14, 1890.

10. *Seattle Post-Intelligencer,* August 21, 1889.

11. *Puget Sound Mail,* November 15, 1888.

12. Ibid., quoting an unspecified issue of the *Skagit News.*

13. *Skagit News,* September 30, 1889; October 7, 1889.

14. Ibid., September 30, 1889.

15. Plat of Gibralter, County Auditor's Office, Skagit County Courthouse, Mount Vernon, Washington.

16. *Skagit News,* May 5, 1890.

17. *Ellensburgh Register,* March [?], 1890, Relander Collection.

18. *Yakima Herald,* August 14, 1890.

19. *Skagit News,* January 5, March 16, October 12, November 2, 1891.

20. Ibid., May 14, 1894.

21. See Charles Miles and O. B. Sperlin, eds., *Building A State: Washington 1889-1939,* vol. 3, pp. 87-88, for a discussion of the effects of the Panic of 1893 in Washington.

22. Assignment of judgment, warranty deed, filed on December 14, 1893, and recorded in Book Q, pp. 605-6 of Real Estate Transactions, County Auditor's Office, Yakima County Courthouse.

23. Sheriff's certificate of sale on foreclosure, filed on January 21, 1891, and recorded in Book M, 487, of Real Estate Transactions, and deed, filed on October 10, 1892, and recorded in Book P, p. 281, of Real Estate Transactions, County Auditor's Office, Yakima County Courthouse.

24. Varinia Allison Freeman to the author, November 4, 1964, states that she was named for Varinia, wife of Spartacus, from a passage her father had underscored in a copy he owned of *The Ancient Lowly* by C. Osborne Ward. There is no evidence that she was

named for Varinia Davis, wife of Confederate President Jefferson Davis.
   25. DeWitt Gilbert, ed., *The Memoirs of Miller Freeman, 1875-1955*, p. 34.

CHAPTER 10

   1. See John D. Hicks, *The Populist Revolt: A History of the Farmers' Alliance and the People's Party*, p. 95, for a discussion of the effects of the end of availability of free land.
   2. *Washington Farmer* (North Yakima, Washington Territory), February 28, 1885.
   3. *Yakima Herald*, February 21, 1895. Freeman had also been criticized for his stand on the Chinese in the issues of February 7 and 14, 1895.
   4. Ibid., September 19, 1895.
   5. Ibid.
   6. Ibid., August 6, 1896.
   7. *Seattle Post-Intelligencer*, August 14, 1896.
   8. Ibid., August 15, 1896.
   9. *Yakima Herald*, December 3, 1896.
   10. Ibid., February 4, 1897.
   11. *Seattle Times*, January [?], 1897, Relander Collection; *Yakima Herald*, February 4, 1897.
   12. *Yakima Herald*, August 12, 1897.
   13. DeWitt Gilbert, ed., *The Memoirs of Miller Freeman, 1875-1955*, p. 35.
   14. *Yakima Herald*, February 18, 1897.
   15. Ibid., June 17, 1896.
   16. Ibid.
   17. Suit on Account, Pioneer Press Company v. R. L. Freeman, June 18, 1896, North Yakima Justice Court, and Judgment, October 27, 1898, Yakima County Superior Court, County Clerk's Office, Yakima County Courthouse, Yakima, Washington.
   18. Legh Richmond Freeman to Colonel C. G. Coutant, April 26, 1897, Hebard Collection.
   19. *Yakima Herald*, November 4, 1897.
   20. *Washington Farmer and Freeman's National Farmer and Turfman*, January 22, 1898.
   21. *Yakima Herald*, June 30, 1898.
   22. *Yakima Democrat*, June 17, August 12, 1899, Relander Collection.
   23. Varinia Allison Freeman to the author, September 16, 1964.
   24. *Yakima Democrat*, August 12, 1899, Relander Collection.
   25. Complaint, Legh R. Freeman v. L. Miller Freeman, September 8, 1899, King County Superior Court, County Clerk's Office, King County Courthouse, Seattle, Washington.
   26. Answer and Cross-Complaint, Legh R. Freeman v. L. Miller Freeman, King County Superior Court.
   27. Complaint, L. Miller Freeman v. Legh R. Freeman, December 14, 1899, and Decree, February 10, 1900, King County Superior Court.
   28. Will, Legh R. Freeman, February 21, 1907, County Clerk's Office, Yakima County Courthouse.
   29. *Yakima Daily Republic*, October 19, 1906.
   30. Judgment, St. Paul and Tacoma Lumber Company v. Legh R. Freeman, February 13, 1900, King County Superior Court Case 28354, vol. 13, p. 110; Judgment, Buell Lamberson v. L. R. Freeman, February 13, 1900, King County Superior Court Case 28353, vol. 13, p. 109.
   31. *Yakima Epigram*, August 13, 1898, Relander Collection.
   32. William Sidney Shiach, ed., in *An Illustrated History of Klickitat, Yakima and Kittitas Counties*, p. 572, lists her birth date as October 31, 1863. No age was published at the time of her funeral. Records at Shaw & Sons Funeral Home, Yakima, Washington, show only a birth date of 1866.
   33. *Yakima Democrat*, January 25, 1902, Relander Collection.
   34. Mrs. F. X. Nagler, private interview, November 6, 1963.
   35. Varinia Allison Freeman to the author, August 3, 1964.
   36. Ibid., September 16, 1964.
   37. Judge's Order, D. E. Lesh v. Leigh [sic] R. Freeman, August 20, 1907, Yakima County Superior Court.

38. Stipulation, William H. Robeson v. Legh R. Freeman, April 12, 1907, Yakima County Superior Court.

39. Judgment, Legh R. Freeman and Mary R. Freeman v. John S. Kloeber and Anna Kloeber, June 6, 1911, Yakima County Superior Court.

40. William Dennison Lyman, *History of the Yakima Valley Washington Comprising Yakima, Kittitas and Benton Counties,* vol. 1, p. 366; *Yakima Democrat,* April 21, 1906. See the *Yakima Republic,* July 3, 1903, for an account of private irrigation plans.

41. *Yakima Democrat,* April 21, 1906, Relander Collection. See David Lavender, *Land of Giants: The Drive to the Pacific Northwest, 1750–1950,* pp. 436–38, for a discussion of the activities of private irrigation companies.

43. *Yakima Morning Herald,* August 11, 1909.

44. *Yakima Democrat,* June 20, 1908, Relander Collection.

45. Ibid.

46. *Yakima Morning Herald,* September 1, 1909.

47. Ibid.

48. Ibid., January 5, 1910.

49. Ibid.

50. *Yakima Democrat,* June 8, 1910, Relander Collection.

51. Ibid., September 7, 1910.

52. Ibid.

53. "Eleventh Biennial Report of the Secretary of State," vol. 1, p. 254.

54. Judgment, American Color Type Company v. Legh R. Freeman and Mary R. Freeman, December 2, 1912, Yakima County Superior Court.

55. "Legh R. Freeman, Candidate for Mayor," undated.

56. *Yakima Morning Herald,* February 8, 1915.

57. Varinia Allison Freeman to the author, September 18, 1964.

58. Ibid., January 24, 1970.

59. Inventory, Legh R. Freeman estate, June 29, 1916, County Clerk's Office, Yakima County Courthouse.

60. Probate records, Mary R. Freeman estate, April 2, 1917, County Clerk's Office, Yakima County Courthouse.

CHAPTER 11

1. H. V. Snively, "Memorial Address," *Washington Farmer* (Seattle, Washington), March 1, 1915.

2. J. Cecil Alter, *Early Utah Journalism: A Half Century of Forensic Warfare, Waged by the West's Most Militant Press,* p. 10.

3. William A. Katz, "The Western Printer and His Publications, 1850–90," p. 709; William H. Lyon, *The Pioneer Editor in Missouri, 1808–1860,* p. 164.

4. Lyon, *Pioneer Editor in Missouri,* p. 165.

5. Ibid., p. 35.

6. Oliver Knight, "The Frontier Newspaper as a Catalyst in Social Change," p. 74. Knight recognizes the personal nature of frontier journalism and states (p. 81) that the frontier newspaper was capable of prompting social change.

7. Cf. Donald F. Carmony, "The Pioneer Press in Indiana," p. 231; Knight, "The Frontier Press as a Catalyst in Social Change," p. 74; Lyon, *Pioneer Editor in Missouri,* pp. 35–36; and Louis B. Wright, *Culture on the Moving Frontier,* pp. 132, 135.

8. James Melvin Lee, *History of American Journalism,* pp. 322–23; Douglas C. McMurtrie, ed., *The History of the Frontier-Index (The "Press on Wheels"), The Ogden Freeman, The Inter-Mountains Freeman and the Union Freeman,* p. 1.

9. Ray Allen Billington, *America's Frontier Heritage,* pp. 63–66.

10. Publications claiming the frontier press served as a mirror of its society include Carmony, "The Pioneer Press in Indiana," p. 231; Robert L. Housman, "The End of Frontier Journalism in Montana," p. 133; Housman, "The Journalist as Historian," in *A Century of Montana Journalism,* ed. by Warren J. Brier and Nathan B. Blumberg, p. 59; James Owen Knauss, *Territorial Florida Journalism,* p. 15; Flora Belle Ludington, *The Newspapers of Oregon, 1846–1870,* p. 3; and Donald W. Whisenhunt, "The Frontier Newspaper: A Guide to Society and Culture," p. 726. Alter, *Early Utah Journalism,* pp. 9–11, and Elizabeth Keen,

"The Frontier Press," pp. 78-79, define the value of the newspaper to historians, yet recognize the personal nature of its content. Publications recognizing frontier journalism as highly personal include Knight, "The Frontier Newspaper as a Catalyst in Social Change," p. 81; Lyon, *Pioneer Editor in Misssouri,* pp. 46-47; Reuben Gold Thwaites, "The Ohio Valley Press Before the War of 1812-1815," p. 352; and George S. Turnbull, *History of Oregon Newspapers,* p. 17.

11. John Myers Myers, *Print in a Wild Land,* p. 255.

12. Lyon, *Pioneer Editor in Missouri,* p. 43.

BIBLIOGRAPHY

PRIMARY SOURCES

Manuscripts

Freeman, Legh Richmond. Hebard Collection. File, Western History Research Center, University of Wyoming, Laramie.
_____. Military service file, National Archives and Records Service, Washington, D.C.
Kemper, James Lawson. File, Alderman Library Manuscripts Department, University of Virginia, Charlottesville.
Relander, Click. Newspaper and manuscript file, Yakima Valley Regional Library, Yakima, Washington.

Letters to the Author and Private Interview

Freeman, Varinia (Miami, Florida). Letters to the author, 1965–1970.
Gabse, Frank J. (clerk, Montana Second Judicial District Court, Butte). Letter to the author, July 8, 1964.
Glass, George W. (Houston, Texas). Letter to the author, March 20, 1967.
Nagler, Mrs. F. X. (Yakima, Washington). Private interview, November 6, 1963.
Schmidt, William F. (archivist, Nebraska State Historical Society, Lincoln). Letter to the author, June 18, 1965.

Public Documents

Auditor's Plat Records. Skagit County Courthouse, Mount Vernon, Washington.
Auditor's Real Estate Transactions. Yakima County Courthouse, Yakima, Washington.
Circuit Court Records. Culpeper County Courthouse, Culpeper, Virginia.
City Council Minutes. North Yakima, Washington Territory, 1886.
County Clerk's Records. Madison County Courthouse, Madison, Virginia.
"Eleventh Biennial Report of the Secretary of State." *Washington Public Documents, 1909–1910*, vol. 1. Olympia, Washington: State Printing Office, 1910.
Population Schedules of the Sixth Census of the United States, 1840, Virginia. Vol. 3, Schedule 1, Free Inhabitants. Washington, D.C.: National Archives Microfilm Publications, 1964.
Population Schedules of the Seventh Census of the United States, 1850, Virginia: Culpeper, Cumberland, and Dinwiddie Counties. Vol. 3, Schedule 1, Free Inhabitants, and Slave Schedule. Washington, D.C.: National Archives Microfilm Publications, 1964.
Population Schedules of the Eighth Census of the United States, 1860, Virginia. Vol. 2, Slave Schedule; Vol. 4, Schedule 1, Free Inhabitants; Vol. 20, Schedule 1, Free Inhabitants, Orange County. Washington, D.C.: National Archives Microfilm Publications, 1964.
Superior Court Records. King County Courthouse, Seattle, Washington.
Superior Court Records. Yakima County Courthouse, Yakima, Washington.
Thorpe, Francis Newton, comp. *The Federal and State Consititutions, Colonial Charters, and Other Organic Laws of the States, Territories, and Colonies Now or Heretofore Forming the United States of America*, vol. 7. Washington, D.C.: U.S. Government Printing Office, 1909.

Newspapers

Legh R. Freeman's Newspapers:
(All known extant copies of Freeman's newspapers were examined. Incomplete files were available from the periods cited. Institutions holding collections are indicated.)
Atlantis (Glendale, Montana Territory), October 27, November 17, 1880: Historical Society of Montana, Helena.

159

Butte City Union (Butte, Montana Territory), November 4, 1883–February 24, 1884: Historical Society of Montana, Helena.

Daily Inter-Mountains (Butte, Montana Territory), July 16–December 6, 1881: Historical Society of Montana, Helena.

Frontier Index (Julesburg, Colorado), July 26, 1867; (Fort Sanders, Dakota Territory), March 6–24, 1868; (Laramie City, Dakota Territory), April 21–July 21, 1868; (Green River City, Dakota Territory), August 11–21, 1868; (Green River City, Wyoming Territory), August 25–October 13, 1868; (Bear River City, Wyoming Territory), October 30–November 17, 1868: Bancroft Library, University of California, Berkeley. (Butte City, Montana Territory), August 23, 1879, January 7, 1881; (Thompson Falls, Montana Territory), April 12–July 5, 1884: Historical Society of Montana, Helena.

Inter-Mountains Freeman (Butte, Montana Territory), April 10, 1881–December 24, 1882: Historical Society of Montana, Helena.

Ogden Freeman (Ogden, Utah Territory), September 5, 1876–June 27, 1879: Bancroft Library, University of California, Berkeley.

Union—Freeman (Butte, Montana Territory), April 1–June 24, 1883: Historical Society of Montana, Helena.

Washington Farmer (Yakima City, Washington Territory), September 20, 1884–January 10, 1885: Holland Library, Washington State University, Pullman. (Yakima City), January 22, 1885: Yakima Valley Museum, Yakima, Washington. (Yakima City), January 24, 1885; (North Yakima, Washington Territory), February 28, 1885–September 11, 1886; (Gibralter, Washington Territory), September 6, 1889: Holland Library, Washington State University, Pullman. (Anacortes and Spokane, Washington), April 29, June 24, 1892: Office of the *Washington Farmer*, Spokane, Washington. (North Yakima and Seattle, Washington), January 22, 1898: files of the author. (Seattle, Washington), March 1, 1915: Holland Library, Washington State University, Pullman.

Other Newspapers:
(Scattered issues were examined from the periods cited.)

Daily Inter Mountain (Butte, Montana Territory), April 20–June 14, 1881.

Deseret Evening News (Salt Lake City, Utah Territory), June 18, 1875–April 3, 1877.

Puget Sound Mail (LaConner, Washington), November 15, 1888–November 21, 1889.

Salt Lake Tribune, December 15, 1875–April 1, 1877.

Seattle Post-Intelligencer, September 6, 1888–October 14, 1889; August 14, 1896–January 27, 1897.

Skagit News (Mount Vernon, Washington), August 19, 1889–October 22, 1894.

Spokane Falls Review (Spokane, Washington), February 28, 1885.

Spokesman-Review (Spokane, Washington), September 4, 1966.

Walla Walla Union, February 17, 1877.

Washington Farmer (Spokane, Washington), January 7, 1917.

Weekly Inter Mountain (Butte, Montana Territory), July 21, 1881.

Yakima Democrat, February 4, 1899–September 7, 1910.

Yakima Epigram, October 30, 1897–December 31, 1898.

Yakima Herald (*Yakima Morning Herald*), May 2, 1889–March 27, 1917.

Yakima Republic (*Yakima Daily Republic*), September 29, 1899–April 24, 1903; March 1–3, 1917.

Books

Alter, J. Cecil. *Early Utah Journalism: A Half Century of Forensic Warfare, Waged by the West's Most Militant Press.* Salt Lake City: Utah State Historical Society, 1938.

Betts, Edwin Morris, ed. *Thomas Jefferson's Farm Book.* Princeton, New Jersey: Princeton University Press for the American Philosophical Society, 1953.

———. *Thomas Jefferson's Garden Book.* Philadelphia: American Philosophical Society, 1944.

Bonney, Orrin H., and Bonney, Lorraine. *Battle Drums and Geysers: The Life and Journals of Lt. Gustavus Cheyney Doane.* Sage Books. Chicago: Swallow Press, 1970.

Cooper, James Fenimore. *The Prairie.* New York: Holt, Rinehart and Winston, 1967.
Dimsdale, Thomas J. *The Vigilantes of Montana.* Norman: University of Oklahoma Press, 1953.
Dodge, Grenville M. *How We Built the Union Pacific Railway,* 1st reprint. Denver: Sage Books, 1965.
Evans, James F., and Salcedo, Rodolfo N. *Communications in Agriculture: The American Farm Press.* Replica Edition. Ames: Iowa State University Press, 1974.
Freeman, Legh R. *The History of the Frontier-Index (The "Press on Wheels"), The Ogden Freeman, The Inter-Mountains Freeman and the Union Freeman,* ed. by Douglas C. McMurtrie. Evanston, Illinois: Published by the editor, 1943.
Gilbert, DeWitt, ed. *The Memoirs of Miller Freeman, 1875-1955.* San Francisco: Miller Freeman Publications, 1956.
Homsher, Lola M., ed. *South Pass, 1868: James Chisholm's Journal of the Wyoming Gold Rush.* Pioneer Heritage Series, vol. 3. Lincoln: University of Nebraska Press, 1960.
Langford, Nathaniel Pitt. *Discovery of Yellowstone Park, 1870: Diary of the Washburn Expedition to the Yellowstone and Firehold Rivers in the Year 1870.* Privately printed, 1905.
Scudder, Horace E., ed. *The Complete Poetical Works of Oliver Wendell Holmes.* Cambridge Edition. Boston: Houghton Mifflin, 1895.
Shearer, Frederick E., ed. *The Pacific Tourist.* New York: J. R. Bowman, 1883.
Topping, E. S. *The Chronicles of the Yellowstone.* Minneapolis: Ross & Haines, 1968.
Twain, Mark. *Roughing It.* Rinehart Edition. New York: Holt, Rinehart and Winston, 1953.
Waldron, Ellis I. *Montana Politics Since 1864: An Atlas of Elections.* Missoula: Montana State University Press, 1958.
Wright, Elizabeth. *Independence in All Things, Neutrality in Nothing: The Story of a Pioneer Journalist of the American West.* San Francisco: Miller Freeman Publications, 1973.

Periodicals and Pamphlets

Carrington, James B. "Across the Plains with Bridger as Guide." *Scribner's Magazine* (January 1929): 66-69.
Dow, James R. "Folklore of the Wyoming Territory from Printed Sources." *Western Review: A Journal of the Humanities* 8 (Winter 1971): 23-28.
Freeman, Legh R. "A Graphic Sketch of Frontier Life." *Northwest Magazine* (August 1899): 12-13.
Jones, Robert R., ed. "The Mexican War Diary of James Lawson Kemper." *Virginia Magazine of History and Biography* (October 1966): 387-428.
"Legh R. Freeman, Candidate for Mayor." Printed brochure, undated.

SECONDARY SOURCES

Books

Allen, Gay Wilson. *The Solitary Singer.* New York: Macmillan, 1955.
Anderson, Nels. *Desert Saints: The Mormon Frontier in Utah.* Chicago: University of Chicago Press, 1942.
An Illustrated History of Skagit and Snohomish Counties. Spokane: Interstate, 1906.
Arrington, Leonard J. *Great Basin Kingdom: An Economic History of the Latter-day Saints, 1830-1900.* Cambridge: Harvard University Press, 1958.
Ashton, Wendell J. *Voice in the West: Biography of a Pioneer Newspaper.* New York: Duell, Sloan & Pearce, 1950.
Athearn, Robert G. *Union Pacific Country.* Chicago: Rand McNally, 1971.
Billington, Ray Allen. *America's Frontier Heritage.* New York: Holt, Rinehart and Winston, 1966.
Black, Robert C. III. *The Railroads of the Confederacy.* Chapel Hill: University of North Carolina Press, 1952.
Blair, Walter. *Native American Humor.* San Francisco: Chandler, 1960.
Bonner, James C. "Plantation and Farm: The Agricultural South." *Writing Southern*

History: Essays in Historiography in Honor of Fletcher M. Green, ed. by Arthur S. Link and Rembert W. Patrick. Baton Rouge: Louisiana State University Press, 1967.

Boorstin, Daniel J. *The Americans: The National Experience.* New York: Random House, 1965.

Botkin, B. A., ed. *A Treasury of American Folklore: Stories, Ballads and Traditions of the People.* New York: Crown, 1944.

Brooks, Juanita. *The Mountain Meadows Massacre.* Stanford: Stanford University Press, 1950.

Brown, Dee Alexander. *Fort Phil Kearny.* New York: G. Putnam's Sons, 1962.

_____. *The Bold Cavaliers: Morgan's 2nd Kentucky Cavalry Raiders.* Philadelphia: J. B. Lippincott, 1959.

_____. *The Galvanized Yankees.* Urbana: University of Illinois Press, 1963.

Bryan, Enoch A. *Orient Meets Occident: The Advent of the Railways to the Pacific Northwest.* Pullman, Washington: Students Book Corporation, 1936.

Burlingame, Merrill G. *The Montana Frontier.* Helena: State Publishing, 1942.

Burlingame, Merrill G., and Toole, K. Ross. *A History of Montana,* vol. 2, New York: Lewis Historical Publishing, 1957.

Caesar, Gene. *King of the Mountain Men: The Life of Jim Bridger.* New York: E. P. Dutton, 1961.

Camp, James E., and Kennedy, X. J. *Mark Twain's Frontier.* New York: Holt, Rinehart and Winston, 1963.

Cash, W. J. *The Mind of the South.* Vintage Books. New York: Random House, 1941.

Catton, Bruce. *U. S. Grant and the American Military Tradition.* Boston: Little, Brown, 1954.

Chaplin, W. E. "Some of the Early Newspapers of Wyoming." *Wyoming Historical Society Miscellanies.* Laramie: Laramie Republican, 1919.

Chittenden, Hiram Martin. *The American Fur Trade of the Far West,* vol. 1. New York: Barnes and Noble, 1935.

Connelley, William E. *History of Kansas Newspapers.* Topeka: Kansas State Historical Society and Department of Archives, 1916.

Coutant, C. G. *The History of Wyoming,* vol. 1. Laramie: Chaplin, Spafford & Mathison, 1899.

Davis, Elmer O. *The First Five Years of the Railroad Era in Colorado.* Denver: Sage Books, 1948.

DeVoto, Bernard, "Ogden: The Underwriters of Salvation." *The Taming of the Frontier,* ed. by Duncan Aikman. New York: Minton, Balch, 1925.

Duke, Basil W. *History of Morgan's Cavalry.* Cincinnati: Miami Printing and Publishing, 1867.

Ellison, Rhoda Coleman. *Early Alabama Publications: A Study in Literary Interests.* University: University of Alabama Press, 1947.

Emery, Edwin, and Smith, Henry Ladd. *The Press and America.* New York: Prentice-Hall, 1954.

Fuller, Wayne E. *RFD: The Changing Face of Rural America.* Bloomington: Indiana University Press, 1964.

Fussell, Edwin. *Frontier: American Literature and the American West.* Princeton, New Jersey: Princeton University Press, 1965.

Gates, Charles Marvin, ed. *Readings in Pacific Northwest History: Washington, 1790–1895.* Seattle: University Bookstore, 1941.

Green, Raleigh Travers, comp. *Genealogical and Historical Notes on Culpeper County, Virginia,* vol. 2, 1900.

Greever, William S. *The Bonanza West: The Story of the Western Mining Rushes, 1848–1900.* Norman: University of Oklahoma Press, 1963.

Griswold, Wesley·S. *A Work of Giants: Building the First Transcontinental Railroad.* New York: McGraw-Hill, 1962.

Hage, George S. *Newspapers on the Minnesota Frontier.* St. Paul: Minnesota Historical Society, 1967.

Hawthorne, Julian, ed. *History of Washington,* vols. 1, 2. New York: American Historical Publishing, 1893.

Hebard, Grace Raymond, and Brininstool, E. A. *The Bozeman Trail,* vol. 1. Cleveland: Arthur H. Clark, 1922.

Hicks, John D. *The Populist Revolt: A History of the Farmers' Alliance and the People's Party.* Lincoln: University of Nebraska Press, 1961.

Higham, John. *Strangers in the Land.* New Brunswick, New Jersey: Rutgers University Press, 1955.

Hooper, Osman Castle. *Ohio Journalism, 1793–1933.* Columbus: Spahr & Glenn, 1933.

Housman, Robert L. "The Journalist as Historian." *A Century of Montana Journalism,* ed. by Warren J. Brier and Nathan B. Blumberg. Missoula: Mountain Press, 1971.

Howard, Robert West. *The Great Iron Trail: The Story of the First Transcontinental Railroad.* New York: G. P. Putnam's Sons, 1962.

Hunt, Herbert, and Kaylor, Floyd C. *Washington West of the Cascades,* vol. 1. Chicago: S. J. Clarke, 1917.

Hyde, George E. *Red Cloud's Folk, A History of the Oglala Sioux Indians.* Civilization of the American Indian Series, 2nd ed. Norman: University of Oklahoma Press, 1957.

Irving, Washington. *The Adventures of Captain Bonneville, U.S.A.,* ed. by Edgeley W. Todd. Norman: University of Oklahoma Press, 1961.

Irwin, Will. *The American Newspaper.* Ames: Iowa State University Press, 1969.

Knauss, James Owen. *Territorial Florida Journalism.* Deland: Florida State Historical Society Publication 6, 1926.

Knight, Oliver. *Following the Indian Wars.* Norman: Univeristy of Oklahoma Press, 1960.

Lamar, Howard Roberts. *The Far Southwest, 1846–1912, A Territorial History.* New Haven: Yale University Press, 1966.

Larson, T. A. *History of Wyoming.* Lincoln: University of Nebraska Press, 1965.

Lavender, David. *Land of Giants: The Drive to the Pacific Northwest, 1850–1950.* Garden City, New York: Doubleday, 1958.

Lee, James Melvin. *History of American Journalism,* rev. ed. New York: Garden City, 1923.

Lee, Robert Edson. *From West to East: Studies in the Literature of the American West.* Urbana: University of Illinois Press, 1966.

Lee, W. Storrs, ed. *Washington State: A Literary Chronicle.* New York: Funk & Wagnalls, 1969.

Leeson, Michael A., ed. *History of Montana, 1739–1885.* Chicago: Warner, Beers, 1885.

Lewis, Lloyd. *Captain Sam Grant.* Boston: Little, Brown, 1950.

Ludington, Flora Belle. *The Newspapers of Oregon, 1846–1870.* Eugene: Koke-Tiffany, 1925.

Lyman, William Denison. *History of the Yakima Valley Washington Comprising Yakima, Kittitas and Benton Counties,* vol. 1. Chicago: S. J. Clarke, 1919.

Lyon, William H. *The Pioneer Editor in Missouri, 1808–1860.* Columbia: University of Missouri Press, 1965.

McCague, James. *Moguls and Iron Men: The Story of the First Transcontinental Railroad.* New York: Harper & Row, 1964.

Mantor, Lyle E. "Brief History of Fort Kearny." *Where the Buffalo Roamed,* comp. by Kearney Business and Professional Women's Club. Shenandoah, Iowa: World Publishing, 1967.

Mencken, H. L. *The American Language: An Inquiry into the Development of English in the United States,* 4th ed. New York: Alfred A. Knopf, 1937.

Miles, Charles, and Sperlin, O. B., eds. *Building a State: Washington 1889–1939,* vol 3. Tacoma: Washington State Historical Society, 1940.

Morgan, Dale L. *Jedediah Smith and the Opening of the West.* New York: Bobbs-Merrill, 1953.

Morton, J. Sterling. *Illustrated History of Nebraska,* vol. 2. Lincoln: Jacob North, 1906.

Myers, John Myers. *Print in a Wild Land.* Garden City, New York: Doubleday, 1967.

Nadeau, Remi. *Fort Laramie and the Sioux Indians.* Englewood Cliffs, New Jersey: Prentice-Hall, 1967.

Nesbit, Robert C. *He Built Seattle: A Biography of Judge Thomas Burke.* Seattle: University of Washington Press, 1961.

Olson, James C. *Red Cloud and the Sioux Problem.* Lincoln: University of Nebraska Press, 1965.

Paul, Rodman Wilson. *Mining Frontiers of the Far West, 1848–1880.* Histories of the American Frontier, ed. by Ray Allen Billington. New York: Holt, Rinehart and Winston, 1963.

Relander, Click. *Drummers and Dreamers.* Caldwell, Idaho: Caxton, 1956.
Rourke, Constance. *American Humor: A Study of the National Character.* New York: Harcourt, Brace, 1931.
Rusk, Ralph Leslie. *The Literature of the Middle Western Frontier,* vol. 1. New York: Columbia University Press, 1926.
Shiach, William Sidney, ed. *An Illustrated History of Klickitat, Yakima and Kittitas Counties.* Spokane: Interstate, 1904.
Smith, Henry Nash. *Virgin Land: The American West as Symbol and Myth.* Vintage Books. New York: Alfred A. Knopf; Random House, 1950.
Splawn, A. J. *Ka-mi-akin, Last Hero of the Yakimas,* 2nd ed. Portland: Binfords & Mort for the Oregon Historical Society, 1944.
Stegner, Wallace. *Beyond the Hundredth Meridian: John Wesley Powell and the Second Opening of the West.* Boston: Houghton Mifflin, 1954.
Stone, Elizabeth Arnold. *Unita County: Its Place in History.* Laramie: Laramie Printing, 1924.
Stratton, Porter A. *The Territorial Press of New Mexico, 1834–1912.* Albuquerque: University of New Mexico Press, 1969.
Trickey, Emily E., ed. *Prairie Paradox.* Lincoln: School of Journalism, Univeristy of Nebraska, 1966.
Turnbull, George S. *History of Oregon Newspapers.* Portland: Binfords & Mort, 1939.
Turner, George Edgar. *Victory Rode the Rails: The Strategic Place of the Railroads in the Civil War.* New York: Bobbs-Merrill, 1953.
Utah, A Guide to the State. American Guide Series, Writers' Program of the Work Projects Administration. New York: Hastings House, 1941.
Virginia, A Guide to the Old Dominion. American Guide Series, Writers' Program of the Work Projects Administration. New York: Oxford University Press, 1946.
Wooster, Ralph A. *The Secession Conventions of the South.* Princeton, New Jersey: Princeton University Press, 1962.
Wright, Louis B. *Culture on the Moving Frontier.* Bloomington: Indiana University Press, 1966.
Wyoming, A Guide to Its History, Highways and People. Writers' Program of the Work Projects Administration. New York: Oxford University Press, 1941.

Articles, Periodicals, and Pamphlets

Berry, Myrtle D. "Fort Kearny." Leaflet 7, Nebraska State Historical Society, undated.
Carmony, Donald F. "The Pioneer Press in Indiana." *Indiana History Bulletin* 31 (October 1954): 187–232.
Coulter, Calvin B. "The Victory of National Irrigation in the Yakima Valley, 1902–1906." *Pacific Northwest Quarterly* 42 (April 1951): 99–122.
"Famous Guide." *Montana Magazine of History* 4 (Summer 1954): 63.
Gower, Calvin W. "Kansas 'Border Town' Newspapers and the Pike's Peak Gold Rush." *Journalism Quarterly* 44 (Summer 1967): 281–88.
Hahn, George C. "Wyoming Statehood Stamp." *Annals of Wyoming* 18 (January 1946): 67–69.
Halverson, Guy, and Ames, William E. "The Butte Bulletin: Beginnings of a Labor Daily." *Journalism Quarterly* 46 (Summer 1969): 260–66.
Heilman, Robert B. "The Western Theme: Exploiters and Explorers." *Northwest Review* 4 (Fall-Winter 1960), 5–14.
Housman, Robert L. "The End of Frontier Journalism in Montana." *Journalism Quarterly* 12 (Summer 1935), 133–45.
Katz, William A. "The Western Printer and His Publications, 1850–90." *Journalism Quarterly* 44 (Winter 1967): 708–14.
Keen, Elizabeth. "The Frontier Press." *University of Wyoming Publications,* 20 (July 15, 1956): 75–100.
Knight, Oliver. "The Frontier Newspaper as a Catalyst in Social Change." *Pacific Northwest Quarterly* 58 (April 1967): 74–81.
Loomis, C. Grant. "A Tall Tale Miscellany, 1830–1866." *Western Folklore* 6 (1947): 28–41.
McAllister, Margaret. "Bear River City." *Annals of Wyoming* 41 (April 1969): 125–26.

McMurtrie, Douglas C. "Pioneer Printing in Wyoming." *Annals of Wyoming* 9 (January 1933): 729-42.
_____. "The Pioneer Press in Montana." *Journalism Quarterly* 9 (June 1932): 170-81.
_____. "The Sweetwater Mines, A Pioneer Wyoming Newspaper." *Journalism Quarterly* 12 (June 1935): 164-65.
McWhiney, Grady. "Controversy in Kentucky: Braxton Bragg's Campaign of 1862." *Civil War History* 6 (March 1960): 5-24.
Pfeiffer, Benjamin. "The Role of Joseph E. Johnson and His Pioneer Newspapers in the Development of Territorial Nebraska." *Nebraska History* 40 (June 1959): 119-36.
Thwaites, Reuben Gold. "The Ohio Valley Press Before the War of 1812-1815." *Proceedings of the American Antiquarian Society* 19 (April 1909): 309-68.
Whisenhunt, Donald W. "The Frontier Newspaper: A Guide to Society and Culture." *Journalism Quarterly* 45 (Winter 1968): 726-28.
Willman, Lillian M. "The History of Fort Kearny." *Publications of the Nebraska State Historical Society* 21 (1930): 213-25.
Yoder, Fred R. "The Farmers' Alliances in Washington—Prelude to Populism." *Research Studies of the State College of Washington* 16 (September-December 1948): 123-78.

Unpublished Material

Bergman, Hermas John. "Progressive on the Right: Marion E. Hay, Governor of Washington, 1909-1913." Ph.D. dissertation, Washington State University, 1967.
Boone, Michael D. "The Washington State Legislature of 1897: A Study in Populism." Master's thesis, Washington State University, 1966.
Breitenstein, William Goodheart. "A History of Early Journalism in Montana, 1863-1890." Master's thesis, University of Montana, 1915.
Jones, Robert R. "Forgotten Virginian: The Early Life and Career of James Lawson Kemper, 1823-1865." Master's thesis, University of Virginia, 1961.
Keen, Elizabeth. "Wyoming's Frontier Newspapers." Master's thesis, University of Wyoming, 1956.
Riddle, Thomas Wayne. "Whitman County Populism and Washington State Politics: 1889-1902." Master's thesis, Washington State University, 1971.
Robinson, H. S. "Leigh [sic] Richmond Freeman and the Frontier Index." Western History Research Center, University of Wyoming, undated.
"Rock Island Prison Barracks." John M. Browning Memorial Museum, Rock Island, Illinois, 1964.

INDEX

Abingdon, Virginia, 16
Adams, James Madison, 98–99, 103, 107
Ahtanum Creek (Washington), 98
Ainsworth, Washington, 98, 105
Alfalfa Saloon, 100
American Color Type Co., 138
The Americans: The National Experience, 144
Anacortes [Ship Harbor], Washington, 25, 114–20, 129
Anacortes American, 117
Anacortes Daily Progress, 117–19
Anacortes Enterprise, 115
Anderson, Lu, 27, 89
Appalachian Region, 16
Appomattox, Virginia, 17
Arapahoes, 77–79
Arizona, 31, 37, 38–39, 69, 90
Ashley, Congressman J. M., 53
Atlantis (Glendale, Montana), 85–86, 88

Barbour, John S., Jr., 10
Bat, Obed, 35
Bayview, Washington, 114
Bear Creek (Wyoming), 28
Bear River City, Wyoming, 25, 37, 39, 48–55, 58, 69, 79, 93, 99, 143–44
Beaverhead County, Montana, 85–86
Bellingham, Washington, 112
Bent, W. B., 53–54
Benton, Dakota Territory [Wyoming], 25
Berkeley, Bishop, 39
Big Horn, 28; Big Horn Country, 47; Big Horn Mountains, 77
Bissell, C. V., 128–29
Black Coal, 77–78
Black Hills, 94
Blair, Walter, 38
Blyman, Joseph, 71
Bogle, Judge W. H., 132
Bond, H. M., 62
Boorstin, Daniel J., 144
Bowman, Amos, 115
Bowman, Anna Curtis, 115
Bozeman, John, 27–28
Bozeman, Montana, 23, 27
Bozeman Chronicle, 93
Bozeman Trail [Powder River Road], 23–24, 26, 47, 93
Bragg, General Braxton, 15
Bridger, Jim, 22–23, 26–28, 35, 39, 89, 93, 145

British Columbia, 69, 90, 133
Brougham, Lord Henry, 5
Brown, Marshal Moroni, 72
Brundage, Hiram, 18–19
Bryan, E. A., 130
Bryan, William Jennings, 124
Bryan, Wyoming, 49
Butte, Montana, 25, 52, 79, 81–82, 84–86, 90–92, 94–95, 98, 115, 129
Butte City Union, 91
Butte Workingmen's Union, 91

Calamity Jane, 92
California, 31, 47, 133
Camp Brown, 70
Canadian Pacific Railroad, 111–12, 114, 133
Capital Publishing Company, 100–101, 103–4, 107–9
Carlton, George W., 89–90
Carrington, Colonel Henry B., 23–24, 26
Cascade Mountains (Washington), 97, 99, 110, 115
Cavalier myth, 6, 7
Chadd, Richard V., 100
Cheyenne, Wyoming, 49, 51, 92
Chicago, Illinois, 46, 58, 70, 131, 133
Chickamauga, Georgia, 15
Chinese, 41, 43–45, 55, 58–59, 63, 84, 93–95, 122–23, 138
Chisholm, James, 51
Church of Jesus Christ of Latter-day Saints, 63
City Creek Canyon, Utah, 68
Civil War, 3, 9, 12–13, 15–17, 29, 45, 123, 145
Clyman, Jim, 35, 37
Coeur d'Alene mining district, Idaho, 91–92, 94–96
Colorado, 69, 90, 137
Colorado River, 38, 42, 59
Coltenbaugh, M., 114
Columbia River, 70, 97–98, 115
Cooke, Jay, 115
Cooley, R. B., 81
Cooper, James Fenimore, 35
Coover, Tom, 28
Coulter, Calvin B., 135
Council Bluffs, Iowa, 61
Coutant, C. G., 53, 129
Cowles, W. H., 140
Credit Mobilier, 52–53
Creighton, Edward, 18, 22

ISBN 978-1-59789-774-7

Produced with the assistance of Christopher. D. Hudson & Associates. Contributing writers include Carol Smith and Stan Campbell.

Published by Barbour Publishing, Inc., P.O. Box 719, Uhrichsville, Ohio 44683, www.barbourbooks.com

Our mission is to publish and distribute inspirational products offering exceptional value and biblical encouragement to the masses.

 Member of the
Evangelical Christian
Publishers Association

S0-BXW-246

matthew
&mark

GOOD NEWS FOR EVERYONE

CONTRIBUTING EDITORS:

DR. IAN FAIR
DR. STEPHEN LESTON

CONSULTING EDITOR:

DR. MARK STRAUSS